Canada's Place
A Global Perspective

Lorne Tepperman
Maria Finnsdottir

Rock's Mills Press
Oakville, Ontario
2022

Published by
Rock's Mills Press
www.rocksmillspress.com

Cover image: Strebe, Azimuthal equidistant projection, based on NASA's "Blue Marble" photograph.

For information about this book, including bulk and retail orders, contact Rock's Mills Press at customer.service@rocksmillspress.com.

Canada's Place

With good wishes,

L.T.

Contents

Preface

This book focuses on how Canada addresses a number of key social problems, including economic inequality, social justice issues, crime, health and addictions, and environmental challenges. We do so by comparing Canada's performance to that of sixteen similar countries. It goes without saying, however, that these are big issues and this is a (relatively) little book. Not surprisingly, there are too many topics to cover all of them thoroughly. As authors, we can only strive to convey an overall vision of the world as we view it. If we were discussing this material with you, face to face, no doubt we could continue for hours with abundant examples and counterexamples. But we do not have this liberty; we are writing a book.

Canada and the other sixteen countries all do pretty well by global standards in dealing with social problems. But no matter how well a country does on a particular issue, acute problems persist and need to be addressed. As we argue throughout this book, the Nordic countries have done an excellent job in reducing income inequality and providing social benefits to disadvantaged people. Yet as we will see, wealth inequality remains high in those countries, as in other prosperous but less progressive countries. Even social welfare regimes like Denmark, Norway, and Iceland fail to eliminate extreme economic inequalities.

Similarly, despite Canada's success in welcoming and integrating a diverse range of immigrants and establishing a multicultural society, acute challenges remain in these and other areas of Canadian society. Such success did not prevent shocking events like the murder by automobile on June 8, 2021 of an Islamic family in London, Ontario. Nor did it prevent or excuse the upsurge in some places of anti-Asian sentiment and behaviour during the COVID-19 pandemic. It did not prevent or excuse the passage of a Quebec law intended to limit the wearing Islamic (or other religious) symbols by public employees.

Most poignantly, Canada's success in dealing—and dealing reasonably successfully—with a wide range of social problems does not excuse its deplorable lack of success in its dealings with its Indigenous peoples. A sad irony exists in the fact that Canada has done as well or better than any other country in the world in welcoming immigrants from other shores and enabling them to become productive members of Canadian society, while all too many of the country's original inhabitants live in conditions of poverty and deprivation. The discovery of large numbers of unmarked graves of children who had attended church-run residential schools is only the latest tragic chapter in a long, often horrific story extending back for centuries.

It seems worth pointing out that, while denunciations of John A. Macdonald, Egerton Ryerson and others who played roles in establishing the residential school system have become commonplace, ill treatment of Indigenous peoples is not simply a dismal historical artifact. It continues today, in such forms as anti-Indigenous hate crimes, the loss of hundreds of missing and murdered Indigenous women, and the decades-long failure to supply clean drinking water to Indigenous communities. Indeed, one of the reasons Canada scores relatively poorly on many societal metrics compared to other high-income countries is because the country's Indigenous peoples have been denied adequate healthcare, effective social services, and the economic opportunities tens of millions of non-Indigenous Canadians view as their birthright.

Canada is, to be sure, not the only country experiencing fraught and fractured relations with its Indigenous peoples. Similar problems exist, to a greater or lesser extent, in Australia, the United States, New Zealand, and other countries. The challenge Canadians face in righting the wrongs done to Indigenous peoples underlines the fact that this book is about real countries where real people make and carry out social policies designed to solve social problems. That those people often fall short of their goals—indeed, often fall short of virtuous or admirable behaviour—is an unhappy but eternal fact of the human condition. It tells us we must strive harder and remain alert for signs that even now we are falling short of the mark. This book is written with the optimistic view that people of good will can do this.

In this book, we make the assumption that national (and provincial) governments are key actors in the solution of social problems. However, in an age of globalization, this is a contentious claim. Most people will agree that governments still take important actions. Yet others might say that we ignore the critical role multinational corporations and capitalists— that is, bankers and investors—play in government decision-making. They would be right. In this short book, we ignore the ways that corporations and powerful investors influence the decision-making process. We do so because different groups of powerful people combine in different ways to influence particular decisions. The group influencing decisions about green energy, for example, will be different from the group influencing decisions about healthcare or prison reform or workplace safety.

Readers looking for a detailed class critique or condemnation of corporate influence may be disappointed by our failure to discuss these influences. They should assume we understand that, behind every public issue we discuss, and every potential change, there are many powerful voices, both inside and outside Canada, influencing the government. Many of these whisper their counsels in the ears of the powerful, unheard by the general public. But that does not mean these voices go unheeded by those making crucial political and economic decisions that will shape the country's future. It is our hope that in writing this book, we can play a small part in enabling every Canadian to think deeply about the social problems facing their country, and how those challenges might be met and overcome.

Canada's Place

CHAPTER ONE

The Success of Nations

Introduction: What You Can Expect

This book is called *Canada's Place: A Global Perspective* because it's about Canada in comparison with the rest of the world and, especially, in comparison to sixteen similar countries. As we will see, Canada is doing better on a variety of social problems than some of these countries but worse than others. In fact, Canada is pretty consistently a middling kind of country—not too good and not too bad. At first glance, this doesn't make for a dramatic or interesting story. But on closer examination, it does. And one with important lessons for leaders and citizens alike.

Imagine you opened your newspaper today and read the headline, "Today's weather: not too hot and not too cold, in fact pretty ordinary." Likely, you wouldn't rush to read the rest of the weather forecast. Or if the headline was "Today's unemployment rate: a little high but not too high; in fact, just about the same as yesterday"—again, not something you would rush to read about. So why read a book about how Canada is a ho-hum kind of a country, not too good and not too bad? In fact, why read a book about Canada at all?

Well, let's back up a bit. Canada is a middling kind of country, but only within the relatively small set of advanced industrial and post-industrial democracies, which among themselves account for a minority of the world's population. If you were to plunk Canada down in South America or Africa, it would top the lists on most if not all measures of economic performance and population well-being. So, it's a bit like an airline passenger saying they have a ho-hum seat in the first-class section of the plane. Nobody stuck in the back of the plane is going to feel sympathetic for them. Yes, Canada may be a bit ho-hum when compared with the other top nations of the world, but it's still worth our close consideration.

There are many good reasons you might read a book about Canada. It's not the world's biggest country or the world's richest country and it arguably doesn't even have the most beautiful geography, although some might disagree. But if you're reading this book, it's probably because Canada is your country. It's the place where you live, where your family lives, and where you make a living. You may have been born here and have a long history—a long memory—of life in this country. Or you may have come here as an immigrant and grown to love the country as a place of safety and opportunity.

Similarly, if you live abroad, you may admire Canada for some reason. You may even envy the 300,000 to 400,000 people who come to Canada every year as immigrants or refugees. These are all good reasons for wanting to read a book about Canada. They're also good reasons for wanting to think about how Canada is doing: whether it's doing well as a country or just ho hum.

People were not always as indifferent to this question as they seem to be today. Fifty years ago, the topic of Canada—how it was doing, how it might do in the future, and how it might do better—was a very hot topic of discussion. Back in the 1960s and 1970s, many young people were concerned about Canada's future and about Canada's independence as a nation. In particular, they were concerned about Canada's relationship with its powerful neighbour. They didn't want Canada to be economically or politically dominated by the United States. That's because they didn't want our future dictated by American policies. Many people—Canadians and others—felt the United States had taken a few too many wrong turns.

If you were alive then, you may remember lively debates at school about the Vietnam War. If you were living in Canada then, or if you were a Canadian studying abroad, you were very keen to distance yourself from American foreign policy—especially the murderous fiasco of the war in southeast Asia. If you had traveled outside the country—for example, had traveled to Europe in that dramatic tempestuous summer of 1968—you might have worn a Canadian flag on your jacket or on your backpack. You wanted to let everyone know that you were a Canadian, not an American.

You knew that Americans were widely disliked because of their government's policies, while Canadians were not. Canadians, at that time at least, were viewed as international good citizens. Canadians didn't make wars; they tried to end wars through diplomacy. Twentieth-century Canada wasn't known for keeping black people in the subordinate role of second-class citizens, punishing people who held progressive political views, celebrating ostentatious wealth, or promoting evangelical religion at the expense of science.

That concern to distinguish Canada from the United States, and to distinguish us as people from Americans, didn't end in the 1970s. After Vietnam, Canadians watched with horror as American CIA agents promoted right-wing dictators in Central and South America. After 9/11, Canadians watched the Americans involve their country in a foolish and unnecessary war in the Middle East. Most recently, Canadians watched the disastrous presidency of Donald Trump undermine the U.S. Constitution, but, more importantly, undermine international relations and the well-being of Canada.

In short, throughout our adult lives, many of us have been interested in preserving Canada's independence and the ways Canada is different from the United States. Yet repeatedly, Canadians have looked with envy as well as curiosity at America's achievements—at its wealth and power—and wondered if we Canadians should strive to copy American strengths.

At the least, a great many Canadians have continued to compare Canada with the United States and to compare Canadians with Americans. So, if you were hoping that we're going to do that kind of comparing in this book, you will be glad to hear that we will. Yes, we are going to compare Canada with the United States on many important dimensions. However, we're not *merely* going to compare Canada with the United States. We're going to compare Canada with various countries that have qualities Canada ought to copy.

As we will see, these are countries that share many of Canada's goals, values, and ambitions. They are countries in which people lead lives much like the lives we lead in Canada. Perhaps most importantly, they are countries that are more similar to us as *moral commu-*

nities. That's because comparisons with the United States have convinced many observers that, in Canada, we are a different moral community from the United States. Many think that this difference should be better understood, highlighted, and strengthened. So, you might say that the purpose of this book is to make clear how Canadians are different from Americans morally as well as socially, politically, and economically. It is to show how we are similar to many other countries in the modern world, and how we could be better—more consistent—as a moral community.

But what do we mean by moral community? What is a moral community and why should we care about it? Why is a sociologist talking about a moral community, and not a philosopher or a minister of religion? And what if any kinds of empirical data can be brought to bear on the study of moral communities? That is, how could we study Canada in a rigorous way, using data as sociologists like to do, to show whether we are doing well as a moral community, compared to other moral communities? And how can we use data from other countries to help us understand how we could do better as a moral community? That is, what can we learn from the study of other countries that would help us improve as a country? How we could move from being a middling, ho-hum kind of country to a country that better expresses our values, goals, and morals?

To summarize, in this book we will compare Canada with sixteen other similar countries—countries with similar levels of economic prosperity and a similar cultural outlook. Like Canada, these are all modern, stable, prosperous countries. We are going to study whether the measured incidence of social problems in these similar countries varies with their populations' homogeneity and economic inequality, among other things. In this way, we hope to find out how successful Canada is as a society in comparison with other similar societies. On this topic of societal success, Hall and Lamont (2009: 2) write

> A wide range of outcomes can be associated with successful societies, including nonviolent intergroup relations, open access to education, civic participation, cultural tolerance, and social inclusion. We see each as desiderata. However, the priority each should be assigned is open to debate and engaging in that debate could easily absorb much of this volume, leaving little room to consider the issues that most concern us, namely, how institutional and cultural structures feed into such outcomes. Therefore, the empirical outcomes on which we have decided to focus the book are those of population health, taken as a proxy for social well-being. We concentrate on the health status of those living in a particular country, region, or community and what we sometimes describe as "health plus."

We agree with this assessment, and in at least two chapters—on health and addictions, and on accidents—we will specifically adopt this public health perspective. Beyond that, however, we will also look at other indicators that tap more directly into measuring how well we live out Canada's values and institutions, in comparison with those of other countries.

We will focus our attention on common and widespread social problems, because by definition, these are issues we all worry about. To jump ahead a bit, in doing so we will find that the smallest, most homogeneous, most civil and egalitarian countries have the lowest rates of social problems. This, we presume, is because they are better able than other nations to oversee, evaluate, prevent and correct social problems, because they have social cohesion, trust, and social capital. But, as we will see, these same countries also have lower rates of immigration than Canada, and deal with more racism and exclusionary politics than we do. We will have occasion to consider that fact at some length and draw conclusions about it.

Remember, we are not going to consider and compare *all* the nations of the world. We are only going to look at seventeen similar countries. Nor are we going to assess the *relative* importance of population size, homogeneity, and economic inequality in their effects on social problems. Even if we wanted to do this, we couldn't make much statistical headway by comparing seventeen similar countries. On the contrary, we would want to compare the largest possible number of very different countries—clearly, a different strategy from the one we have followed in this book.

Similarly, we are not going to consider all the social problems a country might face. We have identified six social problem domains—namely, economic inequality, social inequality, accidents, crime, health, and environment—and ignored many other possible domains. Within each domain, we consider only a handful of problems and ignore many other problems. However, we consider the domains we have selected to be both socially significant and representative of all the domains we might have considered.

We recognize that the statistics measuring these problems change from year to year, but they tend to change only slightly. The rankings of countries on these measures change very little from one year to another, and countries that score at the extremes on a given dimension—very low or very high—tend to change least. So, for example, if we find Canada scoring very high on immigrant integration in 2020, or the United States scoring very high on homicides in 2021, we should not expect to something very different in 2022 or even 2025.

In the end, by using these statistics, we will identify countries that are doing better than Canada and the reasons for that. As well, we will consider how Canada might achieve similar successes and, thus, come closer to achieving its own self-stated goals as a moral community.

That's the task we've set for ourselves in this little book. If you think about it, you will realize it's a big task for such a little book. However, we don't expect this work to answer all the questions that we are asking. In fact, this is a book of questions about Canada—about its goals and its achievements as a moral community. Using data from various other countries, we see that Canada could be doing much better. That leaves you, the reader, with the task of wondering whether and how we might do so.

After reading this book, you may decide that Canada is doing just fine as a ho-hum kind of a country. You may feel it doesn't matter if we meet our own moral ambitions, so long as we are comfortable and lead pleasant, safe, and enjoyable lives as many Canadians do. You may decide that you want to think about this further and maybe even collect some information of your own about other countries that we discuss in this book. You may even decide to discuss some of these issues with your family, your friends, your neighbours, or your elected political leaders.

The point is, we want you to engage with this problem. If you decide that it's not a problem, or you don't care, well, then just put down this book and turn to some other activity. But if you do think as we do that Canada is dealing poorly with many of its problems—moral, social, economic, and maybe even spiritual—then we hope you will continue reading this book. You may end up thinking about some possible solutions and start to reflect on ways that we might bring about important positive changes in our society. So, with this in mind, let's make a start on the agenda of this book; then, you will be better able to see what you're getting yourself into.

Looking at Social Problems

The first thing you'll notice about this book is that it contains chapters in which we discuss various groups of social problems. This book studies social problems because these are issues that many people discuss in everyday life. They are issues that most Canadians—both policy makers and ordinary citizens—consider worthy of public attention and debate. We think they're matters that trouble many Canadians and that need to be fixed.

Take the example of homelessness. Relatively few Canadians are homeless and live on the street; yet most Canadians would agree that, as a wealthy country, we shouldn't have any Canadians living on the street. Most would agree that being forced to live on the street is a dangerous, unhealthy, and degrading condition. We don't want Canada to be a country that ignores people who are forced to live on the street. To use a term we introduced earlier, we, as members of the Canadian "moral community," don't think homelessness is acceptable. It is, for most Canadians, a social problem that needs to be solved. Failing to address and solve

Homelessness is only one of many social problems that Canadians face as members of a moral community.

this problem reveals a flaw in our moral community: homelessness shows Canadians to be, at best, hypocritical about their commitment to compassion and social justice.

Now, as with any social problem, the social problem of homelessness has certain key features. First, homelessness has many causes that are hard to research and understand. Second, partly for that reason, homelessness is hard to prevent. Third of all, eliminating homelessness will need a lot of thought, action, and money. Fourth, this puts homelessness in competition with other social problems—addiction, crime, discrimination, and so on— that also need a lot of thought, action, and money. Fifth, earmarking time and money to this (or any) social problem may mean raising taxes, and many people don't want to hear that their taxes are being raised. That means, sixth, that our elected leaders must spend a lot of time and political capital educating people about why they should pay higher taxes to solve this problem. A failure to do so may result in the politicians being kicked out of office.

So, all social problems are in competition for public attention and concern, because they are in competition for funding. Now, in this book we do not discuss every social problem we could possibly discuss. In fact, we discuss only six social problem "domains" or clusters: as mentioned, they are economic inequality, social inequality, accidental deaths and injuries, crime and victimization, health and addictions, and environmental and population issues. Within each of these domains, we discuss only a few of the more obvious and arguably more important problems. No doubt, we will miss some important problems in doing this, and may even give too little attention to certain domains. However, remember that our goal is to get you thinking about these issues, not to give you the final answers.

Now, the importance of social problems for us is that lots of people care about them and they carry "weight" in our moral community. Beyond that, sociologists also know how to study and measure them. Sociologists and other social scientists have been studying these same problems for at least a century. And since we understand them and can measure them well, we can readily speak about how these problems change over time and how they vary from one country to another.

True, we are better able to measure some of these problems than others. For example, we do much better at measuring poverty and income inequality than we do at measuring racial discrimination. However, we are getting steadily better at studying even poorly measured problems, and in this book, we will confine ourselves to studying problems that are, in our view, reliably measured. We will also warn you when we suspect the quality of some measurements is flawed.

Our plan is to examine six social problem domains to see how well Canada is dealing with problems in each domain, compared to sixteen other countries. After reviewing the national data and then examining provincial variations, we spend the last chapter doing four things. First, we summarize and confirm the conclusion that Canada is doing a ho-hum middling job, compared to many of these other countries. Second, we consider possible reasons that Canada is doing only a ho-hum job. Third, drawing on what we have started to learn about the best of these comparison countries, we ask what changes Canada might adopt to solve its problems more effectively. Fourth and finally, we consider what Canada and Canadians might have to give up, to make these seemingly desirable changes.

In the end, we may decide that Canada can achieve its moral goals simply by adopting the best, smartest ideas to be found in comparison countries. Or we may decide that Canada can only achieve a few of its moral goals this way. We may feel that our country is just too different, or too dominated by foreign interests, to go any further. Or we may decide that Canada can only achieve certain moral goals by turning its back on others. For example, we may decide that Canada cannot reduce economic inequality without significantly reducing its immigration rate or ethnic diversity. Or it cannot reduce environmental pollution without undermining the economic well-being of several Prairie provinces. In short, Canada may have to reckon with conflicts between moral goals. It may have to make certain difficult choices, such as accepting more diversity and inequality to preserve our multicultural tradition and identity.

The Problems We Will Study

In each of the next six chapters, we will consider particular social problems and compare Canada's experiences with these problems to those of sixteen other countries. Here, it is worth saying a few words about each of these domains and the problems they comprise.

First, as mentioned, we will confine ourselves to problems for which we have reliable measurements. So, for instance, we know we have good data on the number of homicides in a given country. Typically, we have much less reliable data about the number of assaults or thefts, so we will give more attention to homicides than to assaults or thefts. Second, we will focus on problems about which we know Canadians are concerned. These are problems which national surveys show to be the concern of majorities or (at least) sizable minorities of Canadians. Third, we will focus on problems that are, therefore, central to Canada's moral community. Each problem—by its nature and by publicly expressed concern—is something that Canadians claim to feel deeply about, whether it is healthcare, the environment, racial diversity, or child poverty.

One problem we should note from the beginning is Canada's enormous regional diversity, in the moral dimension as in others. People simply don't feel the same about a given social issue in one part of the country as they do in another part. No bigger differences in cultural, social, and political sensibilities can be found in Canada than those between Quebec and Alberta, for example. And these regional differences are critical because the legislative power to deal with many of the problems we discuss in this book is provincial, not federal. The British North America Act of 1867, on which Canada's nationhood was originally based, gives critical decision-making powers (in, for instance, education, health, and social services) to provincial governments.

This has several huge implications. First, it means that different provinces can, and do, deal with issues of poverty, social justice, early childcare, and local taxation in very different ways. Canada, where social problems are concerned, is less a single country than a grab-bag of provincial and territorial political systems. Second, and growing out of this, the statistics we collect for Canada do not reveal a single national mindset or moral community. At least, they do not do so in the way they might in a more homogeneous country with a unitary or centralized government such as Norway or France. Third, when we compare a federal country (like Canada or United Kingdom or the United States) with a unitary country (like Norway or France or New Zealand), we are comparing apples and oranges. At the least, we can feel confident it will be harder to bring about large-scale change in a federal country than in a unitary country. For all of these reasons, we have included a chapter that examines the variation among provinces and territories on all of these social problems.

With these warnings in mind, let us briefly consider some of the evidence we will look at in the chapters that follow. In chapter 2, we will examine the social problems of poverty and income inequality. People have always understood that poverty is a social problem, in the sense that it is bad to be poor and good to be rich. No one wants to be poor and, at its extreme, poverty is life-threatening. Only more recently have people come to understand that income inequality is also a social problem, even when the number of people who are poor is relatively small. It is much less life-threatening to be a poor person in a rich country like Canada than in a poorer country like, say, India. However, psychologically, it is just as bad, or even worse, to be poor in a rich country, because there you are constantly reminded of your failure as well as your deprivation. And, as we will see, relative deprivation also has long-term effects for mental and physical health.

We will see in chapter 2 that we have good data on income inequality for Canada and sixteen comparison countries. Of course, there are scholarly disputes about whether to look at income or wealth inequality. And some scholars dispute whether to look at the data before or after the recipient has been taxed and has received government transfers. There are even more disputes about how to measure poverty, although Canada has, in 2018, settled on a particular metric, the so-called market-basket measure. Disputes remain, because the cost of living varies from one part of Canada to another, as well as between city and countryside. So, we will have to navigate these disputes to reach reasonable and reliable conclusions.

Even more important, we will have to try to introduce cost-of-living considerations into all discussions of poverty and prosperity. In some of the smaller, less well-off towns and cities, you can live reasonably well on $3,500 a month because rents are low, as are transportation and even food costs. This is scarcely possible in the larger cities. Similarly, countries in which people pay higher-than-Canadian taxes but receive higher-than-Canadian minimum wages are also hard to compare with Canada. This, as a colleague recently reminded us, immediately comes to mind when you pay $10 or more for a cup of coffee in Reykjavik or Copenhagen.

To repeat, we are interested in studying problems associated with poverty and income inequality. We are doing this because Canadians have shown, through opinion surveys, voting, and government legislation that these issues are morally (as well as economically and politically) important. In each chapter, we will also consider some new and unresolved issues in that domain, for people who want to think "outside the box."

In chapter 3, we will discuss social problems associated with what people have come to call "social justice" issues. These include issues around job discrimination, wage discrimination (or employment equity), and prejudiced and unfair treatment of other kinds (for example, bullying and hate crimes). Where the victims we discuss in chapter 2 are low-income people, the victims we discuss in chapter 3 are so-called minorities: for example, women, seniors, immigrants, and racialized people. Here, in general, reliable measurements are harder to get and often harder to interpret. This is especially true when people have two or more of these statuses. Then, we focus on what is known as intersectionality—the complex combination of disadvantaged statuses we will discuss further in a later chapter.

For example, it will be hard to show decisively, and with comparable data from different countries, the extent of discrimination against hiring and promoting women for executive positions in business. It will also be hard to show, with comparable data from different countries, the extent of wage discrimination against new immigrants or racialized job holders. Here, we may be able to show that immigrants and racialized workers earn less on average than non-immigrants and non-racialized workers. However, it is often hard to know whether they are victims of discrimination, or if there are other factors (for example, immigrants' language skills) that explain the difference, or whether it is a mix of all these things.

All of that said, it is important to try to measure how Canada is doing on these social justice variables. That's because Canada has committed itself, almost above all else, to protecting and celebrating diversity. That's why, for example, the Canadian Charter of Rights and Freedoms provides protections against discrimination for various minority groups and women but does not protect low-income people or people in precarious jobs. That is also why Canada enshrined multiculturalism in law in 1988.

In chapter 4, we discuss crime and violent victimization. These are much less socially contentious topics than, say, economic inequality or even social justice. Few people are willing to make a case for the social merits or fatalistic inevitability of homicide, kidnapping, rape, or child abuse. However, we face difficulties in studying this social problem domain. First, though we probably have close to complete and reliable information on the incidence of homicide and kidnapping, we can be confident this is not true of rape and child abuse. In fact, few victims come forward to report they have been raped, and even when they do, their cases rarely go all the way to trial. We also rarely hear about abuse within family homes. So, data on many types of crime and violent victimization will be inaccurate or uncertain.

There are other complexities we will talk about later, but you may have already started to think about some of them. For example, how can we be certain if a death has been the result of a homicide, suicide, or accident? Often, it's hard to tell. Equally, how can we be certain if a reported rape was not, as is often claimed by the alleged perpetrator, actually a consensual act or a misunderstanding? In short, we will meet measurement issues in this social problem domain, but there will be no doubt that we are discussing issues about which every moral community has strong views.

One element is added to the discussion mix in this chapter, and that is a discussion of the growing importance of global influences. All the social problems we discuss, crime included, have national and international aspects. For example, rich mine owners in Canada help to create poor mine workers in Africa. However, any given social problem may be dominated by national or international causes. Crime, much more than economic inequality and social inequality, falls outside the control of any single state. Said another way, crime is quickly globalizing with the cooperation of many states and police services needed for effective detection and prevention. This globalization of social problems will also be increasingly obvious in several chapters of this book.

Of course, globalization is a complex topic, and the nature of global connections is rapidly changing. We want to avoid simplifying the topic. In the past decade the tendency of the world's politics, economics and culture has been toward protectionism, isolationism and xenophobia, respectively. COVID-19 has only aggravated counter-globalization, making many nations draw inward in their concerns. There is no way of knowing for certain whether these inward-looking nationalisms will persist or retreat with the resumption of increased trade, travel, and communication. But in the pages that follow, we will assume that globalization does resume, since that is implicit in the expansionary nature of world capitalism.

The topic of chapter 5 is health and addictions. As with crime, so too with health and addiction issues. Little moral ambiguity exists about the desirability of certain outcomes compared to others. In every known society, people prefer good health over bad health, life over death. So, societies that maximize the length and health quality of people's lives are obviously doing a better job—a more morally satisfactory job—than societies that do not do so.

Everyone knows the COVID-19 pandemic is a global problem and outside the complete control of any individual state. That is not to say that states are powerless to detect, treat, and control COVID-19 to a great or lesser degree. We saw evidence of that in varying rates of infection and mortality around the world. Some countries, including the U.S., lost control of this epidemic; others, like Japan, did much better. States have also varied in their ability to secure and distribute anti-COVID vaccines. Here, Canada initially did a poor job, compared with the U.S. and other states. A similar point can be made about the opioid epidemic, which rages fiercely in some countries and scarcely at all in others.

International variations are even more marked when we look at health conditions that typically fall under the scope of local and state administration: for example, infant mortality. Rates of infant mortality, throughout the world, are seen as a prime signal of the quality of healthcare but, beyond that, the quality of life in different countries. The same is likely true of some kinds of cancer, of obesity and obesity-related diseases such as diabetes, and of infectious diseases like tuberculosis, measles, and so on. These diseases or conditions do not usually come into the country from elsewhere; they are usually the product of local demographics and public policies.

Issues of interest in this chapter include the incidence of certain conditions in the population and the healthcare that people can access to mitigate those conditions. So, for example, in some societies, death from work-related cancers will be more common than in other societies, largely because workplaces are not regulated to protect workers' health. And in societies where such cancers are common, some people will be more likely to die of them than others because they cannot get the timely treatment they need.

In chapter 6, we discuss accidental deaths and injuries. This is the second of two chapters devoted to public health concerns, the other being chapter 5 on health and addictions. In devoting two chapters to public health issues, we reveal the belief that poor health, whether accidental or not, is a powerful and revealing measure of how well society is working. A country with a high rate of deaths on the job is a country that does not care for, or take care of, its lower income working people. Obviously, we will find accidental deaths and injuries in every country, just as we will find poverty and discrimination in every country. But at the same time, every country can lessen and reduce on-the-job injuries, just as it can minimize and reduce poverty and discrimination.

Not all accidental deaths and injuries occur at work; in fact, many occur at home and even during leisure activities. Again, they cannot all be prevented, but societies, as we will see, vary widely in how diligently and well they prepare and protect their citizens against these eventualities. This is true whether we consider anti-smoking campaigns, seat-belt campaigns, bicycle helmet campaigns, water-safety campaigns, or speed limits and traffic enforcement practices. Societies have life-and-death decisions to make in all of these areas of life, and some societies do so better than others.

Oddly, though almost everyone experiences an accidental injury at one time or another, most people are unaware of safety issues most of the time. For example, it takes a lot of pedestrian deaths before people mount a campaign to lower speed limits, install traffic cameras, and make streets safer for pedestrians, bicyclists and other drivers. That is because, while we are aware that accidents are unpredictable in the individual case, we often fail to grasp how they are predictable in the aggregate. We learn to think of accidents as unexpected and random, therefore uncontrollable, therefore not worthy of serious efforts to reduce incidence and harm.

Often, where accidents are concerned, we simply blame the victim (as many people also like to do with victims of poverty, domestic violence, or unemployment). However, epidemiological research on accidents shows us clearly there are patterns to accidents—for example, some jobs are more dangerous than others, and some highways are more dangerous than others. The rates of accidents in different times and places are what sociologist Émile Durkheim called *social facts*: they tend to be stable over time and tell us a lot about the social environment.

In chapter 7, we discuss problems connected with the environment. As with problems related to crime, health, and addiction, those related to the environment are increasingly global and will continue to be so. They need global cooperation, which some nations are more willing to provide than others; and they also need national and local vigilance.

So, for example, climate change and global warming are global problems and result largely from more than a century of unregulated and thoughtless industrialization. In every country, the profits of the industrial elites have received the greatest attention, at whatever cost to the ecosphere. Besides that, however, there are also more narrow environmental problems: for example, the national treatment of forests, timberlands, and parklands. In some countries, these have been protected against short-term exploitation and preserved for future use. In other countries, they have not been, resulting in deforestation, forest fires, water pollution, and loss of human life.

As Thomas Malthus pointed out over two centuries ago, there is a close and unavoidable connection between environmental issues and population issues. That's because people need food to eat, air to breathe, water to drink, and so on. The link between environmental quality and population survival is permanent and unquestionable. Therefore, we will also briefly discuss population size and density in this chapter. And, as it turns out, both population size and density are relevant to our discussion in the last chapter. Because as it turns out, with societal success as with many other things, size matters.

Malthus aside, it is only within the last few decades that humanity has started to take environmental concerns at all seriously. So, it is hard to say what position environmental concerns occupy in the Canadian moral community. We do know there is huge regional variation on this issue. Alberta has historically and increasingly based its economic well-being on oil and gas extraction. So, for Albertans, environmental issues like climate change are much less compelling than economic issues like job losses if people substitute hydroelectric or nuclear or wind power for oil and gas. By contrast, environmental issues are very important in British Columbia, Quebec, and Ontario, especially to young people, and especially to people who work in the information economy.

With this understanding of regional variation in mind, in Chapter 8 we compare Canadian provinces and territories with one another. Our goal there is to show that, within Canada, there is a great deal of variation—sometimes as much or more variation as there is between Canada and our sixteen comparison countries. This tells us that comparing Canada, as a whole, to other countries is a risky proposition. Some parts of Canada are doing very much better or very much worse than other parts of Canada. Yet, we will persist in the view that we can compare Canada, as a country, with other similar countries, despite this (often wide) regional variation.

The Countries We Will Study

To understand how Canada is doing with its social problems, we will compare Canadian statistics with statistics from comparable countries. But how should we select suitable comparisons? Some possible comparisons would be misleading or irrelevant. For example, if we were to compare Canada with countries having the most similar population size, we would compare it with Iraq, Poland, Afghanistan, and Morocco. However, the economic, social, and cultural differences between these countries and Canada are just too large.

Similarly, low population density is a defining feature of Canadian society. However, it would not be helpful to compare Canada with countries with the most similar population density: for example, with Libya, Guyana, Botswana, and Mauritania. Again, the economic, social, and cultural differences are just too great between Canada and these other countries.

We could focus on economic similarities and compare Canada with the countries that have the most similar gross domestic product (GDP), a measure of the economy's size. If we do so, we will find ourselves comparing Canada with Brazil, Italy, South Korea, and Russia. Here, the population density, social and cultural differences between these countries and Canada are still too large to make comparisons informative.

In this book, we are going to compare Canada with other countries that have similar values as well as similar economic profiles. In effect, we are comparing similar moral communities. Here, we will use the results of research by Ronald Inglehart, who used data from the sixth wave of the World Values Survey. As you can see from the "mapping" of countries in Figure 1-1 on the facing page, doing so allows us to compare Canada with other English-speaking countries (the U.S., UK, Australia, New Zealand, and Ireland). It also leads us to compare Canada with the countries of Protestant Europe: notably, Iceland, Switzerland, Denmark, Norway, Sweden, the Netherlands, and Finland.

What people in these countries all have in common, according to the World Values Survey is, first, a high regard for self-expression, liberty, tolerance, and wide participation in political and economic decision-making. Second, people in all of these countries put less emphasis on traditional social practices and religious values than other people in the world. People living in the Scandinavian countries of Protestant Europe are even less traditional than people in the English-speaking countries mentioned earlier. In short, the data mapping based on the World Values Survey tells us to compare Canada with other English-speaking countries and with the countries of Protestant Europe.

Note that countries of the Confucian tradition—Japan, Hong Kong, South Korea, Taiwan, and China—are all just as committed to secular-rational values as the people in Scandinavia. However, they are much less committed to tolerance and self-expression than people in Scandinavia and the English-speaking countries, making for a significant cultural difference from Canada.

So, if we are looking for suitable comparison countries, we cannot do better than choose other English-speaking countries, the countries of Protestant Europe, and a few of the more liberal, secular countries of Europe. (Arguably we could have included Austria in this list, but it was situated in a different cultural group by Inglehart. Therefore, we followed his lead

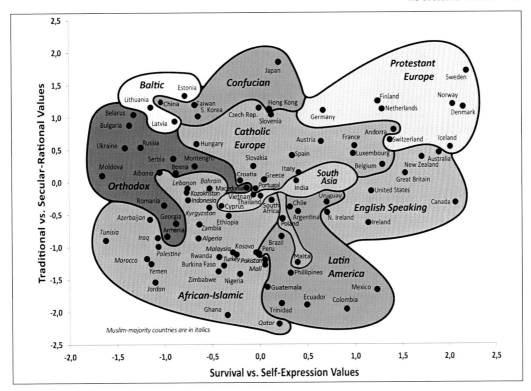

Figure 1-1. The Map of World Values, 2017.

and left it out of our analysis.) Not by coincidence, they are also all classified by Immanuel Wallerstein and his colleagues as similar. Following up on Wallerstein's classic world-system analysis, Babones (2005) has compiled a list that includes only countries that researchers have consistently classified as core societies. If we overlay this list of countries with the English-speaking or Protestant European countries mentioned above, plus France, Luxembourg, and Belgium, we get the following list of comparisons for Canada:

1. Australia
2. Belgium
3. Denmark
4. Finland
5. France
6. Germany
7. Iceland
8. Ireland
9. Luxembourg
10. Netherlands
11. New Zealand
12. Norway
13. Sweden
14. Switzerland
15. United Kingdom
16. United States

Comparing Canada with these other countries makes sense because all of these countries have similar cultural outlooks, similar standards of living, and similar positions in the world economy. This being so, with these comparisons we can hope to learn how Canada is doing, how much better it might do, and how it might go about improving. In short, these comparisons give us a clear idea of Canada's place in the world.

Some social scientists think it would be better to compare countries in a different way, by examining what they call their *cultural tightness* or *looseness*. As Gelfand et al. (2007: 7) tell us, "Societal tightness-looseness has two key components: The strength of social norms, or how clear and pervasive norms are within societies, and the strength of sanctioning, or how much tolerance there is for deviance from norms within societies." As the authors go on to note (2007: 31), the existence of external norms encourages individuals to feel accountable for their actions, further reinforcing those external constraints. Societies that historically found themselves under pressure from the environment or outside forces tended to develop tighter cultures. Jackson et al. (2020) elaborate on this theory:

> Human groups have long faced ecological threats such as resource stress and warfare and must also overcome strains on coordination and cooperation that are imposed by growing social complexity. Tightness–looseness (TL) theory suggests that societies react to these challenges by becoming culturally tighter, with stronger norms and harsher punishment of deviant behaviour. TL theory further predicts that tightening is associated with downstream effects on social, political and religious institutions.

This approach helps to predict how different societies will react to various challenges. In general, the countries we discuss in this book—Canada and sixteen comparison countries—fall on the medium to loose end of the cultural dimension, and are culturally much "looser" than many countries in the developing world.

Figure 1-2 indicates tightness scores for some of the countries discussed in this book. Interestingly, Canada's score indicates it is a relatively "loose" society in terms of social norms. One might speculate that this characteristic helps explain Canada's openness to immigrants from other cultures as well as its ability to sustain the longstanding partnership between English- and French-speaking Canadians.

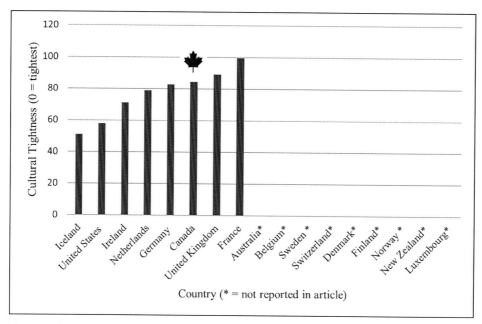

Figure 1-2. Cultural Tightness Scores, Canada and Comparison Countries, 2014.

Some Things We Can Expect to Find

As we will see in this book, many of the problems that afflict Canadians are national in scope and national in origin. They include poverty, crime, illness, and racial discrimination. All of these national problems link, directly or indirectly, to economic inequality. As we will also see, some comparison countries do better than Canada in preventing and solving their social problems. We want to understand how and why they do better. Therefore, we will spend time in the last chapter discussing the countries that do better than Canada in preventing and dealing with national problems.

As we will also see, many of the problems that afflict Canadians today are transnational in origin. They work at a global scale and are outside Canada's immediate control. These problems include certain kinds of crimes, epidemics, environmental issues, and migration issues. Some of our comparison countries do better than Canada in preventing and solving these problems. For example, some do better than others in controlling their borders, some have become global leaders in green energy, and others expend more resources on cybersecurity and education. Again, we will want to understand how and why they do better.

But what should you expect as you dip into this book? To jump ahead a bit, in the end we will consider three main theories about the differences between nations. Call them sameness theory, civility theory, and equity theory. We will compare these three theories as well as seventeen countries.

Sameness Theory: The so-called *sameness theory* focuses on a country's population size and homogeneity. We will consider the possibility that countries with small, homogeneous populations are the best able to mobilize their population to make important changes—changes that help to solve and prevent important social problems.

This prediction is supported by a theory put forward more than 250 years ago by the French political thinker Charles de Secondat, Baron de Montesquieu in a classic book titled *The Spirit of Laws* (1748). According to Montesquieu, small size is necessary if we are to have good laws. Small size also makes it easier to enforce these good laws, to prevent and correct social problems: for example, to catch and punish criminals. However, small size is necessary but not sufficient for good laws and good law enforcement to prevent and solve social problems. Other things (like prosperity) being equal, homogeneous countries can do things that diverse countries cannot. For example, they can mobilize popular sentiment in ways that large, regionally and culturally diverse countries cannot. And small countries are more likely to preserve cultural homogeneity than larger ones.

Let's consider the population sizes of the seventeen countries we review in this book. One (the U.S.) is very large; three (Germany, France, and the UK) are medium-sized, and the rest, including Canada, are small (below forty million people). Ten are in the range of ten million or fewer people (see Figure 1-3 on the next page).

That said, small, homogeneous states typically need other qualities to achieve good laws and good law enforcement. The first necessary quality is internal self-control, or an absence of foreign interference with governance. In fact, Montesquieu saw a susceptibility to foreign conquest and control as the central weakness of small republics. Second, small states also need a reasonable degree of prosperity and stability if they are to prevent and solve social problems. In turn, prosperity and stability are often found in societies characterized by the modern values Inglehart identified in Figure 1-1 earlier: that is, secular-rational and self-expression values.

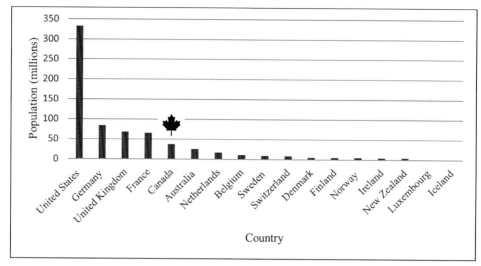

Figure 1-3. Population of Canada and Comparison Countries, 2020 (millions).

Civility Theory: The so-called *civility theory* focuses on a country's norms of politeness and courtesy. It argues that countries will succeed only if they embrace civility and promote civil values to all citizens, would-be citizens, and young children.

A mere celebration of individualistic values—of liberty and self-expression—will not produce civility; indeed, it may often pull in the opposite direction. So, one of the enduring paradoxes of modern societies is that they embrace self-expression and individualized ambitions—as we learned from Inglehart—yet also embrace social forms that tame and civilize rampant self-assertion. People in civilized societies are taught to express their personal sentiments and wishes in ways that neither offend nor frighten other people. We learn that, as citizens, we have responsibilities of respect and politeness to one another, and not merely rights to self-expression.

This learned skill that sociologist Norbert Elias (1978) calls "civility" is a societal accomplishment associated with modernization and nation-building. Civility, Elias shows us, grows up alongside the "rule of law" through written codes, courts, prisons, police officers, and soldiers. Civility is associated with the control and decline of public violence; on the other hand, violence tends to occur in societies that lack stable, accepted, non-violent means of resolving disputes.

Not surprisingly, civility also needs the learning and practice of self-control. As Elias shows, polite manners and strong governments develop together. These two developments make up the so-called civilizing process, which links changes in politics to changes in personal relations (such as table etiquette and good manners). The rise of self-control coincides with the rise of a strong state. It is through the rise of this state that a national culture of civility can develop around matters like good table manners, polite excretion, and private sexuality. A strong nation-state does not guarantee civility, but it makes civility possible.

Equity Theory: The so-called *equity theory* argues that, to be successful, civil (and civilized) values must also be translated into public institutions and governmental actions.

According to Gosta Esping-Andersen (1995), modern societies always promise social improvement and social "solidarity of the people." However, they vary in terms of which particular justice principles they accentuate and which specific notions of social solidarity they pursue. Some states, for example, embrace a notion of equality that invites cooperation and collective well-being. Others, however, embrace a notion that invites competition and the glorification of individual achievement. Because of these different goals, states can have one of three kinds of welfare system, which Esping-Andersen terms liberal regimes, conservative regimes, and social democratic regimes.

Liberal regimes typically provide modest aid to low-income, usually working-class recipients. This aid, which is means-tested and based on strict claim rules, is often stigmatizing. This regime encourages market solutions (like private health insurance) to personal problems (like poor health). It does this either by guaranteeing only a minimum of aid, forcing the recipient to co-pay for services received, or by directly encouraging and supporting private welfare plans, as well as charities.

Conservative regimes also typically provide modest aid to low-income, usually working-class recipients. However, instead of relying on the market to provide the rest, they rely on families to do so. To keep families strong and viable, these regimes encourage family life though traditional family values and family benefits that promote motherhood and through social insurance that excludes non-working wives. They encourage families to care for their own members, with the state stepping in only when the family is no longer able to aid its members. Here too, charities are encouraged as sources of aid to families and individuals.

Social democratic regimes typically provide more generous aid to every citizen. They preserve a high level of basic well-being for all, remove stigma to aid recipients, and give individuals—especially women and children—more agency in their families. By socializing the costs of caring for children, the aged, and the infirm, these regimes relieve many women of what is, often, a crushing burden of care. Doing this, however, means making welfare services such as healthcare and employment insurance into costly public responsibilities to be paid out of general tax revenues. Doing so also encourages states to reduce social problems such as bad health and unemployment through policies that include public health promotion and full employment. Here, charities play only a small role in aiding individuals and families.

As should be obvious, real societies are often a mix of types. Canada, for example, contains some elements of social democratic regimes, such as universal public healthcare. However, it lacks many other elements (for example, universal public daycare for children), leaving these to the market or the family. Thus, it is a mix of social democratic and liberal or conservative regimes.

What's more, wide regional variations are possible within countries. In Canada, for instance, we find variation in welfare regimes from one province to another. That is because education and social services are largely under the control of provinces (not the federal government). So, for example, daycare in Quebec largely follows a social-democratic model, while daycare in Ontario follows a liberal model. Beyond this, many regions or countries of the world, coming out of different cultural and political traditions, have created different welfare regions.

In this book, we will show that societies that do best in preventing and solving social problems are societies that are small and homogeneous. They also put a premium on civility and provide government services that stress equity. These three principles—sameness, civility, and equity—are most evident in the five Nordic countries we examine: Norway, Sweden, Denmark, Finland, and Iceland. They are least evident in the United States and United Kingdom. They are evident to varying degrees in different parts of Canada: for example, more evident in Quebec than in Alberta.

We will argue that each of these three principles contributes significantly to the prevention and solution of social problems. In particular, they contribute by setting the stage for tax collection and an allocation of public funds that is popular, respectful, and equitable. In countries like the United States, where tax collection and the reallocation of funds is shaped by political contention, disrespect for vulnerable minorities, and vast wealth inequality, social problems go largely unsolved and unprevented. In the last chapter of this book, we will go into more detail about the reasons that sameness, civility, and equity are all important principles of social organization. We will also consider how they work together in Nordic countries.

Then, we will consider the difficulties Canada may face in creating this same combination of principles, and therefore why it may have trouble achieving the same success that we witness in the Nordic countries.

Concluding Remarks

This book looks at the relative success of Canada and certain other countries in dealing with some key social problems. In this sense, it looks at Canada's place in the modern world. We will use our three theoretical approaches—sameness theory, civility theory, and equity theory—to try to make sense of why some countries are better than others at handling these social problems.

We recognize that the statistics for each problem and each country we are studying will change slightly from one year to the next. However, what research on such data has shown repeatedly is that for the most part, the rankings of countries will not change much from one year to the next. This is especially true at the ends of each distribution. Middling countries will remain middling countries. From year to year, extremely high-scoring countries will remain extremely high and extremely low-scoring countries will remain extremely low. We can have a high degree of confidence in this outcome.

This book will try to show you how Canada is doing and how it could do better, if it learned from the experience and practices of other, similar societies. However, this is not intended to be a book written for professional politicians and civil servants. We will note some of the main forces militating against higher taxation or a higher minimum wage, free postsecondary education, universal childcare and so on. We will note the federalist political structure is an impediment, but we will not propose a plan to get all the provinces on board. Our goal is not to lay out a detailed framework on detailed issues: How do we overcome Canada's declining union density? How can we bring Alberta to the table to discuss the transition to green energy production? How can we change the minds of most Canadians, who, surveys suggest, oppose more government involvement in the economy and prefer more private consumption to more public goods?

These are all difficult questions to answer, and for the non-expert readers of this book, they would seem confusing and tedious. Instead, we will in the pages that follow argue in favour of taking Scandinavia as a model for solving Canada's social problems. In doing so, we will urge Canadians to think more like Swedes, Danes, Norwegians, Finns, and Icelanders. But if we are successful in this effort, there will still be theoretical and practical work to do. This short book is not the place to undertake that work—only to motivate readers (and voters) to think about and call for such actions by their elected politicians and civil servants.

Finally, in this book we will also consider the possibility there is a strong link between these approaches. Just as certain institutional (welfare) arrangements may need certain cul-

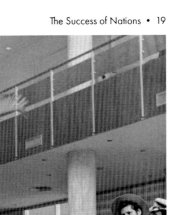

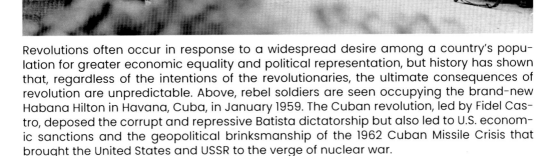

Revolutions often occur in response to a widespread desire among a country's population for greater economic equality and political representation, but history has shown that, regardless of the intentions of the revolutionaries, the ultimate consequences of revolution are unpredictable. Above, rebel soldiers are seen occupying the brand-new Habana Hilton in Havana, Cuba, in January 1959. The Cuban revolution, led by Fidel Castro, deposed the corrupt and repressive Batista dictatorship but also led to U.S. economic sanctions and the geopolitical brinksmanship of the 1962 Cuban Missile Crisis that brought the United States and USSR to the verge of nuclear war.

tural arrangements, so too certain institutional and cultural arrangements may need certain demographic arrangements. Put another way, solving important social problems may call for a particular combination of changes to increase sameness, civility, and equity. Often revolutions take on such major societal changes, as do military conquests; yet often they fail or produce undesired changes, such as political repression. Usually, the most successful efforts at societal change are small and incremental. Thus, we are concerned about how Canada can make many important changes but do so without a revolution.

Canada may not be able to make the important changes needed to prevent and solve our most troubling social problems. Indeed, Canada may have to bear certain demographic, cultural, and institutional costs to make such changes; and some of these costs may be intolerable. We may want to achieve civility and equity, for example, but not at the cost of diversity. With that warning and general outline in mind, we can proceed.

CHAPTER TWO

Poverty and Economic Inequality

As we explore social problems in Canada we'll look first at poverty and the related problem of economic inequality. The two aren't the same, as we will show, but they are related in important ways.

As we will see, Canada is a middling country. Compared to our sixteen similar countries, it has a moderate number of poor people and a moderate degree of income inequality. It also has a moderate degree of wealth inequality and a moderate amount of upward social mobility. On many if not all of these measures, Canada does better than the United States and the United Kingdom, but (with few exceptions) worse than the Nordic countries of Denmark, Finland, Norway, Sweden, and Iceland.

Let's look at the problem more closely and consider why Canada is the way it is. People have been aware of poverty and talked about it for thousands of years. The topic isn't a new one. Poverty isn't something sociologists just discovered, or that policymakers recently started looking at.

Consider some ancient and respected views about poverty. Juvenal, a Roman writer of satires, declared "It is not easy for men to rise whose qualities are thwarted by poverty." People have rediscovered the truth of Juvenal's observation many times over the last two thousand years. If we want society to be equitable and give people the chance to show off their ability, then we cannot tolerate high levels of poverty.

That's because, under such conditions, a great many talented people cannot develop and show their abilities. Poverty prevents them from assuming social roles in which they can benefit society and receive the rewards to which they are entitled. In effect, poverty is unfair. It shortchanges everyone. Poverty robs society of talent that could make everyone's lives better.

Aristotle, a famous Greek philosopher of twenty-four hundred years ago, noted that "Poverty is the parent of revolution and crime." That's a powerful assertion. None of us wants crime and revolution, so we can't want poverty either. If we want to avoid social upheaval and crime, we must do everything we can to prevent poverty.

The ancient Greek historian Plutarch made a similar point: "An imbalance between rich and poor is the oldest and most fatal ailment of all republics." You'll note that to dramatize the problem's extent, Plutarch called poverty the fatal ailment of *all* republics. Even

republics that are otherwise healthy can die of such an ailment.

Frederick Douglass, the American thinker and political figure who made great efforts to improve the condition of Black people in the United States in the nineteenth century, made a similar point. He wrote: "Where justice is denied, where poverty is enforced, where ignorance prevails, and where any one class is made to feel

Although poverty has been a feature of human civilization since ancient times, its persistence in contemporary societies despite vast increases in overall wealth and productive capacity is a tragic social problem. Above, a homeless man walks through downtown Toronto.

that society is an organized conspiracy to oppress, rob and degrade them, neither persons nor property will be safe." A society plagued by endemic poverty will likely see a great deal of violence, instability, crime, perhaps even revolution—and, at the very least, confusion and fear.

Violence, instability, crime, distress—these aren't the only things to be feared when inequality and poverty run rampant. There are other effects we have to consider, too. Mahatma Gandhi, the famous spiritual leader of twentieth-century India, described poverty as "the worst form of violence."

Violence is an interesting word for Gandhi to use. When talking about violence, we normally think about physical abuse and pain. We cannot, however, ignore non-physical—that is, psychological and social—forms of violence. These are the kinds of violent speech or behaviour that degrade other people and undermine their sense of humanity. The sociologist Pierre Bourdieu calls this "symbolic violence." Whatever the physical or economic effects of poverty for poor people, this symbolic violence is harmful. What's more, it doesn't fit with the idea of Canada as a moral community.

Again, these aren't modern concepts. We find them in statements made thousands of years ago. Confucius, a Chinese philosopher who lived about twenty-five hundred years ago, once said, "In a country well governed, poverty is something to be ashamed of. In the country badly governed, wealth is something to be ashamed of." On the one hand, poverty may reflect on the individual who feels ashamed of having missed chances to be wealthier and more successful. On the other hand, a poor person may feel outraged at the failure of society to allow them to show what they can do. Poverty may be a commentary on an individual. But just as surely it can condemn a society as misgoverned and failing to meet its goals as a moral community.

Finally, consider the words of Nelson Mandela, the former president of South Africa and a great leader against apartheid in the twentieth century: "As long as poverty, injustice and gross inequality exist in our world, none of us can truly rest." Mandela reminded us that poverty has practical effects like crime and political unrest we cannot afford to ignore. But he also highlighted the moral effects of poverty, calling on us to live up to our principles as a moral community.

The main problem with poverty is not just that it's harsh and brutalizing. Poverty is also deeply unfair. As the French philosopher Jean-Jacques Rousseau pointed out more than 250 years ago, most social and economic inequality is unfair because it gives some people unjustified privileges or benefits. These privileges, such as inherited wealth, have nothing to do with an individual's merits or talents. It is one thing to lavish praise and wealth on a remarkable scientist, industrialist, artist, or scholar whose work has benefited humanity. It is another thing—a socially unjustifiable thing—to award inherited wealth to the unremarkable child or grandchild of a rich person. It's also impossible to justify celebrating, rewarding, and protecting people who earned their wealth and position through exploitation and duplicity.

There seems to be no Darwinian argument for leaving wealth to one's children. Nor does evidence suggest such inherited wealth is routinely used in constructive, socially beneficial ways. Quite the contrary. Statistics gathered by the nineteenth-century scholar Francis Galton and others show a tendency of merit to regress to the mean over generations. Said another way, talent tends to dissipate and wealth disappear from families over about three generations, taking families from "clogs to clogs" in a century or less. Conversely, the great innovators and fortune-makers of today—for example, the technology giants like Bezos, Jobs, Gates, and Zuckerberg—come from fairly modest families, not from those with inherited wealth.

So, poverty and economic inequality clearly have a moral as well as a practical side. We want to solve the problems of poverty and extreme, unjustifiable inequality because we want to reduce levels of crime and violence, as well as other physical and mental health effects. But we also want to eliminate poverty and inequality because they are unfair. They are morally unjustifiable. They do violence to our moral community.

Explanations of Poverty

Why might societies that claim to be moral fail to deal adequately with poverty and economic inequality? Well, we can draw at least three possible explanations from the theories of sameness, civility, and equity that we discussed earlier. First, a society may be too large and diverse to be able to mobilize public opinion on this topic. As Montesquieu pointed out, in large societies we are likely to find classes of powerful people who oppose changes meant to reduce poverty. Economic inequality may actually benefit an elite which therefore has little interest in solving social problems. This elite tends to oppose high taxes (and the social safety net such taxes might pay for) and a strong state that would regulate their economic interests.

The economic inequality that develops within a large republic also undermines civic virtue and democratic decision-making, according to Montesquieu. A small republic runs more risk of being dominated by outside powers, but a large one is more likely to dominate *other* countries, increasing economic inequality in the world as a whole. In short, small republics are more likely to be peaceful and egalitarian than large ones. On this, Montesquieu writes:

In an extensive republic there are men of large fortunes, and consequently of less moderation; there are trusts too considerable to be placed in any single subject; he has interests of his own; he soon begins to think that he may be happy and glorious, by oppressing his fellow-citizens; and that he may raise himself to grandeur on the ruins of his country. In an extensive republic the public good is sacrificed to a thousand private views; it is subordinate to exceptions and depends on accidents. In a small one, the interest of the public is more obvious, better understood, and more within the reach of every citizen; abuses have less extent, and of course are less protected.

Second, consider the theory of civility and incivility. Societies with too much commitment to individualistic principles tend to show incivility to people who are poor or do not succeed economically. They "blame the victim," on the premise that, had the poor person tried harder, they would have succeeded. Such attitudes are rooted in a worldview called the "just world belief," which holds that a person's own actions will likely bring morally just or fair results to that person. If so, all meritorious actions will be rewarded and all non-meritorious actions will be punished or, at least, not rewarded. Research shows this view is more widespread in the United States than in Canada or Europe. It is also more widely held by rich people and religiously pious Protestants and East Asians than by poor people and the non-religious.

Third, we must consider the degree to which a culture is committed to notions of equality or liberty. Nineteenth-century philosophers recognized two different ways of thinking about freedom. One focused on the theme of liberty—the right to do what one wanted unless specifically proscribed from doing so. This raised the principle of individualism—including freedom of speech, belief, and assembly—to its highest possible degree. The other focused on the theme of equality, if necessary at the expense of personal liberty. For example, the state would have to raise taxes and redistribute wealth to ensure a minimum standard of well-being for all members of society. Only in this way could everyone have some access to education, safety, and health. In the United States, as already mentioned, there is much more resistance to taxation and redistribution than in any of our other comparison countries.

Thus we would expect to find the poverty rate in the United States to be higher than in any of the other comparison countries. Figure 2-1 shows that this is, in fact, the case. Australia, Luxembourg, Canada, the UK, and New Zealand also have relatively high poverty rates, but those rates are still at least one-third lower than the U.S. rate. By contrast, the lowest rates of poverty are found in the three Nordic countries of Iceland, Finland, and Denmark.

Poverty rates track shifts in the overall economy. When the economy worsens, the number of poor people increases. They suffer most from downturns like the Great Recession of 2008–09 and that which was brought about by the COVID-19 pandemic. We still don't know the long-term economic effects of the pandemic and probably won't for several years. Nonetheless, the evidence so far suggests that working in low-paying, part-time jobs put low-income Canadians at greater risk of becoming poor even if they were not poor already (Gaetz et al., 2013).

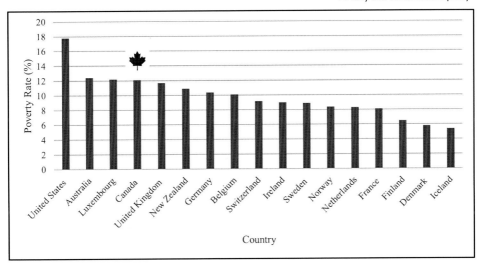

Figure 2-1. Poverty Rate, Canada and Comparison Countries, 2019.

Measuring Poverty: A Continuing Problem

One thing—and perhaps the most important thing—that distinguishes our current understanding of poverty from that of Aristotle, Plutarch, and others mentioned at the start of this chapter is *measurement*. The hallmark of modern scholarship, and especially modern science, is the ability to measure the key ideas about which we make theories. So, to do our job, we must be able to measure poverty well.

We can all agree that poor people do not have enough of what they need for life—that is, not enough food, clothing, and shelter. People without enough money may experience poverty in different ways. But what they share in common is too little money to meet their needs, and a view that they are "failing" in the eyes of society. But what exactly do we mean by this? Without an exact, agreed-upon definition, we cannot make scientific measurements.

We can agree that low-income or poor Canadians are people whose individual or family income lies below a specific level. But how and where do we draw that line? Until recently, three methods were widely used to measure poverty in Canada. The most common measure was the so-called *low-income cut-off* (LICO). It set income thresholds below which a family would likely spend more of its income on basic needs than would an average family of similar size (Statistics Canada, 2013). In principle, poverty could be eliminated, using this measure, if only every household were to spend the exact same fraction of its income on necessities.

A second method was the *low-income measure* (LIM). It recognized that families with different numbers of members, in different-sized cities, will have different cut-off points for poverty. So, this measure counts households according to their *relative* poverty—in other words, not by what they can or cannot afford to buy, but by how much less they have than others. Thus, by this measure, there will always be poor people in any community, because there will always be people with either higher and lower incomes. More important, this measure recognizes what sociologists call "relative" deprivation: how one household compares financially with its neighbours.

A third method of measuring low income, and now Canada's officially accepted measure, is the *market-basket measure* (MBM). The MBM calculates how much income a household needs to feed and house itself, in absolute terms. The MBM looks at the cost of a "basket" of food, clothing, shelter, transport, and other basic needs, considering these costs as necessary for a modest standard of living (Heisz 2019). Such costs are then used to set thresholds of poverty. Those vary depending on region and family size. Those with incomes below the threshold for their region and family size are considered to live in poverty.

It's difficult to find detailed Canadian information on the budgets of poor people: what they earn and what they buy. However, we know from Statistics Canada that, in 2017, families in the bottom income quintile (i.e., the lowest 20 percent of the population) spent an average of $33,764. Of this, 34.8 percent went for shelter, 15.1 percent for transportation, and 14.3 percent for food.

These subsistence items also include goods needed to satisfy at least some community norms—for example, the kinds of clothing worn in a community. Parents no matter how poor cannot send their children to school in rags. Thus, this measurement of poverty takes into account to some degree relative deprivation. However, the MBM is mainly a measure of absolute deprivation: what fraction of households can afford the minimum needed to survive in a given community.

Depending on how we define and measure poverty, the number of Canadians deemed to be "low income" will vary (as we see in Figure 2-2 below), leading to political and social confusion.

Measurement Method	Reported Poverty Rate (%)
Low-income measure (LIM) (after tax)	14.20
Low-income cut-off (LICO) (after tax)	9.20
Market-basket measure (MBM)	12.90

Figure 2-2. Reported Poverty Rate in Canada by Measurement Method.

On the one hand, governments want to show low and declining poverty rates, which is harder to do with the (relative) LIM measurement. On the other hand, the market-basket measure comes closest to people's common sense understanding of poverty since this measure allows people to imagine spending an income. Largely to quell this confusion, in August 2018 the federal government officially adopted the MBM as its official way of measuring poverty.

Unfortunately, the MBM has flaws. The current MBM was last updated in 2008–10 (Heisz 2019). But since then, a so-called affordability crisis has swept through major cities including Vancouver and Toronto. Housing and childcare, as just two examples, cost much more today than they did in 2010. And the skyrocketing cost of rental housing hit low-income Canadians hardest, since they are least likely to own their homes. That means the MBM may not be doing Canadians justice as the official poverty line.

Stapleton and Yuan (2019) note at least six "externalities" that raise the actual cost of eating far beyond what estimates of poverty usually suggest:

> Externality #1: Public transit, biking, and walking are the normal modes of transport for low-income people. But even the smallest subcompact car can cost 37 cents a kilometre to run. So, the transportation they rely on raises the cost of the diet.

Externality #2: Staples (like rice and potatoes) in economy sizes and tinned goods are heavy. A single person without access to an automobile likely would need at least two trips to safely carry or roll even the most inexpensive diet to their home. That could raise the cost of the diet by $10 a month.

Externality #3: For low-income adults living in a safe and secure apartment, storing canned and dry goods is easy. However, for single people living in rooming houses, items left in common spaces or unsecured rooms can easily disappear, adding to the cost of the diet.

Externality #4: To safely store more than 30 kilograms of dairy products, meat, fruits, and vegetables, you need a refrigerator. Many rooming houses do not allow small fridges and insist instead that tenants share large, central fridges. Freezer space in a central fridge is almost always shared among rooming-house tenants and space is limited, so people may not be able to buy in large, lower-cost quantities.

Externality #5: People who live in safe, shared accommodation usually have access to a stove and oven. Those who do not are likely to use a hot plate, a toaster oven, or a microwave. However, all of these cooking devices draw costly electricity. As well, hot plates are dangerous to run, especially in buildings with old wiring.

Externality #6: Low-income people usually know what nutritious food is. However, what they value most is a full stomach. Without the means to buy enough healthy, fresh food and the worry there won't be enough of it, they are likely to buy inexpensive and filling food with less nutrition: yet another food externality.

Beyond this, the MBM is hard to use if our goal is to compare countries. This problem gets even worse when we compare seventeen countries. Therefore, the Organization for Economic Co-operation and Development (OECD), a group whose thirty-seven members are mainly high-income countries, does not use a market-basket measure when assessing poverty in its member nations. Instead, it uses something closer to the (relative) LIM measure. That's essentially the measure used in Figure 2-2 above.

Reviewing the published literature on poverty rates, Morelli et al. (2014: 25) write

If a "less poor" country is one with a "single digit" poverty rate (where between 5 and 10 percent of its population are poor), 17 countries have hit that target in the mid- to late-2000s…. The Scandinavian and Nordic nations are generally lowest, along with a number of "middle" Western, Central, and Eastern European nations who have joined the EU 27 (from Belgium and the Netherlands west to Luxembourg, Germany, France, Austria, plus Switzerland, the Czech Republic, Slovakia, Hungary, Slovenia, and Romania). This pattern has been more or less the same since the first LIS measures appeared 20 to 25 years ago, though the number of nations has now expanded considerably. Taiwan weighs in with the 17th lowest poverty rate—about 9.5 percent. Another nine nations have relative poverty rates from 10 to 15 percent, including Italy, Spain, Greece, Poland, Estonia, Canada, Australia, Ireland, and South Korea. Three rich nations are between 15 and 19 percent: the United Kingdom (15), the United States (18), and Israel (19). Moving to the MICs, six countries overlap the three rich nations in the 15 to 20 percent range, with Russia having a poverty rate below the United States and Israel, and Uruguay and Mexico more or less even with the United States. Finally, Colombia, India, and Brazil were all at 20 percent poverty. Poverty rates are 25 percent and above in Guatemala, China, South Africa, and Peru. In short, the range of comparable relative poverty rates from the most comparable source extant varies by a factor of five.

The OECD defines "poverty" as the share of people living on less than half the median disposable income in their country. The OECD report notes, "The use of a relative income threshold means that richer countries have the higher poverty thresholds. Higher poverty thresholds in richer countries capture the notion that avoiding poverty means an ability to access to the goods and services that are regarded as customary or the norm in any given county." By this measure, the average relative poverty rate was 11.7 percent in 2016 for the entire OECD group of countries. Poverty rates were highest in United States at almost 18 percent and lowest in Denmark and Finland, where poverty affected only 5 percent to 6 percent of the population.

Merely measuring something as basic as "poverty" takes painstaking work. Beyond that, many measurements contain more or less hidden political and ideological assumptions. They can also have political effects. Many assumptions and potential biases enter the measurement, no matter how we measure an idea like poverty or inequality. We need to keep all of these matters in mind when examining and interpreting the data in this and other chapters.

Poverty and Mobility

Often, low-income people try to solve the problems of wealth inequality through upward social mobility. When the economy is doing well, most people prosper, and many are upwardly mobile. But social mobility by itself does not create economic equality. Vast inequalities of wealth and power persist even in societies with many opportunities for advancement, like the United States and Canada in the mid-twentieth century. And when wealth is shared unequally, there are fewer opportunities for upward mobility even if the economy is thriving.

When the economy is growing, education opens the door for many poor and middle-class people to enter positions of authority and esteem. Some even earn a high income, and a few may become wealthy. Intergenerational economic mobility is much higher in Canada than in many other countries, including the United States. It is nearly as high in Canada as it is in Nordic countries like Denmark, Norway, and Finland.

The OECD devised an ingenious way of measuring and discussing intergenerational social mobility. The results are displayed in Figure 2-3 below. They ask, with current rates of intergenerational mobility, how long it would take for a member of a low-income family to reach the average income of that country. In countries with the most opportunity for upward mobility, low-income people will take the least number of generations to reach the average income. By this measure, in our comparison group, the countries with the highest rates of mobility are four Nordic countries—Denmark, Norway, Finland, and Sweden—followed by New Zealand and Canada. The United States and United Kingdom fall around the middle of the pack.

Germany and France have the lowest rates of social mobility among our comparison countries. As Figure 2-3 shows, it takes about six generations for low-income people to reach the average income. It takes a low-income family an estimated five generations to move up to the average in the United States and United Kingdom, and four generations in Canada. The same move takes only two generations in Denmark and three in Norway, Finland, and Sweden.

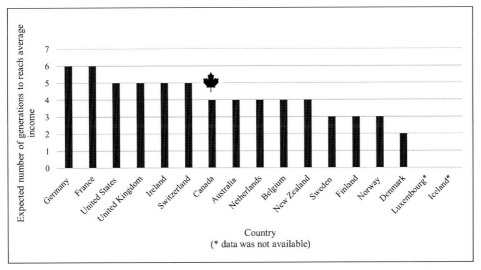

Figure 2–3. Estimates of Intergenerational Mobility, Canada and Comparison Countries, 2018.

For the most part, different rates of mobility speak to differing access to formal education. Formal education brings low-income people major benefits in all industrial societies. However, students born into higher-income families benefit the most from education, because they already possess cultural and social capital. These are the valuable visible and invisible skills and knowledge learned from parents and peers. Thus children from higher-income groups do better in the classroom and are more motivated to continue on to higher education.

Among the most notable beneficiaries of formal education in Canada are immigrants and their children. The influx of highly educated, skilled immigrants benefits Canada in many ways, but it hasn't reduced wealth or income inequality. In fact, it does not even erase the competitive advantage of trained native-born people. Despite our commitment to a prosperous multicultural society, Canada suffers from "brain waste." Skilled immigrants face systematic barriers such as the devaluation of their foreign credentials and work experience, despite a Canadian immigration policy that invites educated foreign professionals to apply.

As a result, many skilled immigrants experience downward mobility in Canadian society, at least for a while. Many former lawyers and doctors, because of their unrecognized credentials, end up in low-paying, less skilled jobs. Failure to adequately recognize foreign qualifications raises many barriers for skilled immigrants. Rather than fully using their skills and education and being integrated into Canadian society, far too many immigrants languish in jobs for which they're overqualified.

Other things being equal, young people born abroad, who receive their education and work experience in Canada, fare better than those who immigrate as adults. Yet many international students leave the country after graduation, due in part to visible and invisible social barriers. For example, some don't want to report repeatedly and provide documents to the immigration authority. Some dislike the mismatch between public holidays in Canada and those back home, making it hard to visit their family and friends. Some feel excluded from public and social activities because of difficulties speaking English or French. Others complain about the cold climate, or report that they face discrimination during their stay in Canada.

Income and Wealth Inequalities

By *wealth*, we mean all the property and financial assets that belong to a family or individual. This will include the ownership of homes, real estate, stocks and bonds, savings, and physical property such as cars, jewelry, art, and furniture, to name a few. If we look at the range of wealth in our society, we find that it is even more extreme than the range of incomes.

The wealthiest 1 percent of Canadians command far more wealth, influence, and power than the bottom half of the Canadian population combined (see, for example, Hastings and Domegan, 2013). What's more, the share of wealth held by the world's wealthiest citizens rose steadily in the last fifty years. French economist Thomas Piketty notes that, as a result, economic inequality today is as high as it was just before the Great Depression of the 1930s (Piketty and Saez, 2003; Piketty, 2013).

Inequalities in wealth are different from those based on income. For example, although the Waltons are the wealthiest family in North America, family members do not earn an income, salary, or wages for hours of labour worked. Instead, their income comes from invested capital. Most enjoy a high standard of living based on the wealth they received or inherited from the founder of Walmart. Similarly, by converting their income into capital, even modestly wealthy Canadians can preserve and expand their wealth through property ownership, stocks, and other investments. By contrast, unless they were born into wealthy families, even the highest-earning doctors, dentists, and lawyers will need to work for years to pay off student debts and cover other living expenses.

Wealth inequalities preserve a country's class system by ensuring that wealthy families keep control over huge sums of wealth and power. By contrast, *income inequalities* divide the working population into status groups with different earning levels and lifestyles, based on different types of work. Data from the World Bank show that wealth inequality is very high throughout the world, and uniformly higher than income inequality (which we discuss in detail below). As we see in Figure 2-5 below, Gini indexes for wealth inequality are much higher than those for income inequality. The *Gini coefficient* gives a measure of inequality on a scale from 0 to 1. A Gini coefficient of 0 would represent a country with complete equality, while a Gini coefficient of 1 would represent a country with complete inequality.

The Gini coefficient of wealth inequality for the world as a whole was 0.885 in 2019. Canada recorded a Gini coefficient of 0.728. For Finland the figure was 0.742, for Denmark 0.838, for Norway 0.798, and for Sweden 0.867. For the United States, the Gini coefficient of wealth was 0.852. As happens many times in the course of this book, Canada comes in around the middle of the pack. Nine countries in the comparison group posted higher Gini coefficients and were more unequal than Canada in how wealth is distributed. Seven posted lower figures and were more equal in that regard.

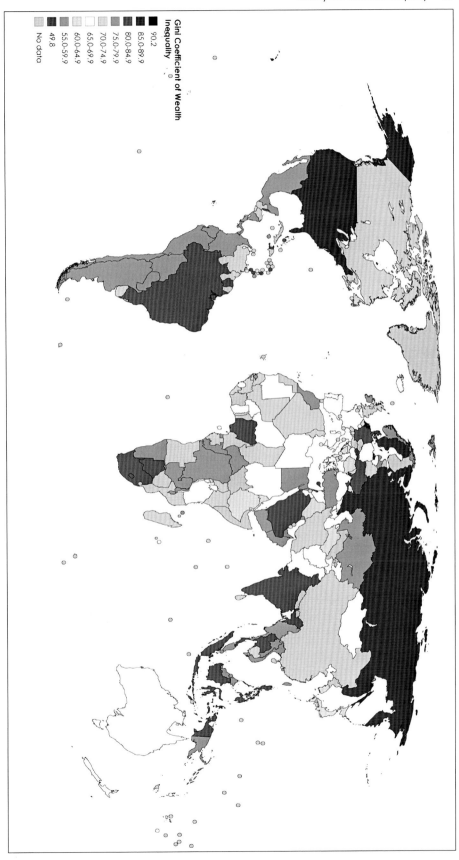

Figure 2–4. World Map of Gini Coefficients of Wealth Inequality.

Gini Coefficient of Wealth Inequality

90.2
85.0–89.9
80.0–84.9
75.0–79.9
70.0–74.9
65.0–69.9
60.0–64.9
55.0–59.9
49.8
No data

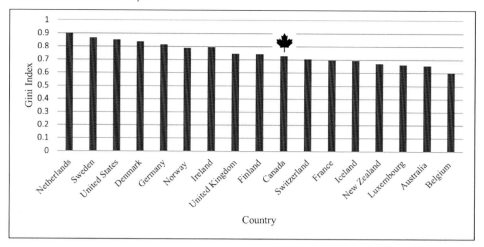

Figure 2-5. Gini Coefficients for Wealth Inequality, Canada and Comparison Countries, 2019.

You might expect the Nordic countries to have low levels of wealth inequality, but this is not the case. They do have low levels of *income* inequality, meaning that incomes are relatively equal for everyone. However, wealth inequality in these countries is very high, and a small minority of the people owns most of the wealth. Since the Gini coefficient for wealth for the world as a whole is 0.885, evidently Canada and its comparison countries are somewhat less unequal than many other less industrialized, lower-income countries.

In short, income and wealth are linked, but they are not the same. Income describes how much money an individual or household earns in a year, while wealth describes how much an individual or household's possessions are worth. Wealth includes property, stocks, and other investments. As the OECD defines it, "Wealth data refers to net private household wealth, that is the value of all assets owned by a household less the value of all its liabilities at a particular point in time."

Earlier we referenced economist Thomas Piketty. In his book *Capital in the Twenty-First Century* (2013), Piketty shows that wealth inequality is higher today than at any other time in the last hundred years. After 1929, the Great Depression, the Second World War, and the rise of welfare states throughout the industrial world interrupted two centuries' worth of growing wealth inequality. But in the last fifty years, with globalization and market deregulation, wealth has reasserted itself, and imbalances of wealth have regained their historically high levels. On this, the OECD (2019) reports

> Household wealth is much more unequally distributed than income. On average, households in the top 10% of the wealth distribution own more than half (52%) of all total household wealth, and as much as 79% in the United States. In comparison, the richest 10% of income earners get on average around a quarter (24%) of all cash income, ranging from 20% in the Slovak Republic to 36% in Chile. While wealth inequality is higher than income inequality in all countries reviewed, countries with lower income inequality levels are not necessarily those with low wealth concentration, as witnessed by the examples of Denmark, Germany and the Netherlands.

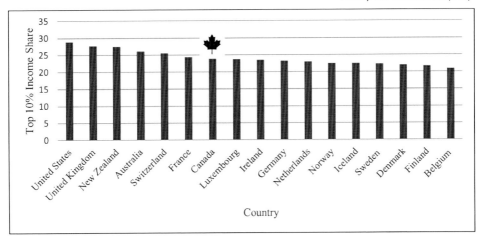

Figure 2-6. Income Share of the Top Ten Percent of Income Recipients in Canada and Comparison Countries.

The OECD data shown in Figure 2-6 reveal the top 10 percent of Canadian income recipients accounted for one-quarter of all income that Canadians earned. Wealth is even more concentrated. The top 10 percent of Canadian wealth-holders control about one-half of all wealth. By contrast, the top 10 percent of Belgian earners laid claim to only about 20 percent of all income, while the top 10 percent of Belgian wealth-holders controlled about 42 percent of the nation's wealth. The numbers are similar for Finland (20 percent of incomes, 45 percent of wealth) and Norway (22 percent of incomes, 52 percent of wealth). Thus, Belgium, Finland, and Norway are close to the OECD averages on both counts. Canadian wealth was more concentrated than in those countries, though less concentrated than in the United States.

Through various inheritances—economic, cultural, and social—people born into wealth will likely stay wealthy. And if they are smart, they convert that advantage into even more financial, cultural, and social power. They also collaborate with other powerful and well-placed groups to influence lawmaking and promote political views and public policies tailored to their interests. They promote this dominant ideology through various means, including ownership of media outlets and donations to political parties and movements meant to influences public policy.

Huge inequalities of wealth cause significant social and political problems. First, people who have *not* amassed wealth rightly feel society is unjust. Often, this sense of injustice translates into support for populist movements that challenge the status quo, but frequently hurt other poor and disadvantaged people. Second, the wealthy use their wealth and power to influence and even undermine democratic decision-making and skew legislation in their favour.

Measuring Income Inequality

Though we may have trouble defining and measuring poverty and wealth, we can measure income inequality well. Earlier we mentioned a widely accepted measure of inequality, the Gini coefficient or index. When measuring income inequality, a perfect score of 0 on this index represents complete equality across a society, while a score of 1 reflects total inequality. To picture this, imagine dividing $1,000 among 1,000 people. If every person received $1, the Gini index would be 0. If one person received $1,000 and the remaining 999 people received nothing, the Gini index would be 1.

Using this measure, we know for certain that income inequality increased in Canada over the past twenty years. During the 1980s, Canada's Gini index was about 0.281. By the late 2000s, it had risen to about 0.32. This score is far lower than the highest Gini scores on record. To put it in context, the current Gini index for the U.S., according to the OECD, is 0.414. On the other hand, the Gini index for Iceland is only 0.25. In general, we find the highest Gini scores—ones in the range of 0.5 to 0.6—in the least developed nations of Africa and South America. By contrast, the states of North America, Europe, and the rest of the developed world are wealthier, have fewer desperately poor people, and are more equal in how income is shared.

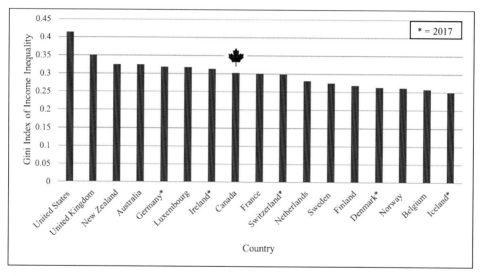

Figure 2-7. Income Inequality across Canada and Comparison Countries, Using the Gini Index, 2018.

Figure 2-7 shows that, even after taxes, income inequality in Canada is higher than in the Nordic countries and much of Western Europe. However, it is lower than in most other English-speaking comparison countries, including the United States, Britain, Australia, and New Zealand. The Nordic countries show the highest rates of income *equality*, while the United States and United Kingdom showed the highest rates of income *inequality*.

Another way to measure income inequality is to look at how much income is earned by the top tenth percentile of the income distribution. The data we examined earlier, in Figure 2-6, show that we get a slightly different view of income inequality using this measure than by using the Gini index. In fact, the cross-national differences are more extreme when we measure inequality this way. However, except for the United States, the main outliers in this regard are lower-income or "developing" countries like South Africa, China, Colombia, Brazil, and India. They are far more unequal in their income distributions than Canada and our sixteen comparison countries, even including the U.S.

In recent years, researchers have debated the merits of discussing income inequality as opposed to wealth inequality. Of the two, wealth inequality is probably more important.

After all, wealth underlies power and prominence in a society. The most influential people are usually the wealthiest people, not those earning the most in a given year. However, data on incomes are easier to come by than data on wealth, so income inequality is easier to measure. And as we have said, there is some connection between wealth and income, however imperfect.

Income inequality grew in many countries over the past quarter-century. It increased most in rapidly growing and industrializing countries like India, China and South Africa. It grew slightly in the United States and even in the Nordic countries of Finland, Denmark and Norway. As we see in Figure 2-8, it decreased slightly in Canada between 2007 and 2018.

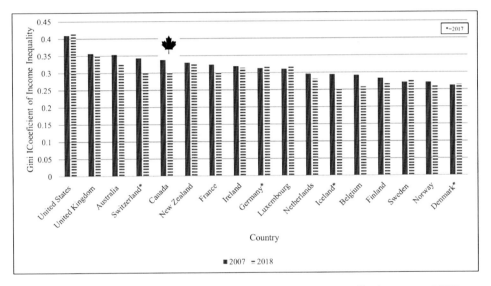

Figure 2-8. Change in the Gini Coefficient of Income Inequality between 2007 and 2018 in Canada and Comparison Countries.

Attitudes to Poverty and Redistribution

As noted earlier, there exist different ways to measure and explain poverty. Some people blame internal causes, such as laziness, addiction, or lack of intelligence. Others blame external causes, like discrimination or high unemployment rates. Yet a third group blames chance, bad luck, or fate. Most people recognize that many factors control a person's financial success or failure. However, opinions begin to differ when individuals discuss which cause is most significant. In Canada, for instance, people usually consider external social forces—for example, downturns in the economy—as more significant in causing poverty than internal or personal flaws. It is largely because Canadians do not blame the victims that we support government intervention and the creation of social safety nets, such as welfare.

On the other hand, people in the United States tend to think that, no matter what external forces are working against individuals, the final cause of poverty is individuals themselves. The American credo declares individuals responsible for their own opportunities. American values—such as the idea that people need freedom, not welfare—reflect this credo. Americans more often view freedom in terms of liberty to succeed (or fail) than as equality of treatment.

That's why Americans are less likely than people in Canada and the Nordic countries to support government redistribution of wealth, higher taxes, or better social programs (such as universal healthcare). As we see in Figure 2-9 below, countries differ markedly in their efforts to reduce poverty through taxes and transfer payments. Not surprisingly, the United States puts the least effort into decreasing poverty in this way—a stark contrast to the Nordic countries. For its part, Canada resembles the U.S. more than the Nordic countries. As Figure 2-9 shows, Canada reduces poverty only by about 44 percent through taxes and transfer payments.

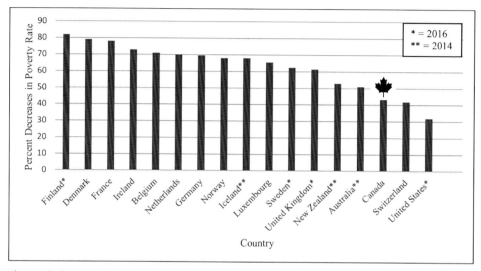

Figure 2-9. Percent Decrease in Poverty Rate through Taxes and Transfer Payments, Canada and Comparison Countries, 2015 or Most Recent Data Available.

Social benefits "in kind" serve as one way in which governments help ease poverty. "In kind" means benefits are given as services, rather than as cash transfers. For example, they might include a school lunch program for students who need it, or free medical care for seniors and veterans. As we see below in Figure 2-10, France offers the highest rate of benefits in kind at more than 19 percent of the country's total gross domestic product. By contrast, Canada, Iceland, and Ireland commit less than 10 percent of their respective GDP to these social benefits.

Sharp and Capeluck (2012: 2) note that

> Among the 35 OECD countries for which data are available, Canada ranked 24th in terms of after-tax income equality in the late 2000s. Canada also had the 25th lowest income inequality offsets among 30 OECD countries; the effect of taxes and transfers on income inequality in Canada was 0.030 points or 20.4 per cent below the OECD average. If Canada's redistributive effort were to be raised to the OECD average, nearly two thirds of the increase in after-tax inequality that has taken place in Canada since 1981 would be eliminated. Equally, if the level of redistributive effort that was in place in Canada in 1994, the year where redistribution was greatest, had still been in place in 2010, one half of the rise in after-tax inequality between 1981 and 2010 would be reduced. Canada thus has much room to increase its redistributive effort. What is needed is political will.

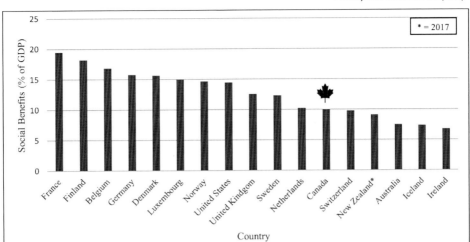

Figure 2-10. Social Benefits to Households as Percentage of GDP, Canada and Comparison Countries, 2019 or Most Reccent Data Available.

Because of different beliefs and policies, people in different countries pay different amounts of taxes. One way to measure this difference is to look at taxes as a percentage of a country's total economic output (or GDP). In Sweden, taxes account for 51 percent of GDP, compared to 43 percent in Finland, 34 percent in Canada, and only 24 percent in the United States. The average for member countries of the OECD is 35 percent. Societies that support government intervention, like Sweden, accept higher levels of taxation, while the opposite is true for nations like the U.S.

Governments influence wealth inequality largely through tax policy, including different tax rates for different sources of income. Canada taxes capital gains (net proceeds from selling an asset) and dividends from Canadian companies at lower rates than employment income. Wealthy people tend to earn much more of their incomes from capital gains and dividends than non-wealthy people, and therefore get to hold onto a much larger share of their income as wealth than others do. Marx might say this is a legal mechanism to ensure that one's relationship to means of production determines class position.

Taxation has a dramatic effect on Gini indices for different countries. First, progressive taxation regimes work to equalize after-tax incomes in a country because not only do you pay more total taxes the more you make but you also pay more tax as a proportion of your total income. Second, governments provide after-tax benefits in kind that (begin to) equalize living standards between rich and poor. Typically, countries with high levels of inequality *before* taxes also have the top (though lowered) levels of inequality *after* taxes. By both measures, the United States and the United Kingdom display high levels of income inequality. Canada has medium levels and the Nordic countries low levels of inequality.

However, there are some important exceptions to this rule. For example, Ireland uses taxation as a way to reduce income inequality through transfer payments and benefits. Similarly, Nordic states have long used taxation as means for indirect redistribution through free education, unemployment benefits and social housing. As noted, both Canada and the Nordic countries have lower levels of inequality than the U.S. Compared to the U.S. and UK, Canada does well. But the Nordic countries have been even more successful in setting up social policies that benefit people in need. There are many reasons for this difference.

Overall, the Nordic countries developed more successful social policies to invest in human capital, welfare, and gender equality.

The U.S. did not always place behind these other countries on poverty rates. In the 1970s, Canada, Norway, and Sweden all posted higher rates of absolute poverty than the United States. But over the last twenty years, all three recorded lower rates of poverty. The U.S. experienced an economic boom in the 1990s, reducing poverty levels. But without a satisfactory social safety net, poverty rates rebounded when economic conditions deteriorated. By contrast, countries that worked to provide sustainable aid, like Norway and Sweden, saw steadily improving conditions for the poor.

When governments fail to address poverty, political and social problems fester and spread. Beyond the effects of inequality on health, crime, and limited educational opportunity, inequality also weakens social solidarity. In particular, economic hardship—like that faced by the poor in an increasingly unequal society—undermines people's confidence in civil institutions (Lamprianou and Ellinas, 2017). The Brexit vote in 2016 shows this trend. Impoverished regions of the UK that saw deep cuts to welfare programs and infrastructure spending as well as a loss of good jobs voted to leave the EU, while prosperous regions mainly voted to remain. This shows how people's confidence in the status quo falls when they are victims of inequality. Ironically, the political and social policies that harmed the economic well-being of these regions had little if anything to do with the EU. But that nuance was lost in the sound and the fury of the Brexit campaign.

The view that immigrants and big government pose a threat to well-being has turned voters all across the West towards far right and populist movements. These include supporters of Donald Trump's Republicans in the United States, Alternative for Germany (AfD) in Germany, and the Leave campaign in the 2016 UK Brexit referendum. What these voters share is dissatisfaction with economic inequality and their declining status, which they think results from globalization.

In short, when people are angry and frightened by the prospect of downward status mobility, they tend to support antidemocratic actions by their leaders. Ironically, the leaders they support often fail to correct the problems of economic inequality. They may even, through tax cuts for the rich as in the U.S., make things worse.

The Rise of Precarious Work

Over the past fifty years, many unionized, well-paying manufacturing jobs vanished in Canada and other high-income countries. Causes include automation as well as the movement of plants and jobs to countries with lower wages.

A shift also occurred from permanent to temporary work—that is, employment lasting six months or less, often referred to as the *gig economy*. Since 1998–99, the growth in temporary and short-term jobs outpaced growth in the number of permanent jobs (Statistics Canada, 2018). The percentage of Canadians employed temporarily rose from 12.0 percent in 2016–17 to 13.6 percent in 2017–18 (Statistics Canada, 2018). While this one-year increase may sound small, think about what ten or twenty such increases would add up to, and you get a clear idea of what young workers face.

Temporary work is sometimes called contract work, because employees must rely on a chain of short-term contracts to cobble together a living wage. In 2016–18, around 20 percent of employment gains came from such temporary work (Statistics Canada, 2018).

The rise of precarious employment can be symbolized by the transition from high-paying industrial jobs like those held by the steelworker (right) to part-time, modestly paying positions like those of today's coffeeshop barristas (above). People still work with their hands but in different ways and for lower pay. The steelworker was photographed by noted film director Stanley Kubrick when he worked as a photographer for *Look* magazine in 1949.

Temporary work falls into a broader category of work known as *non-standard or precarious employment*, which is the fastest-growing type of employment in developed countries, including Canada. It includes jobs with one or more of the following features: part-time employment, self-employment, fixed-term work, temporary work, on-call work, homework, and telecommuting. Non-standard work accounts for about one-third of all jobs in Canada. As well, many people are overqualified for the jobs they hold.

With the rise of precarious employment, more Canadians work irregular hours, and not by choice. Between 1994 and 2014, the percentage of the labour force with "standard" Monday-to-Friday work hours fell from 74.5 percent to 66.5 percent, with more Canadians working for pay on evenings and weekends. This means fewer people can synchronize their daily routines with needed services and programs as well as family and community activities. Low-income households suffer the greatest impact from this shift.

Income inequality has also increased, up by almost 10 percent since 1994. Much of the increase occurred in the 10-year period from 1994 to 2004. The level of inequality since then has remained relatively stable. Even as incomes rise, the top 20 percent of Canadians pull in the lion's share. According to the Conference Board of Canada, the gap in real after-tax average income between the richest and the poorest grew by over 40 percent between 1994 and 2009.

We can, however, offer some good news to conclude this section. First, the overall incidence of poverty declined by 44 percent between 1994 and 2014. The poorest Canadians benefited from real increases in income over this period, although these increases were not equally enjoyed by all. Those still most at risk from poverty include children, older adults, Indigenous people, people with disabilities, and single-parent families—especially those led by women. In fact, despite changes in the tax system that benefit seniors, the poverty rate among Canada's seniors has risen since the 1990s, and, again, is most pronounced among women.

As well, fewer Canadians today work more than 50 hours per week. The percentage of Canadians in the labour force working more than 50 hours per week fell steadily after hitting a peak in 1994 of 14.6 percent. This downward trend reduces the risk of work-related injuries and poor health associated with long hours. Finally, more employers now offer flexible work hours. Workers can better determine when their workday begins and ends. While such flexibility does not typically reduce total number of hours worked, it does provide employees with a greater sense of control over how they use their time.

Concluding Remarks

We can measure poverty and economic inequality in many ways. Typically, governments decide where to draw the poverty line, so the meaning of poverty varies by society, within societies, and over time. On the other hand, the Gini index of inequality is used universally.

Having said that, where does Canada rank in comparison with the sixteen other countries we considered in this chapter? On the measures used here to assess the handling of poverty and inequality, we would rank Canada thirteenth out of seventeen countries. Canada does better on rates of upward mobility, but on other measures it performs more poorly. Canada always does better than the United States and, usually, better than the United Kingdom. But Canada does worse than the Nordic countries on nearly all measures of poverty and economic inequality.

Poverty and inequality are thorny issues. They involve not just economic hardship but also cause physical and mental health problems. The last few decades have seen many changes in the Canadian workplace. The 2008 global financial crisis resulted in a spike in the unemployment rate, which is the measure of the number of Canadians who are not employed and looking for work. Even today, workers feel the aftereffects of this recession.

After 2009 and until the onset of the COVID-19 epidemic, Canada's unemployment rate steadily declined. However, this economic recovery occurred alongside a drop in the size of the labour force and an increase in precarious jobs. So, while the lower unemployment rate suggests that more Canadians have jobs, many people gave up trying to find work and dropped out of the labour force. From June 2017 to June 2018, around 126,500 Canadians remained unemployed despite searching for a job for a year or more (Statistics Canada, 2018).

By 2018, the overall unemployment rate fell to pre-recession levels, although the number of long-term unemployed workers remained stubbornly high (Statistics Canada, 2018). The quality of available jobs also declined. And with the shutdown of many workplaces because of the COVID-19 pandemic, Canada faced record high rates of unemployment in the spring of 2020.

Canada cannot improve its standing among comparison countries unless it makes work more stable and better paying for those who must rely on weekly or monthly paychecks. It must also do more for those who cannot get or keep a job. For example, it could put in place permanent programs like the Canada Emergency Response Benefit (CERB) as a supplement for those in the gig economy who cannot rely on employment insurance.

However, to do this, Canada must show an extraordinary and so far, unprecedented commitment to making important changes. Can Canada make changes of this magnitude without the sameness, civility, and equity observable in the Nordic countries? For example, can it increase tax rates (and in this way redistribute income) under the current conditions of social diversity and individualistic sentiment? Or will more cohesion based on cultural and social consensus be needed? We will say more about these issues in the last chapter.

Finally, it is worth noting the similarities between Canada and the Nordic countries, even though Canada's economy is so interdependent with that of the United States. Clearly, Canadians aspire to be more Nordic than American and have enough sovereignty to pursue such a path. But there is much more to be done, to close the gap between inequality in Canada and in the Nordic countries.

CHAPTER THREE
Social Justice

Social justice is a broad, somewhat vague term meaning fair and just relations between the individual and society. It is purposely vague because it covers a large variety of situations about which many people agree in general but disagree on specifics—for example, on the idea that "Black lives matter." As well, "justice" is not a simple idea, nor is "fairness." We will discuss both terms in this chapter, but neither is as intuitively simple as "poverty" or even "equality."

Maybe that's why we don't find simple, punchy sayings about justice and fairness like those of the ancient thinkers we cited in the last chapter. It took quite a while for people to figure out what they meant by justice and fairness. Indeed, they still argue about it today.

Before plunging ahead, let's consider a few wise things people did say about justice. Consider first the words of Alexander Solzhenitsyn, a fighter against communist totalitarianism in Soviet Russia in the last century. He wrote, "Justice is conscience, not a personal conscience but the conscience of the whole of humanity." Solzhenitsyn suggested that anyone can understand what is just. To do so, they only need to consult their own conscience. If everyone did that, then the conscience of humanity as a whole would be awakened.

Now, consider the views of Albert Einstein, mathematician, physicist, and philosopher, who argued that "In matters of truth and justice, there is no difference between large and small problems, for issues concerning the treatment of people are all the same." The sentiment is similar, when you think about it, to Solzhenitsyn's. Problems of conscience are universal. Anyone can understand them if they open their minds. In this sense, big moral questions and small ones are the same. Likewise, issues of justice affecting men and women, racialized people and non-racialized people, young people and old people are all the same. As humans, we all have the capacity to understand the moral issues involved if we simply look to our consciences.

Perhaps the same universality of "justice" led Benjamin Franklin, the philosopher, writer, and constitution-maker of eighteenth-century America, to declare that "Justice will not be served until those who are unaffected are as outraged as those who are." By this, Franklin meant that there is something universally understandable about justice and about fairness. Even people not personally affected by a particular injustice can understand the hardships of victims of injustice and unfairness.

Twentieth-century philosopher and historian Arnold Toynbee declared that "The best safeguard against fascism is to establish social justice to the maximum extent possible." Said another way, if we want to live in a society that is just and fair—a society that is democratic and not fascist—then, as much as possible, we must support social justice for everyone. Even if we do not directly, immediately, and personally gain by doing so, in the long run we will all benefit.

James Baldwin, the twentieth-century American writer and philosopher, offered some insights on how to decide whether a society is in fact just and fair. "If one really wishes to know how justice is administered in a country … one goes to the unprotected—those precisely who need the law's protection most—and listens to their testimony." We can all understand the general meanings of justice and fairness. These are universal ideals. But the people who have been most directly harmed by injustice are, without doubt, experts on the topic and those whose input we need most.

Finally, here is a saying that you may have already heard: "The arc of the moral universe is long, but it bends towards justice." Here Theodore Parker reassured us that, perhaps because we all understand and crave fairness and justice, in the end the universe will be just. Morality, fairness, and justice will prevail. This optimistic view may embody the same sentiments expressed by Einstein, Franklin, and Solzhenitsyn—that fairness and justice can be understood by everyone and that they benefit everyone. We can all strive to bring about a just society, and this effort will prevail.

Justice and fairness do not mean the same thing as equality, however. Nor do they mean that all people have to be treated in the same way. You can treat different people differently and still be fair.

Take the notion of *employment equity*. Canada's Employment Equity Act asserts that treating people fairly may mean treating them differently. For example, not everyone needs a wheelchair ramp, and people who do need and use them benefit unequally from the cost of installing them. But think about this matter a little more deeply, and you'll realize that installing wheelchair ramps merely levels the playing field.

With this in mind, in the 1970s the government of Canada began to address the fact that the composition of the public service did not reflect the composition of the country. White, English-speaking, non-disabled men vastly outnumbered all other public service employees. A debate began—and continues today—about the best way to address those differences. This debate revolves around divergent understandings of equality.

Consider the nature of this problem. Using the simple example of schoolchildren in a classroom, sociologist Christopher Jencks (1988) has shown there are at least five different interpretations of justice and fairness where "equal" opportunity is concerned. He does this by asking us to imagine how a schoolroom teacher, Ms. Higgins, should split her time among better and worse readers. Jencks suggests five different ways she might do this. Each way is fair in one way, though arguably unfair in another.

1. *Democratic equality* (this is Jencks' term) requires Ms. Higgins to give everyone equal time and attention. She must disregard how well they read, how hard they try, how deprived they have been in the past, what they want, or how much they or others will benefit.
2. *Moralistic justice* requires Ms. Higgins to reward virtue and punish vice. In the classroom, this means rewarding children who make the most effort to learn what Ms. Higgins is trying to teach and giving them more of her time.

3. *Weak humane justice* requires Ms. Higgins to give some students—especially those who have been shortchanged at home or in their earlier schooling—more time than she gives other students.

4. *Strong humane justice* requires Ms. Higgins to give more of her time to students who, in the past, have been shortchanged by life in any way.

5. *Utilitarianism* means that competitions must be open to all, run on a level field, and judged solely on the basis of performance. This requires Ms. Higgins to simply give most of her time to the best readers, since they will profit most (adapted from Jencks 1988: 519–20).

As you can see, only one model of justice—democratic equality—suggests we must treat everyone the same way. In a schoolyard race, this might mean lining up all the kids at the same starting line before blowing the "go" whistle. Other models of fairness urge us to take extra steps to help those who lag behind or to give more attention to the most talented. In that same race, the former approach might mean allowing younger, smaller students to start at a line set a little ahead of the bigger, faster students. That way, they all have an equal chance to finish the race together. The latter approach might mean selecting only the most talented students to participate in the race and concentrating coaching and training resources on them.

Now, in this chapter we are going to focus first on gender justice and, second, on racial justice. We could examine many other kinds of social justice issues, but for reasons of space we will limit ourselves. We will find that, where gender and race are concerned, Canada does better than some comparison countries but worse than others. We will look for differences across the seventeen countries of interest and draw conclusions about whether Canada is fair and just enough.

Data on Gender Inequalities

Let's start with a fairness issue that seems simple. Do women earn as much money as men do? If not, is the gap between men's earnings and women's earnings larger in some countries than in others? And if it is, where does Canada stand? On the next page, Figure 3-1 shows that Canada has the third highest gender gap in earnings, behind the United States and Finland. The gap is lowest in Luxembourg, followed by Belgium and Denmark.

The gender wage gap shown here is calculated simply as the difference between the median earnings of women relative to median earnings of men in a particular country. However, as in the last chapter, we have to ask questions about measurement issues. For example, can we rely on this gender gap measurement to tell us what we want to know? Does it prove that Canadian women are treated less fairly than men in the workplace, where wages are concerned, compared to other countries?

In fact, we *can't* be certain this is the case, using this particular measurement. For example, the earning gap between men and women may be larger in Canada than, say Belgium, because more women in Canada work part-time. This, in turn, might reflect a stronger tendency among Canadian women (compared to Belgian women) to bear children and stay home with them during their early years.

If so, this particular way of measuring a gender pay gap may tell us more about the different age structures and fertility practices of Canadian women than about wage dis-

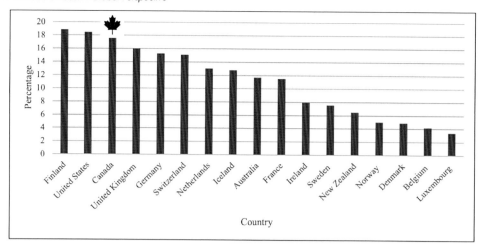

Figure 3-1. Gender Wage Gap (%), Canada and Comparison Countries, 2019.

crimination. Compared to Belgian women, Canadian women may be younger and bear more children. Or Belgium and Canada may offer different childcare and parental support services, which would allow Belgian women to work full time more easily even as mothers. Unfortunately, we have no way to find the right answer from only the data in Figure 3-1. But we should be aware of this problem as we go forward.

Of course, gender wage gaps carry consequences, however they originate. That's why, although women generally make up at least half of a nation's population, sociologists tend to refer to them as a "minority group." Women aren't a *numerical* minority, but compared to men they are somewhat marginalized and disadvantaged in society. In fact, women are overrepresented among the poor people of the entire world, a fact referred to as the *feminization of poverty*. The feminization of poverty stems, in large part, from women's occupational disadvantages and their subordination to men in most spheres of social and economic life.

Women are underrepresented not only at high occupational levels but in positions of economic and political power in society. When we say that women are underrepresented, we mean that they make up a smaller proportion of a certain sector than we would expect given their numbers in the general population. Figure 3-2 (below) gives us one example of this, showing the representation of women in politics, which is generally a male-dominated field throughout the world. As the figure shows, women make up significantly less than half the members of parliament in our comparison countries.

Canada, here, ranks somewhere in the middle, with less than one-third of our parliamentary seats being held by women. Canadian women are far less likely than women in the Nordic or some other comparison countries to hold elected parliamentary seats but do better than women in the United States and United Kingdom, as well as several European countries.

Western politics—indeed, politics everywhere—has historically been male dominated. This has proven an obstacle for women who run for office. Canadian women won political rights in bits and pieces, receiving the right to vote federally in 1918 and in the provinces in the years between 1916 and 1940. Since then, they have continued to make gains in the political arena, increasing their representation steadily since the 1980s. However, they remain significantly underrepresented.

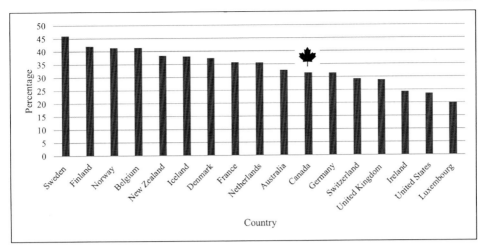

Figure 3-2. Percentage of Parliamentary Seats Held by Women, Canada and Comparison Countries, 2018.

The Nordic nations, like Canada, are liberal democracies, but women there enjoy more success in politics. Sweden and Norway boast legislatures with (near) gender parity. This may reflect differences in political culture between Canada and the Nordic countries. For example, the Swedish government heralds itself as "the first feminist government in the world," and claims gender equality as one of its central priorities in policy- and decision-making.

Low fertility rates, the Swedish welfare system, and women's equal opportunity to study and gain employment all helped women increase their numbers in the Swedish parliament (Freidenvall, 2003). On top of this, Swedish culture makes a good work-life balance a priority. This leads many women (as well as men) to work part-time, making room for other parts of their lives, such as family, friends, and personal interests—and political participation (Freidenvall, 2003).

In Canada and its comparison countries, women are still underrepresented in high level occupational positions and generally earn less than men in these positions. This means that women end up concentrated in lower paying jobs. It also means that when women do manage to secure high-status employment, they tend to be paid less than men doing the same work (Blau and Kahn, 2017).

In large part, women's unequal role in public life reflects their unequal role in their households. Women who work outside the home still tend to assume most of the responsibility for household work and care work. This household labour done (generally) by women is sometimes called "the second shift," a term coined by Arlie Hochschild (Milkie, Raley and Bianchi, 2009). The term refers to the idea that women work one shift at work, and then come home and work another shift's worth of domestic labour. This work also goes by the name of "social reproduction," because of its importance in keeping society going. But because of the extra pressures on their time, many women—especially those with children—prefer part-time work over full-time work. They also tend to leave the workforce earlier and more often than men (Bisello and Mascherini, 2017).

Taken together, these trends in social inequality result in a significant and enduring wage gap between men and women. On average, women in Canada earn 18 percent less than men. The gap in Belgium and Luxembourg is only 3.5 percent.

Violence against Women

Personal violence—especially domestic violence—ranks among the biggest disadvantages women face everywhere in the world. Women suffer disproportionately as the victims of physical and sexual violence. Compared to men, women who experience intimate partner violence also report higher rates of injury caused by abuse. As a result, more women than men experience long-term PTSD-like symptoms (Canadian Centre for Justice Statistics, 2016).

Figure 3-3 documents the lifetime incidence of violence for women in Canada and our sixteen comparison countries. It shows the percentage of women who have experienced interpersonal violence at any point in their adult lives. According to this figure, Canadian women report the lowest lifetime incidence of violence. The United States, meanwhile, reports the highest incidence, with 36 percent of women reporting the experience of violence in their lifetime.

Often, violence against women is perpetrated by domestic or intimate partners. However, as we see in Figure 3-4, Canadian women report low rates of intimate partner violence, compared with the sixteen similar countries.

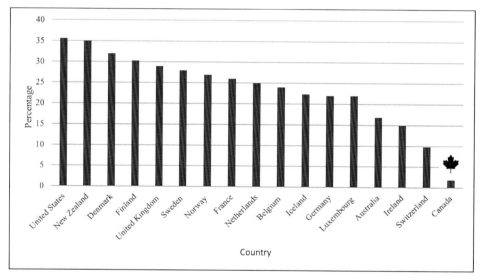

Figure 3-3. Lifetime Incidence of Violence against Women (%), Canada and Comparison Countries, 2019.

In large part, this is because Canadian women will not stand for it. They do not condone interpersonal violence. It runs counter to Canadian culture. As we see in Figure 3-5, few Canadian women condone men beating their wives. In this respect, they are far less to condone such intimate partner violence than women in the U.S. or United Kingdom, though more likely to do so than women in Denmark, Ireland, or Belgium.

The common experience of violence, by women in Canada and elsewhere, holds a wide range of consequences. Women victimized by violence may need to secure emergency housing for themselves and their children. Yet victims of domestic violence who are not financially independent often find few housing choices. Mothers who are victims of violence "are at an increased risk of having their children removed by child welfare authorities because of housing that is unsuitable because of violence or poor living conditions" (OHRC, 2008).

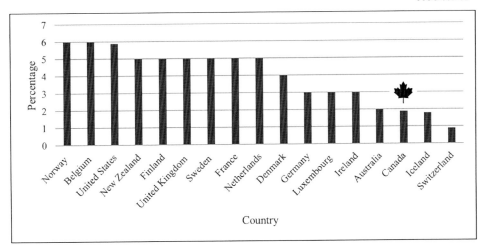

Figure 3-4. Percentage of Women Experiencing Domestic Violence in the Last Twelve Months, Canada and Comparison Countries, 2017.

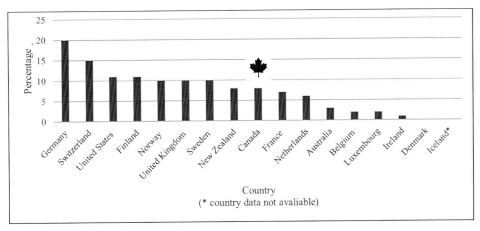

Figure 3-5. Percentage of Women Condoning Violence against Women, Canada and Comparison Countries, 2019.

Indigenous women, who suffer higher-than-average rates of domestic violence in Canada and face more barriers to safe and secure housing alternatives, run the highest risk of having their children taken away (Boyce, 2016; OHRC, 2008). Several factors account for the heightened vulnerability of Indigenous women, including differences in community social and economic resources, and access to services. Researchers also point to the harmful legacies of colonization and the residential school system as contributing to these outsized rates of violence (Daoud et al., 2017).

With few means of escaping sexual, physical, or emotional abuse, many low-income women remain in unsafe living conditions. Women with disabilities who are victims of domestic violence find even fewer choices. Emergency shelters often can't house women with mobility impairments. Renting also poses challenges. Landlords may hold discriminatory beliefs about women escaping abusive relationships. They may fear domestic violence will follow these women to the new accommodation. Even homelessness in Canada is gendered. Studies show that men's homelessness likely results from mental health problems, addictions, or the loss of employment. For women, homelessness more likely results from domestic violence, eviction, and poverty (Peressini, 2007).

Immigrant women do not, apparently, face a higher-than-average risk of partner violence in Canada. However, they are frequently unable or reluctant to report abuse or access supports and services. Language proficiency often serves as a barrier for immigrant women (Jayasuriya-Illesinghe, 2018; Sharma, 2001.) Those who lack fluency in English or French may fail to access services or discuss their problems (Sharma, 2001). Some lack awareness of their rights or what institutions can do to help (Shalabi et al., 2015; Sharma, 2001; Shirwadkar, 2004.)

Because of the widespread threat of violence, many women fear walking alone at night. As we see in Figure 3-6, Canadian women feel somewhat less fear in this regard than American women, but more than women in Norway, Switzerland, or Iceland. Women's fear of walking alone is greatest of all in lower-income, less-developed countries such as Chile, Mexico, and South Africa.

Even teenage and younger girls experience more danger than same-aged boys. As we see in Figure 3-7, everywhere more girls than boys report the experience of cyberbullying. Canadian girls are less likely to experience cyberbullying than girls in Ireland, the UK, or

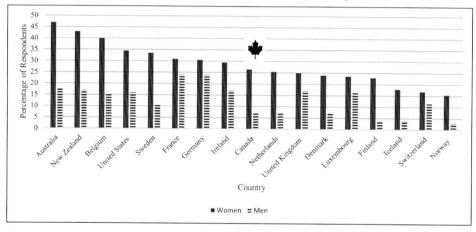

Figure 3-6. Fear of Walking Alone, Canada and Comparison Countries, 2017.

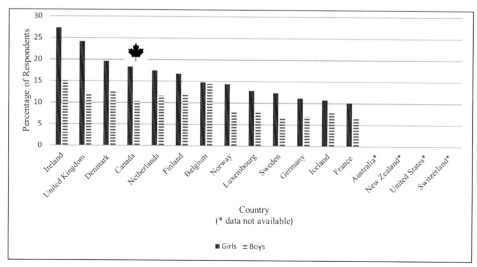

Figure 3-7. Experiences of Cyberbullying, Canada and Comparison Countries, 2014.

Denmark. However, they are more likely to report experiencing it than girls in France, Germany, Iceland, and Sweden.

Measuring Violence against Women Cross-nationally

Women face disadvantages and dangers everywhere. Violence against women also comes in a variety of forms, some more common than others.

The extent of violence against women is moderate in Canada. Because comparing Canada with other countries is the goal of this book, and measurement is so central to this comparison, we will spend time considering efforts to measure violence against women throughout the world. Doing so, we will find that Canadian women are less subject to many types of violence than women in many other parts of the world; and we can say this with considerable confidence in the measures used.

Homicide is an important cause of mortality around the world, but until recently, estimates of the number of homicides by intimate partners have been rare. Stöckl et al. (2013) set out to estimate the prevalence of intimate partner homicide by analyzing published findings. A systematic search of databases revealed that, around the world, 13.5 percent of all homicides are committed by an intimate partner. Women are six times more likely to be killed by an intimate partner than men. No less than one-third of all female homicides are carried out by an intimate partner. High-income countries post unexpectedly high rates of intimate partner homicide. That's true of the countries we study in this book as well as in southeast Asia.

Homicide, however, is far from the most common form of violence against women. Other forms include human trafficking, forced prostitution, female infanticide, genital mutilation, rape in war, sex-selective abortion, sexual abuse by non-intimate partners, and physical and sexual violence against sex workers. WHO estimates that more than 30 percent of all women worldwide have experienced either physical or sexual violence by a partner. About 100 million to 140 million girls and women worldwide have undergone female genital mutilation (FGM) and more than three million girls are at risk for FGM every year in Africa alone. Nearly 70 million girls worldwide marry before the age of 18 years, often against their will (cited in Ellsberg, 2015).

Again, consider the category of intimate partner violence (IPV), which itself comprises a variety of violent acts. On average, IPV affects nearly one in three women worldwide in their lifetimes. However, the distribution of IPV varies widely from one country to another, with a one-year prevalence of less than 4 percent in many high-income countries compared to at least 40 percent in some low-income countries. ("One-year prevalence" is the percentage of ever-partnered women aged from 15 years to 49 years who suffered at least one act of violence within the past twelve months.)

To find the societal factors that predict IPV, Heise and Kotsadam (2015) compiled yearly prevalence data from 66 surveys in 44 countries. The resulting database comprised nearly half a million surveyed women in total. The researchers found that local norms were strong predictors of IPV. These included norms related to male authority over female behaviour and those that justified violence towards women. Remember that in many countries, even some women condone domestic violence, though fewer than 10 percent do so in OECD countries. As well, local laws and practices that give women less access to land, property, cash and credit also predict IPV.

By contrast, poverty (as measured by GDP per capita) is not a strong predictor of IPV. On the other hand, certain aspects of economic growth correlate with levels of IPV. For example, IPV occurs less frequently in countries with a high proportion of women in the formal work force.

Using data from the WHO Multi-Country Study on Women's Health and Domestic Violence (ten countries) and other surveys, DeVries et al. (2013a) sought even better prevalence estimates of IPV. Their results show that, in 2010, 30 percent of women worldwide aged 15 and over had experienced physical or sexual IPV during their lifetime. As we have already seen, great regional variation exists in the prevalence of physical and/or sexual IPV.

Victimization surveys indicate that sexual violence is severely underreported to law enforcement and health officials. However, Watts and Zimmerman (2002) judge that self-reports of violent victimization are reliable. Their review of studies finds high rates of sexual IPV and forced sexual initiation among women in low- and middle-income countries, as well as in the U.S.

Despite warranted concern over measurement accuracy, research into sexual violence is advancing rapidly, aided by behaviorally specific terminology instead of general descriptions such as "forced or unwanted sex." Specific definitions of sexual violence or force are especially helpful in gathering more reliable statistics. When specific terminology is used, the measured prevalence of sexual IPV increases. Not only does the use of specific language increase the accuracy of measurement for trends and cross-national differences, it also allows for a more accurate measurement of correlates.

For decades, researchers have known that violence against women is not, typically, violence perpetrated by a stranger against another stranger. On this, Dahlberg and Krug (2002) note that violent victimization is most often perpetrated by peers, intimate partners and family members. Where IPV is concerned, the abuser and abused may even share a home and interact every day, providing plenty of opportunity for violence. Peers and family members may also play an important role by encouraging, excusing, or ignoring such behaviour.

Similarly, the neighbourhood institutions in which abuse occurs—such as schools and workplaces—may also promote, excuse, or ignore violence against women. The values people hold in these communities of violence often encourage, excuse, or ignore violence against women. They may tolerate violence, remove checks against violence, and even promote violence by increasing tensions between different groups. And the same values that support high rates of homicide also support high risks of violence against women. These include cultural norms that support violence as an acceptable way of resolving conflicts, as one finds in communities without rule of law. Overtly patriarchal values also increase the risk of violence against women. These include norms that justify male dominance over women and children and norms that give priority to parental rights over child welfare. As with homicide, high levels of economic or social inequality also predict high rates of violence against women.

Sexual assault is a global concern for women, with PTSD being a common result. To document this, Scott et al. (2018) drew on data from twelve surveys of community-dwelling adults in eleven different countries. They find that PTSD resulted for 20 percent of sexually assaulted women in their sample. Women who suffered repeated victimization more commonly suffered PTSD. It was also positively associated with prior damaging events and childhood misfortunes. The researchers identified a group at especially high risk of PTSD, featuring women with a history of mental disorder and more-than-average numbers of damaging events. Among the 10 percent of women with the highest predicted risk, 40.3 percent developed PTSD.

Another cultural factor predicting a high risk of violence against women is rape-myth acceptance. Russell and Hand (2017) note that rape (i.e., intrusive sexual assault) is underreported because many women blame themselves or are blamed by others. However, men more typically blame the victim. This tendency displays itself most strongly among men who think women bring rape on themselves by teasing or seducing men. Men who subscribe to the just world belief we discussed in the last chapter tend to adopt this point of view. Such people think the universe is fair. They think that good things happen to good people and bad things happen to bad people. People get what they deserve, and women who suffer violence against them—in this case, rape—must have brought it on themselves.

To find other correlates of violence against women, Abramsky et al. (2011) used data from ten countries included in the WHO Multi-country Study on Women's Health and Domestic Violence. Women aged 15 to 49 years who had ever had a male partner were asked about their experiences of physically and sexually violent acts within the past twelve months. Despite wide variations in the prevalence of IPV, common influences were found. Many factors, including cohabitation, alcohol abuse, young age, attitudes that support violence among women, experiencing childhood abuse, and growing up with domestic violence, increased the risk of IPV. By contrast, more education, a higher socioeconomic status, and formal marriage reduced the risk.

To conclude, women everywhere face many dangers, as well as unfair treatment. Canada is far safer for women than many countries of the world, but not as safe, just, and fair as it might be. In 2014, Canadian women were over six times as likely as men to be sexually assaulted (Statistics Canada, 2017). Specifically, women who were single, young, attended evening outings or had substance-abuse issues tended to report higher rates of sexual assault (Statistics Canada, 2017). While violent victimization has declined in Canada, the victimization rate of sexual assault remained constant over the past decade (Statistics Canada, 2015).

Issues around Immigration and Racialization

We turn now to issues of immigration and racialization. Around the world many people perceive Canada as tolerant, welcoming, and accepting of disadvantaged or marginalized people. For that reason, every year hundreds of thousands of people immigrate to Canada. This results in ethnic diversity or what researchers sometimes call *ethnic fractionalization*.

Figure 3-8 shows where Canada stands in comparison with more than a dozen other similar nations in this regard. Fractionalization is defined as "the probability that two individuals selected at random from a country will be from different ethnic (or cultural) groups" (Fearon, 2003: 208). We can see that any two individuals selected at random in Canada will more likely hail from different ethnic groups than in any of our comparison countries. Simply put, Canada is much more diverse, ethno-culturally, than any of the other countries we are considering. The Nordic nations are the least diverse among our comparison countries. Data were not available for France, Iceland, and Luxembourg.

Every year, between 200,000 and 300,000 people come to Canada to live and to work. In 2018–19, Canada admitted 313,580 immigrants, one of the highest levels in history (Statistics Canada, 2019). Data from Statistics Canada show that about 21 percent of people residing in Canada are either immigrants or permanent residents (Grenier, 2017). Most of those coming Canada between 2006 and 2011 came from Asia. Many others came from Africa, Central and South America, and the Caribbean (Statistics Canada, 2013).

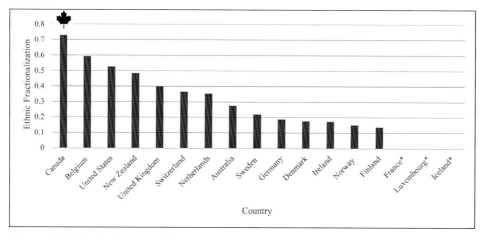

Figure 3–8. Ethnic Fractionalization, Canada and Comparison Countries, 2013.
Note: The closer to 1.0 a country's fractionalization index, the greater the degree of ethnic diversity.

Immigrants come to Canada holding many types of visas and immigrate for many reasons. Some come as family-class immigrants to rejoin their loved ones. Others arrive as refugees, as students to study at Canadian schools, or on work visas. Economic immigrants come to Canada for the specific purpose of working and are generally admitted on the basis of having the necessary skills and experiences to contribute to Canada's economy, whether as skilled workers, businesspeople, or professionals. "Family class" refers to immigrants who are sponsored by close relatives already living in Canada. They may or may not have useful job-related skills, but are supported by a Canadian family member. Finally, refugees come to Canada to flee persecution in their home country. They too may or may not hold job-related skills (Vancouver English Centre, 2014).

According to public opinion surveys, Canadians hold a generally positive view of immigration. The country's immigration laws tend to favour younger immigrants. The federal government decided in 2012 that applicants would receive twelve points towards their acceptance if they were ages 18 to 35 but no points if they were 47 years old and over (Curry, 2012). The government made this change because of the benefits a younger population brings to Canada's economy.

Canada relies on immigration to fill key labour roles. Since the early years of immigration policy, Canada has selected most immigrants based on labour market need. (In some periods, ideas about racial superiority and inferiority also influenced the selection.) Today, most immigrants are more academically qualified than their Canadian-born counterparts. Most people think academic qualifications are the key to finding a good job. However, this is often not the case for recent immigrants. Many are underemployed, meaning that they are overqualified for their jobs. As Figure 3-9 shows, foreign-born residents face higher unemployment rates than native-born residents in most of the comparison countries. The employment gap looms largest in Sweden. In Canada, only a negligible gap in employment between the two groups exists.

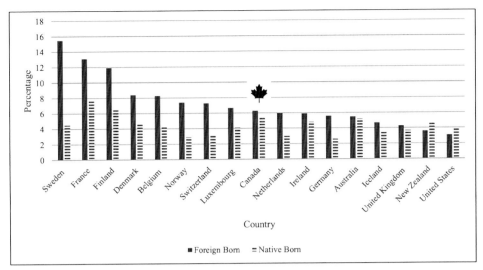

Figure 3-9. Unemployment Rates for Foreign- and Native-Born Individuals, Canada and Comparison Countries, 2019.

Attitudes towards in immigrants in Canada are better than in any of the comparison countries, as we see in Figure 3-10 below. Data from Pew Research shows that Canadians are more likely to view immigrants as making a positive contribution. Canadians also express more positive attitudes toward immigrant values and behaviours on a variety of inclusiveness dimensions. (See Figure 3-11 on the next page.) As a result, immigrants to Canada are more likely than those to other countries to seek and attain citizenship (see Figure 3-12 above on the next page).

Immigrants to Canada not only take out citizenship. They also encourage their children to participate and excel in Canadian society. As we see in Figure 3-13 on the next page, children of immigrants to Canada do better in their cross-national PISA tests of reading than do the children of immigrants in any comparison country.

Problems Facing Immigrants and Racialized Minorities

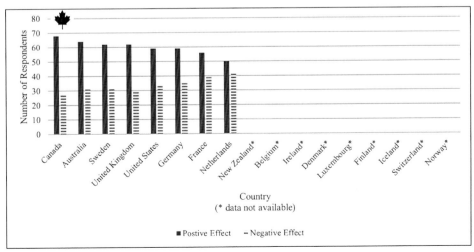

Figure 3-10. Views of Whether Immigrants Have a Positive or Negative Effect on Society, Canada and Comparison Countries, 2018.

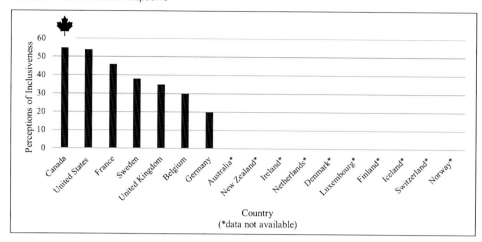

Figure 3-11. Canadian Perceptions of Immigrants on Six Domains of Inclusiveness, Canada and Comparison Countries, 2018.

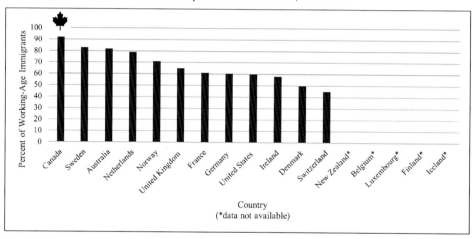

Figure 3-12. Percentage of Working-Age Immigrants Who Have Citizenship, Canada and Comparison Countries, 2015.

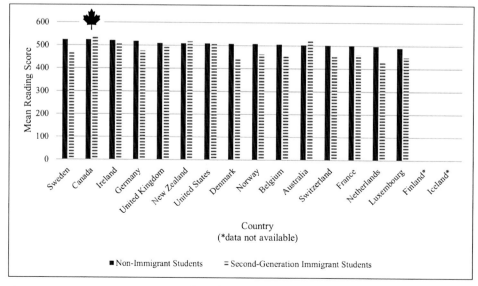

Figure 3-13. Mean Performance (PISA) of Children, Canada and Comparison Countries, 2018.

Our generally positive observations about Canada come with some caveats, however. While immigrants don't face a particularly high risk of unemployment during normal economic times, they do often face underemployment, forced to work in jobs they're overqualified for. The tendency for immigrants to secure work that fails to reflect their experience and qualifications is called *de-professionalization*.

De-professionalization often results because Canadian employers refuse to recognize foreign qualifications and experience. Studies that try to quantify this gap suggest an overseas education is treated as equivalent to three-quarters of a comparable Canadian education. One year of overseas work experience equals only four months of Canadian experience (Finnie and Meng, 2002). Most people who immigrate to Canada do not speak English as their first language. Some jobs also require fluency in French, a skill many immigrants lack.

Canada's job-market expectations make finding a suitable job difficult for many immigrants. Some professional institutions reject licenses from certain other countries, requiring re-licensing, which may be an expensive and lengthy undertaking. A person in a de-professionalized job may lack time to retrain, re-license, and find a better position. As well, studies show that some employers insist on Canadian work experience even when the job doesn't need it (Fleras, 2010). Finally, visible-minority immigrants who complete their education in Canada and gain Canadian credentials still face significant gaps in their earnings compared with Canadian-born white workers (Pendakur and Pendakur, 1998; Lightman and Gingrich, 2018).

A significant pay gap between native-born Canadians and immigrants also exists. This gap is most pronounced among workers holding university degrees. In 2008, university-educated immigrants earned, on average, five dollars less per hour than their Canadian-born counterparts (Statistics Canada, 2009b). The longer an immigrant lives in Canada, the higher their value to Canadian employers.

Besides working in jobs for which they are overqualified and underpaid, immigrants are more likely to work part-time involuntarily. They would prefer to work full-time, but for various reasons they cannot. Recent immigrants work under short-term contracts twice as often as the Canadian-born. They are less likely to belong to unions in their occupation (Statistics Canada, 2009b). New immigrants run a higher risk of non-fatal injury in their workplace (Marni and Kosny, 2012). These data paint an overall picture of Canadian immigrants working in more dangerous jobs for which they are overqualified.

Beyond issues of employment and income, many recent immigrants to Canada face discrimination. A sizeable portion are people of colour who report experiencing discrimination. Figure 3-14 (next page) focuses on the issue of discrimination. About 13 percent of immigrants report experiencing discrimination themselves or say they are part of a group that is discriminated against. This puts Canada in the middle of the pack. Iceland, Ireland, and the U.S., on the other hand, report the lowest levels of discrimination.

This feeling of exclusion may help explain why immigrants are slightly less likely than native-born citizens to participate in local and national elections. But the immigrant-native gap in Canada is much smaller than it is in the Nordic countries such as Norway, Finland, and Iceland (see Figure 3-15 on the next page).

At any given time, Canada is home to several hundred thousand temporary foreign workers through the Temporary Foreign Worker (TFW) program. This program enables employers in Canada to hire individuals from other countries temporarily to fill labour

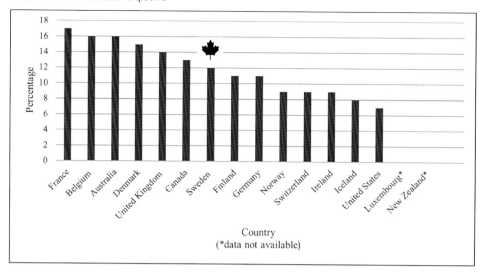

Figure 3-14. Percentage of Immigrants Reporting Discrimination, Canada and Comparison Countries, 2018.

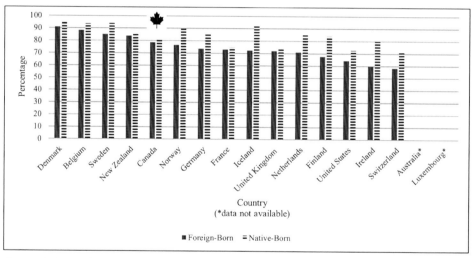

Figure 3-15. Self-Reported Participation of Immigrants in the Electoral Process, Canada and Comparison Countries, 2018.

shortages they cannot fill with Canadian workers. Once the workers' contracts are up, they must leave the country.

Unfortunately, the TFW program creates room for exploitation. For example, many temporary workers find positions through hiring agencies, some of which charge high fees. Some agencies even take a sizable cut from the workers' wages. As well, some employers require temporary foreign workers to live in housing they provide, charge unreasonably high rent, and may even withhold workers' passports.

Non-status workers make up another category of immigrant worker. They work in Canada without the official documentation that affords them the rights and privileges of being a permanent resident or a Canadian citizen. Many people pay non-status workers "under the table." This means the pay they receive is not formally documented. Often, their wages do not meet provincial minimums because the employer is not held legally accountable. And when the work is undocumented, workers are not eligible for employment insurance if laid off or worker's compensation if injured on the job. Finally, non-status workers tend not to complain about working conditions, as doing so makes them vulnerable to deportation.

Despite this evidence of mistreatment, immigrants to Canada are generally successful in integrating, economically and socially. This applies to racialized as well as non-racialized immigrants.

In a study of immigrants to the U.S., Canada, UK, France, Germany and the Netherlands, Richard Alba and Nancy Foner (2015) note similar successes (and failures) in integrating immigrants. However, successes are mixed. Greater success on one outcome (e.g., avoidance of poverty) is usually offset by negatives on others (e.g., lack of employment opportunity). A large body of work by Jeffrey Reitz documents this similarity among countries (for example, see Reitz 2016, 2017, 2018). Not only Canada promotes multiculturalism and offers a friendly welcome to immigrants, these researchers note.

Alba and Foner find little value in trying to explain the success of immigrant assimilation in terms of economic models—for instance, liberal welfare regimes (like Canada) versus social welfare regimes. Similarly, they find little benefit in comparing settler societies (like Canada) with older societies (like France or Germany). In every instance, abstract models fail to capture the nuances of on-the-ground experience. They also fail to capture the significance of seemingly small historical and institutional differences. So, for example, they write (2015: 233) that

> lumping Canada and the United States together as settler societies ignores crucial differences between them that have consequences for integration. Canada needs to be treated as a distinct case, as we have stressed, because of the selectivity of its immigration policies since the late 1960s. They have meant that during the past half-century Canada has avoided the mass immigration of poorly educated workers from the global South that elsewhere has given rise on a large scale to the groups we have described as "low status."

Equally important, both Canada and the U.S. institutionalized openness to immigrants from a wide diversity of origin countries. In both countries, as Irene Bloemraad has put it, the "civil rights and diversity gains [that] were institutionalized through law, bureaucracy, policy, and educational systems, [had] … real effects on national culture." Some trends in the treatment of immigrants in mature industrial societies converge, but divergences also persist. Every case is different. Historical and institutional happenstance creates a structure that, at any given moment, makes immigrant assimilation easier or harder than in another country.

Racialized immigrants pose unique problems in Canada and elsewhere. Sociologists use the term "racialized" because of the suffix: the "-ized" implies that we are speaking of a process, not a stable state. Race is a social construction. Its character and importance are socially determined and constantly changing. Establishing and maintaining racial identity requires symbolic work. While race is not a biological certainty, however, it is an important social fact that holds deep implications for society and for individuals.

Canadians who identify as racialized concentrate in some parts of the nation more than others. Most live in Ontario, British Columbia, Quebec, and Alberta. Fully 96 percent of racialized people live in metropolitan areas, compared to 69 percent of the overall population.

Most Black and Indigenous Canadians say they are treated unfairly because of their race, at least occasionally. However, this mistreatment does not go unnoticed by other Canadians, a majority of whom recognize that Indigenous Canadians, Black people, South Asian people, and Chinese people are discriminated against from time to time. And a majority of Canadians also feels confident these conditions will improve. Likewise, only a minority of people in the discriminated groups feels pessimistic this will come to pass.

Perhaps that is because ever more members of these different groups are meeting and mingling with one another, as neighbours, classmates, workmates, friends, and even spouses and in-laws. Many Canadians have social connections with the members of other racial and ethnic groups. Nearly four Canadians in ten say they have a lot of contact with people outside their own racial group. Inevitably, this is most true for the smallest racial groups, who are bound to mix with others outside their own group at school, work, and elsewhere. However, it is also true of three white people in every four (Environics Institute, Race Relations 2019 Survey of Canadians).

Most important, many Canadians marry people from other racial and ethnic groups. Again, this is most true for the smallest racial groups (like Japanese Canadians), which, logically, offer the smallest pools of marriage partners from which to choose. However, the rates of outgroup marriage (or exogamy) are high (i.e., over half) for certain other small racial groups, such as Blacks, Indigenous people, and Latin or Hispanic Canadians. Asian women—including Japanese, Chinese, Southeast Asian, Filipino, and Korean—are especially likely to marry outside their racial group. By contrast, rates of outgroup marriages are much lower for white Canadians, at around 6 percent for men and 5 percent for women. Still, a large and growing fraction of children in Canadian society now bring two or more racial and ethnic heritages to their lives and those of their friends and colleagues.

Concluding Remarks

We saw in the last chapter that Canada is a middling, ho-hum kind of nation when it comes to dealing with poverty and economic inequality. In this chapter, however, we saw that Canada places in the top tier when it comes to social justice.

Where ethnic diversity, the assimilation of immigrants, and the acceptance of racial diversity is concerned, the data available show that Canada performs better than comparison nations. And Canadians indicate they hope and desire to do even better. This inclination is revealed not only in the responses of Canadians to survey interviews, but in their actions. Many Canadians choose friends and mates from outside their own ethnic and racial group. Meanwhile, the children of immigrants do well at school and, increasingly, at work.

In general, a country's success with inter-group relations depends on the criterion applied. If the criterion is social peace, Canada does well. Indeed, Canada does well on all of the outcomes affected by the selectivity of our immigration policy. These include perceptions of the value of immigration and the proportion of immigrants doing things that require education. However, if the criterion is fair treatment in access to jobs or other valued positions, based on qualifications rather than origins, Canada fares about the same as the other comparators. How you combine these two into an overall "success indicator" depends on the relative weight you give to fairness or social peace.

As well, we need to remember that the countries with immigration problems have immigration either because of the legacy of colonialism (the UK and France, for example) or a

Though work remains to be done, Canada has achieved a good deal in building a diverse society and welcoming large numbers of immigrants to the country.

nearby poor country the border with which is difficult to control (the United States). Their immigrants are different because they find it harder to select and control the immigrant flow as Canada and Australia have done.

The institutional setting of the host society—whether a liberal regime or a social welfare regime, for example—makes a difference too. As Jeffrey Reitz (2018: 223) points out:

> Where institutions have been structured in more individualistic patterns, immigrants encounter greater obstacles to a realization of their economic potential.... These institutional forces create problems for immigrants because they tend to compound and magnify the adversities inherent in the process of migration and adjustment to a new environment. By the same token, the implications are most negative for racial minority immigrants. Previous research shows us that immigrants of non-European-origin to societies dominated by European-origin populations very often have entry-level earnings which are substantially lower than would be predicted based on their observable skills.

However, Canadians seem to be surmounting problems of racial injustice and striving to do even better. (This ignores issues around French-English relations or Indigenous peoples, where it would be somewhat more difficult to speak with complete confidence.) The

Canadian cultural commitment to tolerance, diversity, and multiculturalism pays a dividend. While this commitment may display itself more strongly in some parts of the country than others, overall Canada is moving to solve its historical problems of racism.

Where women are concerned, Canada still needs to close the gender gap in jobs and earnings. Women already take advantage of opportunities for higher education. However, an unequal division of domestic labour translates into an unequal playing field in the workplace, especially for women with children Many feel obliged to trade off full-time work, and the opportunities for advancement this brings, for part-time or periodic work. This means not only less career advancement but smaller pensions and lower pay.

Turning to violence against women, we find Canadian women less victimized and less fearful than women in other countries. On some dimensions, Canadian women do better than women in comparison countries. In general, Canadian women are as safe as women in any of the sixteen comparison countries. Moreover, and contrary to some Canadians' fears, little evidence exists to suggest immigrants from the Global South are importing violent and patriarchal practices from their home countries. For the most part, immigrants to Canada assimilate to Canadian values about gender, as they do for other values.

Having said that, where does Canada rank in comparison with the sixteen other countries we considered in this chapter? Looking at the measures employed here to assess the handling of gender and racialization, we would have to give Canada a mixed rating. On measures of ethnic diversity, integration, and participation, we rate Canada in first place. This is marred only by frequent reports of discrimination and medium to high rates of foreign-born unemployment. On measures of gender equality, Canada rates near the top with low measures of violence against women but nearer to the middle or even bottom on other measures such as the gender wage gap, women's representation in Parliament, and fears of walking alone. Given Canada's mixed scores on different aspects of social justice, we rank Canada sixth out of our seventeen comparison countries.

In short, social justice presents us with a variety of problems that Canada is handling in a variety of ways, with better and worse results. In absolute terms, Canadians should be concerned about the evidence of discrimination against racialized people. In relative terms, Canada is doing better than many comparison countries in dealing with high levels of diversity and high rates of immigration.

CHAPTER FOUR

Crime and Victimization

Studying crime sociologically forces us to examine societies, communities, organizations, and situations. And some of these are simply riskier—more likely to produce crimes—than others. What's more, in sociology, as in life, there is never just one cause of an effect. Instead, there are always many causes and many effects. The sociologist must untangle this web of social causes and effects.

Let's begin this examination of crime—and punishment—with some intelligent and provocative insights from the past. In general, people who are liberal or left-wing view crime as a display of social injustice, not individual failure. So, for example, English historian, philosopher and novelist H.G. Wells wrote, "Crime and bad lives are the measure of a State's failure, all crime in the end is the crime of the community." Along similar lines, playwright George Bernard Shaw noted that "Crime is only the retail department of what, in wholesale, we call penal law." Blurring the state's complicity but stressing the criminal's blamelessness, Mahatma Gandhi declared, "All crime is a kind of disease and should be treated as such." Friedrich Nietzsche would have agreed: "Our crime against criminals lies in the fact that we treat them like rascals."

However, people who hold politically conservative views will more likely blame the victim: that is, hold the individual and not society responsible. So, for example, the Baltimore journalist and essayist H.L. Mencken asserted that "The common argument that crime is caused by poverty is a kind of slander on the poor." He made a good point. After all, not all poor people commit crimes or become career criminals, even if society deals them a bad hand. Then again, not everyone who drives on a dangerous highway dies in a car crash. Similarly, not everyone exposed to a room drenched in coronavirus catches the disease. Yet we don't ignore the influence of environment in either case.

On the related matter of punishment, French sociologist Michel Foucault rightly noted that our reactions to crime often prove ineffective and counterproductive. He labelled prison "a recruitment center for the army of crime." That's because of what sociologists call *prisonization*. As Friedrich Nietzsche more elegantly stated the case, "All in all, punishment hardens and renders people more insensible; it concentrates; it increases the feeling of estrangement; it strengthens the power of resistance." In the end, English essayist Samuel Johnson pointed out that "The power of punishment is to silence, not to confute."

As we will see, Canada ranks as exceptional neither in its prevention nor its punishment of crimes. Other comparison-societies do better. Nordic societies report less crime and resort to punishment less often than Canada. The United States, for reasons we will make clear, reports far more crimes and punishes far more people than Canada. Let's begin our discussion with violent crimes, especially homicides.

Homicides: The Rare Crimes We Know Best

For comparative purposes, there is no better crime to study than homicide. True, homicide is not especially common, but it is important and revealing. In particular, homicide rates help us compare societies (Oberwittler, 2019). First, every society views homicide as consequential. Second, homicide rates can be tracked more easily than many other crimes. Finally, the rates of homicide range widely from one country to another. The global rate of roughly 6 homicides per 100,000 population is an average of widely divergent national rates. These range from 0.25 homicides per 100,000 population in Singapore to roughly 100 homicides per 100,000 population in El Salvador—a gigantic difference!

Historians tell us that rates of homicide and other violent crime were higher in the past. They dropped dramatically in Europe and North America during early modern times. After 1960, rates first increased and then declined again, in response to social, demographic, and economic influences. In East Asia and the Pacific rates decreased in tandem with rising scores on the Human Development Index. In general, industrialization, modernization, and prosperity play a huge role in decreasing homicide rates. Firearms also play a part, but by "pushing" in the opposite direction. Leaving aside Eastern Europe, the frequency of homicide is strongly linked to the spread and use of firearms, which account for 44 percent of homicide cases worldwide. In large part, this accounts for high rates of homicide in the U.S. and rising rates of homicide in Latin America.

Longitudinal studies prove what other studies merely hint at: that poverty and inequality increase deadly violence, while social welfare policies decrease it. Similarly, the existence of state institutions that people view as legitimate and trustworthy acts to decrease homicide rates. We will say more about this connection between political order and homicide shortly. So, despite concerns about some of the available data, the global pattern is clear. To reduce the number of homicides, we must reduce poverty and income inequality and make investments in social welfare. We also need to ensure public confidence in the legitimacy of state institutions.

As we see in Figure 4-1, murder rates are not high in our seventeen comparison countries. They peak in the Global South, especially South America and Africa. They are also high in the Middle East, Russia, and China. In these regions, we find countries that, rightly, lack a high degree of public confidence in public institutions. They also display high rates of poverty and income inequality.

Homing in on the key factors responsible for reducing crime, Tuttle, McCall, and Land (2018) examined data from a sample of 82 nations collected between 1980 and 2010. They found that rates of serious crime declined in many prosperous countries. Over the same period, however, rates of serious crime increased in less prosperous nations. In fact, the wealthiest and most economically developed nations experienced the greatest decline in serious crime. Tuttle, McCall and Land (2018) highlight several social factors that are important in lowering the homicide rate. These include a high GDP per person (that is, a low rate of absolute poverty); a low rate of income inequality; and low infant mortality (largely a proxy for poverty).

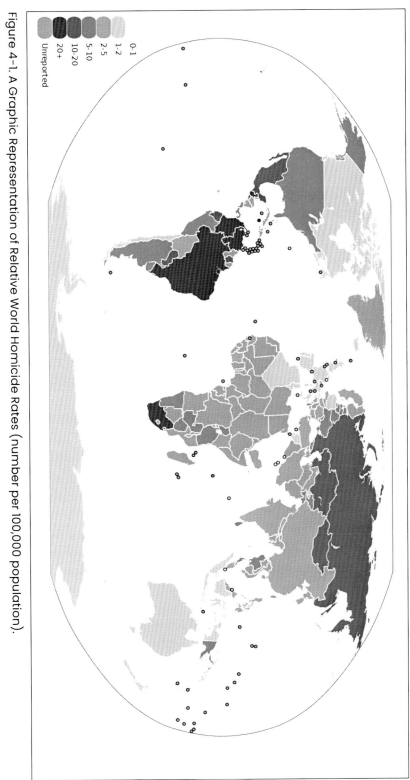

Figure 4–1. A Graphic Representation of Relative World Homicide Rates (number per 100,000 population).

Other important factors include a relatively small criminal or black-market economy (a correlate of poverty), and the presence in the population of relatively few males ages 15–29. We discuss the role of young men in crime shortly. First, however, we will speak to the importance of poverty and economic inequality in shaping crime patterns.

The Roles of Poverty and Economic Inequality

Why do poverty and economic inequality increase the risk of crime, including violent crime and homicide? Most sociological studies find that economic inequality predicts the incidence of both property crime and violent crime (see, for example, Kelly, 2000; Hipp and Yates, 2011). In fact, this argument can be traced back as early as 1938. Then, sociologist Robert Merton first argued that unequal opportunity encourages certain people to commit crimes by denying them access to traditional means of earning a living. There is a "strain" or gap between people's goals and the means available through which to chase those goals (Pratt and Cullen, 2005; Pare and Felson, 2014).

An early view in sociology suggested that crime occurs because of social disorganization: an alleged failure of the social order to restrain individual criminal impulses. Merton's (1938) concept of *anomie* stood in stark contrast to these previously held views (Murphy and Robinson, 2008; Chamlin and Sanders, 2013). In short, Merton proposed that society itself breeds crime and pushes people to break the rules. According to Merton, people learn to aspire to goals that are culturally desirable. They also learn the accepted means by which to gain those ends. For example, North Americans learn to aspire to make enough money to live comfortably and support their families. Ideally, they will reach this goal by securing a good job. But as we have seen, not everyone enjoys equal educational and occupational chances in life. For disadvantaged people, socially unacceptable routes to wealth—such as theft or fraud—may be more readily accessible.

Societies discourage these deviant routes to success through punishments such as fines, imprisonment and other types of formal social control. These efforts to deter crime, however, often prove inadequate. In a society like ours, people put more emphasis on the goal than on the means by which it is won. Our popular culture celebrates "winners" and mocks "losers." As a result, many people come to believe the possible rewards of crime outweigh its potential risks (Murphy and Robinson, 2008). This is especially true for the desperately poor, who have little to lose if they are caught (Janko and Poplin, 2015; Wu and Wu, 2012).

Despite stereotypical conceptions of the criminal poor as morally bankrupt, crime (according to Merton) is not the result of some inborn drive or lack of morals (Featherstone and Deflem, 2003). The broad societal goal of financial success, combined with unequal access to conventional means of achieving that success, promotes crime, according to Merton's classic analysis (Merton, 1938). By denying significant numbers of people an opportunity to succeed through socially acceptable channels, we create conditions that result in high crime rates (see also Murphy and Robinson, 2008; Chamblin and Sanders, 2013).

Recent studies confirm the truth of Merton's theory. Consider the connection between unemployment and crime rates. When people lose their jobs, some turn to crime to meet their expenses (Fougere et al., 2009; Gronqvist, 2013). Young people are especially likely to engage in crime if the economy is in recession when they complete their schooling. One study found that young adults were 5.5 percent more likely to land in jail if they graduated during high rates of unemployment (Bell et al., 2018). At the same time, increased wages at the bottom end of the income distribution have been shown to reduce crime rates (Machin and Meghir, 2004).

Survival-motivated crimes aside, studies show that burglary and auto-theft rates soar as the gap grows between the rich and the poor (Dahlberg and Gustavasson, 2008; Reilly and Witt, 2008). This shows a link between inequality and crime, as well as between absolute poverty and crime. While the desperately poor steal out of material need, better-off but still comparatively disadvantaged people commit property crimes at a higher-than-average rate, even though they already own the means to survive. The poor have more incentive to steal than the rich: financial desperation motivates property crime (Chester, 1976; Ehrlich, 1973; but see also Jacobs et al., 2003; Brookman et al., 2007). Even white-collar forms of theft result from inequality and relative deprivation, since rich people measure their status against people who are even richer. But if people commit thefts out of material need, what motivates violent crime?

Robert Agnew's *general strain theory* (1985, 1992) aims to answer this question by focusing on the emotions evoked by strains outlined in Merton's original theory. When people fail to gain socially valued goals (like money or status), they develop coping strategies to manage the negative emotions that result. Not everyone who experiences these strains turns to delinquency as an outlet, leading Agnew to suggest that criminality follows only in certain circumstances. Specifically, when conditions are unjust, unfair or beyond a person's control, feelings of anger and frustration often result, causing aggressive outbursts. Agnew proposed that social and income inequalities are especially likely to elicit these negative reactions. Low-income earners living in unequal societies tend to become more frustrated with their circumstances.

Agnew suggests that some people cope with their frustration through escapist coping measures, such as alcohol or drug use. Others turn to retaliatory behaviors, committing violent offenses as an outlet for their anger. Young men are especially likely to act this way. They may be less able to access the substances typically used by escapists, and feel less bound by responsibilities—romantic partners, children, mortgage payments—that discourage violent outbursts among adults.

To test this theory, Boggess et al. (2014) examined how gentrification affects crime rates. The study revealed that if several bordering neighbourhoods all underwent economic improvements, fewer assaults occurred in each community. But if one isolated neighborhood began gentrifying, surrounded by communities that remained disadvantaged, aggravated assault rates rose. The same increase did not produce property crimes, such as burglary and robbery. This fact suggests the rise in aggravated assault rates may be due to heightened feelings of hostility rather than efforts to gain valuable possessions.

Violent crimes against middle- and upper-class people usually cluster in neighborhoods where wealthy lifestyles are visible and contrast starkly with surrounding poverty. We can see these patterns on a larger scale as well. Homicide rates in Britain and the U.S.—countries with large income inequalities—are higher than in the more egalitarian Nordic countries (Lappi-Seppala and Tonry, 2011).

While social inequality drives crime rates up, social stability lowers them. As noted earlier, confidence in the stability and legitimacy of state institutions affects crime rates. Testa et al. (2017) use two measures to examine the influence of rule of law on homicide rates. Specifically, they consider whether there an independent judiciary exists, and whether there is a "law and order tradition." They find that stable rule of law drives down homicide rates. Where people think lawfulness prevails, homicide rates are low. The work of sociologist Norbert Elias helps us understand this link between rule of law and violent crime.

What Elias calls the historic "civilizing process" leads to an increased rule of law and thus a decline in violence as societies modernize, for two reasons. First, as nation-states modernize, the state comes to monopolize order-keeping and violence. This civilizing process makes it unnecessary and unlawful for people to use violence for purposes of revenge and makes punishment a matter of public interest. Second, this civilizing process inserts anti-violence norms into the culture. Citizens know they must control their aggressive impulses. Once they internalize new, civilized attitudes, a new restraint lessens violence.

As a result, societies with an independent judiciary—a judiciary that is seen to be apolitical and fair—have lower homicide rates than societies without such a judiciary. Values that support judicial independence and encourage self-restraint tend to discourage criminal violence. Instead, they define peaceful relations as desirable and violent actions as offenses against public order. As the legitimate rule of law strengthens, people increasingly conform. As well, attitudes about law, the courts, and other public institutions change. Citizens come to have more and more confidence in all of these state institutions.

Researchers such as Lachaud et al. found a correlation between homicide rates and poverty by analyzing Ontario census data. On the other hand, although economic inequality has increased in Canada since the 1980s, rates of violent crime have fallen. Social problems are caused by a multitude of factors, and any analysis must take that fact into account.

Public health researchers are also interested in the role of poverty and inequality in producing homicides. Lachaud et al. (2017) launched a population-based study of homicides in Ontario over the period 1999–2012. Specifically, they wanted to compare the effects of economic inequality on homicide rates with the effects of inequality on two common health problems: cardiovascular disease and cancer. To do this, the researchers linked statistics from the Office of the Registrar General's deaths registry with census data for all Ontario residents.

To study socioeconomic status (SES), they used two measures from the Ontario Marginalization Index (ON-Marg): material deprivation and residential instability. Doing so, they find that males aged 15–29 years old are the main victims of homicide, and that homicides in this age group showed an upward trend over the study period. Even more interesting, socioeconomic status proves to have an even larger effect on the incidence of homicide than on cardiovascular disease and cancer. What's more, the loss of life is significant. Researchers estimate the person-years lost to homicide at 63,512 for males and 24,066 years for females. "Person-years" measure the number of people killed multiplied by the estimated number of years each person will have lost from their expected lifespan. Even in Canada, homicides are clearly an important cause of death among young males—especially those living in impoverished neighborhoods.

So far, we have noted that homicide rates decline with modernization and a growth in rule of law and civility. They increase with poverty and socioeconomic inequality. As well,

Papachristos et al. (2018) note that, despite a decline over the last two decades, violent crime continues to concentrate in socioeconomically disadvantaged urban neighborhoods. But what about the role of the age distribution? Is there an association between national homicide rates and the proportion of the male population that is young? Many criminologists think the percentage of young people in the population—especially young men—predicts homicide victimization rates within and across nations. Second, and related to this, many think the percentage of young people accounts for a large fraction of the overall variance in homicide victimization rates across nations.

The crux of the argument is that a positive association exists between the proportion of young men in a population and homicide rates. That is because young men are most at risk of becoming offenders and victims of violence.

To evaluate this theory, Rogers and Pridemore (2017) carried out an extensive review of the research literature. They then used data for the years 1999–2004 from a sample of fifty-five nations to test the two common beliefs noted above. Their review of the literature did not, however, support the prevailing beliefs. First, they noted that, of the 146 statistical models that used a cross-national sample, only nineteen found the expected positive association between the percentage of young people and homicide rates. Said another way, 82 percent of the models revealed no statistically significant association of young men with national homicide rates, and another 5 percent showed a negative association. In fact, including the percentage of young men in statistical models of cross-national homicide rates muddies or weakens the models.

Why, then, did criminologists think that the percentage of young men raised the homicide rate? Rogers and Pridemore (2017) think it is because the percentage of young men may be a proxy for poverty. As we have seen, poverty and inequality increase homicide rates. They also produce, or at least correlate with, high fertility rates, which over time produce large numbers of young people. As a result, high proportions of young people—specifically, young men—produce high rates of homicide because large numbers of these young people are poor. By including measures of both poverty and youthfulness in a model, researchers are measuring the same trait with two different variables, "overfitting" the model and making it less reliable.

That said, the demographic explanation of homicide—the theory that having more young men means having more homicides—still has appeal if our goal is to explain patterns of homicide in Canada. In 1961, the homicide rate was even lower than it is today—about 1.3 homicides a year per 100,000 people (Beattie and Roy, 2018). Around 1966, the homicide rate rose dramatically, by 1976 reaching a peak about twice the level it is today. Then, gradually and with many interruptions, the homicide rate fell to its present, relatively low level (Beattie and Roy, 2018). The simplest explanation is there was a growth in the number of potential killers. In Canada, young men increased in both absolute and relative numbers after 1966 because of the so-called "Baby Boom." This was a burst of births that started in 1946, shortly after the end of World War II. By 1966, the oldest of these Baby Boomers would have been in their late teens and early twenties, the prime ages for violent crime.

The Baby Boom, which continued for twenty years, resulted in a higher-than-usual proportion of young men in the population for roughly another twenty-five years—between 1966 and 1991. This also explains the decisive decline in homicide rates that began in 1991. And so, change in Canada's violent crime rate is explained by the proportion of young men—a proxy for poverty—in the population. By contrast, socioeconomic inequality is a weaker explanation of variations in homicide. After 1976, socioeconomic inequality increased in Canada, as it did in other high-income societies. This should have increased homicides, but it didn't.

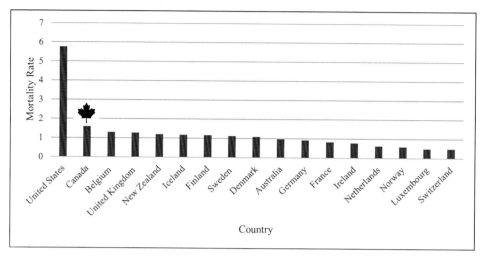

Figure 4-2. Rates of Intentional Homicide per 100,000 Population, Canada and Comparison Countries, 2019.

Figure 4-2 (above) shows homicide rates in various economically developed countries. By international standards, Canada has modest rates of homicide. Your risk of dying from a homicide in Canada is much lower than it would be if you lived in the United States. However, it is much higher than if you lived in (say) Norway, Switzerland, or Luxembourg. Of the seventeen countries in the chart, the United States has a far higher rate of intentional homicide than any other—in fact, more homicides than all the other countries combined.

First, let's start with the demographic explanation of these national variations: more young men. Societies with high birth (or fertility) rates will have a higher fraction of young people than countries with lower birthrates. So, for example, for a long time the United States has had higher birth rates than Norway, Switzerland, and Luxembourg, especially in poor and rural communities.

Consider, also, the related roles played by poverty and economic inequality. The United States has a higher rate of economic inequality than these three comparison countries, so we would predict higher rates of homicide in the former than in the latter. And don't forget the easy availability of handguns in the U.S., compared with these other countries. Handguns are far more common in the U.S. than in any comparison country. Their availability predicts high rates of homicide, as witnessed by the data in Figure 4-2. Half the handguns in Canada come in illegally from the U.S. Other comparison countries do not run this risk, as they do not share a border with the U.S.

Finally, civility and the rule of law have been less secure in the U.S. than in many of our sixteen other comparison countries. Americans and others often discussed this absence of civility and rule of law during the presidency of Donald Trump. However, it has been obvious in other, earlier periods of American history. The tradition of "frontier justice" and vigilantism is stronger and more loudly celebrated in the U.S. than in any of the other countries we discuss.

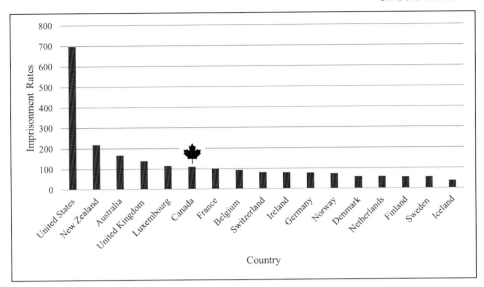

Figure 4-3. Imprisonment Rates in Canada and Comparison Countries, 2018.

Not surprisingly, high rates of crime predict high rates of imprisonment. However, as we see in Figure 4-3, rates of imprisonment in the U.S. go well beyond what one might expect. We find the lowest rates of imprisonment among comparison countries in Iceland, Sweden, Finland, and the Netherlands.

As well, countries vary in the number of offences for which they imprison criminals. The U.S. gives out prison sentences for a wider range of offences than most other countries. For example, the American War on Drugs has resulted in high levels of imprisonment for drug offenses and nonviolent offences.

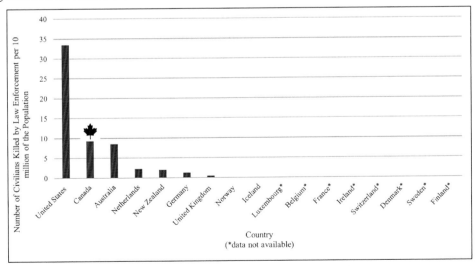

Figure 4-4. Number of Civilians Killed by Law Enforcement (per 10 million of the population), Canada and Comparison Countries, 2017.

Finally, countries vary in the rate at which police kill civilians. Again, as we see in Figure 4-4, the U.S. tops the list, with Norway and Iceland at the end.

Indigenous people are among the most likely to suffer criminal victimization in Canada. As we will see, they are also among those who are most likely to commit and be punished for crimes. Throughout the world, Indigenous people in post-colonial countries entered the twenty-first century at a disadvantage. This disadvantage, built into the capitalist economy, is not limited to Canada. Nor have its results been different in Canada than in other high-income countries. Indigenous people who live in distinct rural communities all report higher than average rates of poverty, unemployment, addiction, poor health, and suicidal plans (Axelsson et al., 2016). This is true whether we look at Canada, the U.S., Australia, New Zealand, Norway, or Finland.

A long history of discrimination and poverty helps explain the disproportionate effect of crime on Indigenous peoples. This photograph of children at the Fort Simpson Indian Residential School—heartbreakingly holding up letters that spell out the word "Goodbye"—was taken in 1922.

Why are Indigenous people, and other vulnerable and disadvantaged people, more likely than average to commit crimes and be victimized by crimes? The answer has to do with social inequality and the long-term privation, harm, and resentment that such disparities produce. Indigenous people are, on average, more likely to live in impoverished conditions than non-Indigenous people in Canada, and poverty can lead to an increased crime rate. These disparities also appear on a global scale. Low levels of education, income, and health persist among Indigenous people in Australia and New Zealand despite the economic development of these countries (United Nations, 2009).

Thus, like Canada, the Indigenous populations of Australia and New Zealand face significant challenges that increase their vulnerability to criminality. The unexpectedly high number of Indigenous people in prison is not unique to Canada. To put matters in context, 27 percent of the Australian prison population comprises Indigenous Australians, despite their accounting for only 2 percent of the adult population in 2016 (Australian Bureau of Statistics, 2018). In New Zealand, the Maori account for 50 percent of offenders, while comprising only about 15 percent of the total New Zealand population (Tauri, 2005; Corrections Department NZ, 2018).

Prejudice may also play a part in these statistics. A possibly significant influence on crime and imprisonment statistics is the role of racial profiling by police and courts (Tator and Henry, 2006; Wortley and Tanner, 2004; Wortley, 2003). Racial profiling leads to over-policing, making certain populations seem more inclined towards crime than they really are. Indigenous people are often simultaneously over- and under-policed. This means that police are more likely to arrest them for a crime and less likely to protect them.

The Ontario Human Rights Commission found in a 2015 survey of 1503 Ontarians that many survey respondents thought they had experienced racial profiling or other forms of racial discrimination. This discrimination might have been based on dress and appearance, such as wearing a hijab; certain types of activities and travel; accents; being an immigrant or newcomer to Canada; and having a racialized name.

The Ontario Human Rights Commission defines racial profiling in a widely inclusive way. It is "any action undertaken for reasons of safety, security or public protection, that relies on stereotypes about race, colour, ethnicity, ancestry, religion, or place of origin, or a combination of these, rather than on a reasonable suspicion, to single out an individual for greater scrutiny or different treatment." Racial profiling occurs when law enforcement officials assume that just because someone is, for example, Black, they are more likely to commit a crime. Critics often accuse the police of racial profiling when police officers watch, search, or stop and question racialized people for no clear reason. Racial profiling might also explain a judge's refusal to grant bail to a person because of a race-based belief that he or she will violate the terms.

As mentioned, Black (as well as Indigenous) people are overrepresented in Canadian prisons. In fact, Black inmates account for nearly 10 percent of the total prison population despite accounting for a mere 3 percent of the total Canadian population. This particular population is one of the fastest growing in federal prisons (Sapers, 2013). Many Black people, and other racialized minorities, feel like victims of prejudice and discrimination by the justice system. For example, in 2011–12, the Office of the Correctional Investigator conducted a study of the unique experiences of Black inmates. Nearly all the Black inmates interviewed for the survey reported experiences of discrimination and covert racism by prison staff. This included being ignored, isolated, or neglected.

Respondents reported noticing a "different set of rules" for Black inmates and greater-than-average difficulty securing a prison job. There were reports of Black inmates being the victims of harmful stereotyping. For example, correction officers labeled many of them "gang members," yet over 80 percent had no gang affiliation.

The study also revealed that Black inmates were overrepresented in "discretionary" prison charges such as disrespecting staff and disobeying orders. They are underrepresented in prison for charges that need proof of infraction (such as a charge of having stolen property). As correctional investigator Howard Sapers (2012) notes, the experience of racial profiling "follows Black Canadians into prisons." Discrimination of this sort feels unfair because it *is* unfair. A sense of being victimized by prejudice and discrimination may lead Black rule-breakers to nurse grievances that lead to further crime and imprisonment. If so, at this point they will be once again targets of harmful, racist treatment.

Human Trafficking and Organized Crime

Unlike the crimes discussed so far, human trafficking is largely transnational or global in nature. It is also nearly invisible, and most Canadians know little about it.

Labour migration is an economic and social mobility strategy that benefits millions of people around the world. Human trafficking and the exploitation of low-wage migrant workers accompany such migration. Human trafficking poses a public health problem for the entire world (Zimmerman and Kiss, 2017).

Extreme economic inequality in the world makes it possible for those in power to dominate people without power (Barner et al., 2014). Arising from unequal power relations, human trafficking exploits many people, but mostly women and children.

Human trafficking displays three aspects. Often, it involves transporting or holding a person. Second, the traffickers do this against the victim's will, usually by using force or threats. Third, they do it to exploit the victim. There are different kinds of human trafficking, such as sex trafficking, organ trafficking, and trafficking in slavery (UNODC). Human trafficking can occur anywhere and to anyone. Reportedly, there is a strong link between drug trafficking and human trafficking. Shelley (2012) notes the link is enormously complex. Many types of drug trafficking intersect in different ways with the many forms of human trafficking. Together, they play an important role in recruiting and keeping human trafficking victims for all forms of sexual exploitation. Traffickers use drugs to compel individuals to perform sexual acts or engage in pornography. Smuggled individuals often pay to be taken to their destination by acting as drug couriers, either by swallowing or transporting drugs. Traffickers also use drugs to recruit new victims and keep them vulnerable to exploitation.

The more complex the business, the larger the network that supports it. Traffickers use various networks, both formal and informal, to carry out their crimes, including transportation and communication networks. Many traffickers work a "circuit." The circuit may consist of certain cities or locations within a city with which a trafficker might be familiar or have connections.

During transit, victims must be housed. Large organized networks use known safe houses or private homes, or arrange with lodging establishments along the route to house victims temporarily without raising suspicion. Internet and mobile technologies allow traffickers to connect with clients, communicate with other members of their network, find and secure transport and lodging, and conduct financial transactions.

Traffickers build networks with secrecy in mind. As a result, reliable statistics about human trafficking are hard to come by. With this in mind, we should view the official statistics presented in Figure 4-5 as tentative.

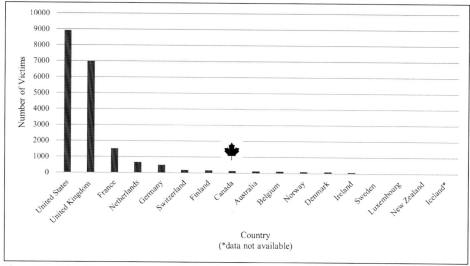

Figure 4-5. Victims of Human Trafficking, Canada and Comparison Countries, 2018.

Apart from secrecy, other factors explain why the prevalence of human trafficking is so uncertain. One reason is that, in a sense, instances of human trafficking are *social constructs*. They rest on certain assumptions about reality which, if changed, would produce different results. Consider research by Feingold (2011) in Burma. He highlights the problem that male-dominated societies treat adult women like children, denying them agency. Thus, people view sex workers who are away from their home community as having been trafficked. Too often, governments' first response to trafficking is to focus on controlling migration, rather than controlling compulsion, deception and exploitation. The society protects adult women from "trafficking" by depriving them of the right to unsupervised movement. Analyzing the unintended effects of well-meant but ill-conceived migration or development policies is critical for a comprehensive approach, which avoids fixing one problem while aggravating another.

Farrell and Reicher (2017) offer a more mundane, institutional account for why we have poor estimates of human trafficking offences. They base their analyses on two police departments, one in Chicago and the other in Tennessee, noting that over the past decade, law enforcement has increasingly been called on to look into human-trafficking offences. There have been numerous efforts to track incidents, arrests, and criminal offences related to trafficking. However, despite the promises of standardized data from law enforcement about human trafficking, the numbers of reported human-trafficking offences and arrests remain low.

Through interviews, the researchers identify four major challenges to accurate human trafficking reporting. First, it's difficult to distinguish between prostitution offences and trafficking for sexual exploitation. Often, victims are also reluctant to aid police in prosecuting traffickers because of their reliance on, and personal connection with, their trafficker or pimp. Second, there are problems training officers to both identify new offences and to report these offences using standard crime reporting procedures. Many U.S. states passed laws requiring police be educated about human trafficking, but the states vary widely in the curriculum and instruction they provide.

Third, specially trained personnel are needed to identify and explore human trafficking crimes. To discover a sex worker's agency, one must ask the right questions. But all too often, caregivers and people in authority—including teachers, doctors, nurses, social workers and police—fail to do so. Deshpande and Nour (2013) note that in 2004 the U.S. Department of Health and Human Services set up a campaign to increase awareness of human trafficking among healthcare workers. Healthcare providers represent one of only a few groups of professionals who may meet with victims of sex trafficking. In fact, one study found that 28 percent of trafficked women saw a healthcare professional while still in captivity.

Sex trafficking begins with targeting and manipulating vulnerable women as young as 13. It is likely that a culture of gender inequality that over-sexualizes women plays a role in the number of women affected by this crime. Not surprisingly, the International Labour Organization considers trafficking to be modern-day slavery. Pimps sell victims as belongings, even branding some with the pimp's street name. Sex trafficking is profitable. A pimp can earn between $168,000 and $336,000 a year for one woman.

The rise of social media makes it even easier to lure and entrap victims. Social media allow pimps to post job advertisements or pose as eligible singles on dating websites. In 2018 classfied ad site Craigslist shut down its "personals" section in response to American legislation meant to hold websites responsible for promoting trafficking. The problem is growing steadily in Canada, commanding the attention of legislators (De Shalit, Heynen, and van der Meulen, 2014: 386).

The demand for sex workers and vulnerable women encourages criminal organizations to exploit victims by taking advantage of global economic inequalities. Criminals associated with these organizations may lure their victims with promises of a better future, financial gain, and the appeal of moving to a high-income country. Hughes (2006: 626) argues that traffickers often exploit women who are looking for employment, luring them with seemingly legitimate job offers as nannies, nurses, companions, or escorts. Besides direct recruitment, criminals also exploit women by using marriage agencies or mail-order-bride services (Hughes, 2006: 634).

Different countries play different roles when it comes to human trafficking. Stewart and Gajic-Veljanoski (2005: 25) note that Canada is both a destination and a transit country. That is, Canada serves both as a market for the victims of human trafficking and a staging ground for the transport abroad of those victims. A report commissioned by the RCMP estimates that at least 800 individuals are trafficked into Canada each year. Between 1,500 and 2,200 people are trafficked out of Canada to the United States (Hanley, Oxman-Martinez, Lacroix and Gal, 2006: 82). Those numbers will likely continue to rise.

Poverty, exclusion, and underemployment increase the likelihood of human trafficking of Canadian women, and especially Indigenous women. Poverty makes this population vulnerable to abduction and forced entry into human trafficking. Many Indigenous women choose to enter the sex trade—to be trafficked—to escape poverty and an often abusive environment. So Indigenous women and others are likely to cross national borders to do sex work.

According to the *Globe and Mail* (Grant, 2016), Indigenous youth make up over half of the victims of sex trafficking in this country. Many blame this situation on the history of violence, racism and discrimination against these Canadians. According to Indigenous representatives, the damage done by residential schools and colonization may have weakened identity and family bonds among Indigenous youth. This makes them easy targets for exploitation. In 2014 alone, there were 206 reports of human trafficking in Canada.

Experts say the number of victims can be even higher. Some have called the crisis a "hidden epidemic" because it remains mostly out of the public eye. Some Indigenous victims lack stable family and home environments (Grant, 2018). Human traffickers may also exploit people from other countries by luring them here, but 90 percent of victims come from within the nation's borders. Most trafficked people are women and young girls, commonly around 15 to 24 years old (Statistics Canada, 2018).

Canada has taken significant steps to deal with these problems. However, it may never be possible to end trafficking because of the ongoing demand for "slaves," and the porous boundaries of Canadian society. Lack of accurate data with which to shape policymaking also poses a problem. Even setting up a common framework to address the issue remains difficult. The media, nongovernmental organizations, and the governments involved affect the way that we define human trafficking. As a result, communities prosecute and look into these crimes in different ways, and in the end few individuals are charged and imprisoned.

Human trafficking occurs alongside, or because of, political corruption. Smith et al. (2014) point out that human trafficking is a profitable crime industry. The $32 billion in revenues each year exceed those brought in by the trade in illegal drugs and arms dealing.

Through globalization and easy mobility, sexual labour and enslavement flourish. This makes human trafficking both a national problem and a transnational crisis. Victims are found in both high- and low-income countries, and in countries regarded as corrupt and those which are not. But higher levels of corruption predict higher levels of trafficking.

Human trafficking involves a source for a product (the victim) and a method of getting that product to its consumers (Konrad et al., 2016). In sex trafficking this can mean a pimp finding a vulnerable victim on the street and forcing her to advertise herself online for commercial sexual exploitation, then helping her complete that business transaction. Alternatively, it may be a complex, transnational organized network that lures victims with false job promises. It brings them to a foreign country, takes their documents, and forces them into exploitive work.

It should come as no surprise that organized crime plays a part in much human trafficking. The World Economic Forum publishes a report every year ranking the global competitiveness of every country. As a part of this report, they survey business owners on the costs and challenges they face because of organized crime. Countries are then ranked on a scale from 1 to 7. A score of 1 means there are enormous costs to business because of organized crime, while a score of 7 means there are no real costs. As Figure 4-6 shows, Finland, Iceland and Switzerland report the lowest costs of organized crime imposed on business, whereas the United States, the United Kingdom and Germany report the highest. Canada, again, finds itself around the middle of the pack.

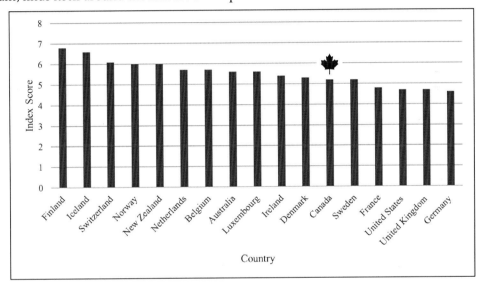

Figure 4-6. Costs on Business Imposed by Organized Crime, Canada and Comparison Countries, 2019.

Organized crime is also involved in trafficking and selling illegal substances. Its involvement with drugs ranges from street-level dealing of marijuana, to the international smuggling and importation of heroin and fentanyl, to the production of methamphetamines. About 80 percent of organized crime groups in Canada take part in the drug trade (CSIS 2007). Despite common assumptions about people involved in organized crime, many drug traffickers lead otherwise respectable lives. They rely on people skills as much or more than blackmail, bribery and force to get their way and cover their tracks (von Lampe, 2007).

Networks of organized crime also work beyond national borders. In the European Union, the free movement of EU citizens across national borders simplifies matters for organized crime (Töttel, Bulanova-Hristova and Kleemans, 2012). According to Töttel et al. (2012), in Germany in 2010 around 85 percent of criminal charges tied to organized crime had international links. Like many of the problems studied in this book, then, organized crime needs an international solution.

While the number of individuals and groups that take part is relatively small, organized crime accounts for a disproportionate share of victimization and crime in Canada. Organized crime groups in Canada number roughly between 500 and 900, and include ethnic gangs, such as the Asian Triads, motorcycle gangs, like the Hell's Angels, and others (Stys and Ruddell 2013).

With organized crime comes violence. One example involves the continuing fight over tow truck businesses in Toronto. The so-called "tow truck wars" have entailed more than fifty incidents of arson, multiple shootings, and four homicides. In early 2021, investigations of the matter resulted in over 200 charges against suspect organized crime offenders and the arrest of at least three police officers on charges of corruption (*Toronto Star*, 2021; Goodfield, 2020).

To end on a positive note, Stys and Ruddell (2013) find that recidivism rates—rates of reoffending—are much lower for offenders from organized crime than among other offenders. This suggests Canada is succeeding to some degree in rehabilitating organized crime offenders.

Concluding Remarks

What a society defines as a crime is socially constructed and culturally relative. Current concepts of morality and responsibility, religious ideals, and competing scientific claims all influence crime's definition and supposed causes. As well, rates of crime vary over time. Even "official" crime rates are socially constructed since they leave out many hidden (or ignored) crimes. All crime is socially relative. We understand it only within the given historical context.

In Canada, law enforcement as well as the monitoring and measurement of crime are complicated by the fact that, while criminal law is a federal responsibility, its enforcement falls mainly to provincial, regional and municipal police forces and court systems. For example, the Ontario Provincial Police is Canada's second-largest police service, responsible for providing policing over an area of more than a million square kilometres. Above, an OPP detachment in Sebringville, Ontario.

How we measure crime and punishment varies widely, depending on how different countries deal with sameness, civility, and equity. Societies with a strong focus on equity will moderate their punishments and try to address the conditions (such as poverty) that produce crime. Societies with a strong focus on civility may emphasize rules protecting public order over those safeguarding private property. Societies with a strong focus on sameness may also be concerned about public order and, beyond that, may exercise a high degree of police vigilance in immigrant and ethnic communities.

As we have seen, though Canada and its comparison countries face similar challenges when it comes to crime, they respond differently in their responses. Canada reports less crime than the U.S. and punishes crime with lengthy imprisonment less frequently. However, crime rates in Canada exceed those in some comparison countries, especially the Nordic countries. Canada relies more on probation, parole, and restorative justice than the U.S., but it does less to prevent crime—and offers less help to disadvantaged population—than the Nordic countries.

Today criminals and criminal organizations work across every border. We must understand problems like human trafficking, cybercrime, and gun violence as global issues that individual countries can combat only by cooperating with other countries. So far, that cooperation has been halting and incomplete.

Having said that, where does Canada rank in comparison with the sixteen other countries we have considered? We rank Canada in the bottom third of the nations that we are studying, around twelfth out of seventeen. Canada fares poorly on such measures as homicide and the killing of civilians by police officers. It does only slightly better in such areas as human trafficking. All in all, criminal justice leaves much room for improvement in Canada. And, as we will see in a later chapter, crime rates vary widely from one province or territory to another. This is not only because the demographic makeup of the provinces and territories varies. It is also because in Canada, although the Criminal Code is federal legislation, provincial and local police forces play the biggest role in enforcing it.

CHAPTER FIVE

Health and Addictions

Health and illness affect everyone. Yet disparities in health and healthcare are not merely personal problems. They are social problems, because improving the health of the whole population depends on governments and other large institutions. And that also makes them national problems, which some nations handle better than others.

No Canadian who has lived through the COVID-19 pandemic can doubt the social significance of health, healthcare, and illness prevention. A recent survey by Environics Institute documented the extent of the harm done by COVID-19 in a national random sample of nearly 6,000 Canadians. In answer to the question, "Have you experienced any of the following as a result of the COVID pandemic?" roughly six in ten reported specific consequences. Some experienced very specific health consequences: for example, 3 percent reported contracting the virus and 6 percent reported the death of a family member from the virus. Others reported significant economic consequences: for example, 6 percent reported they were unable to pay their rent or mortgage, 9 percent reported missing a major bill or credit card charge, 12 percent had been asked to reduce their number of hours at work, and 13 percent had been unemployed or laid off. Since many people with jobs had to work from home, 17 percent reported difficulty balancing their work and family responsibilities. Not surprisingly, 32 percent of respondents—roughly one person in three—said they had trouble sleeping as a result of the pandemic, and 34 percent reported experiencing more depression and anxiety than before the pandemic.

Research reveals that, often, the biggest influences on our health are *social determinants of health* (SDOH) such as income, education, working conditions, housing, and nutrition. As we have (again) learned from the COVID-19 pandemic, some people—people with less education and lower incomes—find themselves more exposed to the risk of illness and are more likely to lose working hours or become unemployed. Without good housing, enough income, good quality education, safe working conditions, and healthy food, people's health suffers. Sociologists focus on these social determinants of health to call attention to social factors—factors other than genetics and personal psychology—that contribute to our well-being.

We will see in this chapter that Canada does moderately well in various health domains in comparison with our sixteen other countries. It does especially well on some addiction issues, such as smoking prevention, but poorly on other health issues such as obesity. Canada has done moderately well in dealing with the COVID-19 pandemic. Through mid-2021, nine of the comparison countries reported higher death rates per capita from the pandemic than Canada. Years earlier, Canada had done even better dealing with SARS and HIV-AIDS. That said, Canada's life expectancy at birth is not as high as it might be, to judge from similar countries. So, on balance, Canada could stand to learn things from our comparison countries, leaving aside the United States and the United Kingdom.

As usual, let's begin this discussion with some insights into the topic of illness offered by thinkers of previous generations. Hippocrates, the father of medicine, called our attention to the close connection between bodily health and mental health. He noted that "persons who have a painful affection in any part of the body and are in a great measure sensible of the pain, are disordered in intellect." In other words, a physical sickness can disorder our thinking. Of this, the poet Alexander Pope wrote, "Sickness is a sort of early old age; it teaches us a diffidence in our earthly state." Said another way, sickness is deeply humbling. The Jewish European thinker Sholem Asch suggested that "an illness is like a journey into a far country; it sifts all one's experience and removes it to a point so remote that it appears like a vision."

No one understood illness and incapacity more intensely or poetically than the (often bedridden) French novelist Marcel Proust. "It is in moments of illness," Proust wrote, "that we are compelled to recognize that we live not alone but chained to a creature of a different kingdom, whole worlds apart, who has no knowledge of us and by whom it is impossible to make ourselves understood: our body." Along similar lines, Soviet-era Russian poet Anna Akhmatova wrote, "I seem to myself, as in a dream, / An accidental guest in this dreadful body."

Sickness disrupts our lives in every way. As Susan Sontag put it, "Illness is the night side of life, a more onerous citizenship. Everyone who is born holds dual citizenship, in the kingdom of the well and in the kingdom of the sick. Although we all prefer to use the good passport, sooner or later each of us is obliged, at least for a spell, to identify ourselves as citizens of that other place." French novelist Francoise Sagan expressed a similar sentiment: "Illness is the opposite of freedom. It makes everything impossible."

However, it is equally important to understand that personal sickness is, often, the symptom of a sick society. On this, 1960s radical David Dellinger argued, "This is a diseased world in which it is impossible for anyone to be fully human. One way or another, everyone who lives in the modern world is sick or maladjusted." And suitable for the present-day COVID-19 pandemic are the words of Albert Camus in his book, *The Plague*: "The pestilence is at once blight and revelation; it brings the hidden truth of a corrupt world to the surface." Put less poetically, illness exposes all of our social inequalities: for instance, the poor working conditions, lack of access to healthcare and disproportionate risk of illness faced by low-income and working-class Canadians.

In his book *The Conditions of the Working Class in England*, Friedrich Engels ([1845] 2009) showed how social disadvantage affected the death rate in the industrial city of Manchester, England. He recognized the importance of social conditions in producing these horrible results. Workers there endured substandard housing, lack of sanitation, inadequate diet and clothing, and harsh working conditions. Three years later, the German doctor Rudolf Virchow, often credited as the father of modern pathology, declared the root causes of a typhus epidemic in Prussia were regional poverty, poor education, and inept government. Virchow famously remarked that "medicine is a social science" and asked, "Do we not always find the diseases of the populace traceable to defects in society?" (quoted in Rather, 1985).

Seeing the link between social injustice and ill health forces us to examine the social inequalities of health. These social inequalities vary in kind and degree from one society to another and are all subject to change through legislation. These are conditions that all modern societies can regulate, change, and improve, if the political will to do so is present. But, as we have seen throughout this book, societies vary in their political will and their ability to institute important social changes. As a result, in some societies, people lead healthier, longer lives than in other societies.

So, for example, look at the data in Figure 5-1, then consider which social practices allow Switzerland to have a higher life expectancy at birth than Canada, when we average across the sexes. Are these the same practices that allow Canada to have a higher life expectancy at birth than the United States? If we can answer questions like that, we can better understand what Switzerland is "doing better" with social determinants than Canada. We can also understand what Canada is "doing better" than the United States.

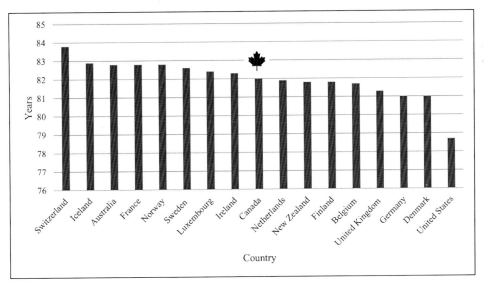

Figure 5-1. Life Expectancy at Birth (Men and Women), Canada and Comparison Countries, 2019.

Endogenous Causes of Death and Disability

The main causes of death in Canada and other high-income countries are what we call *endogenous diseases*. Unlike *exogenous* (also called *infectious* or *communicable*) *diseases*, which are carried mainly by viruses and bacteria, endogenous diseases are genetic in origin, though often stimulated (or slowed) by external conditions. The main endogenous diseases include cancers, heart and circulatory diseases, and lung or respiratory diseases. They can cause death and almost invariably, reduce a person's quality of life.

The genetic risks associated with these diseases often reveal themselves slowly and gradually. However, as a population gets older, more people die from these diseases. Of course, some people do not die from these diseases and lead increasingly long lives but do so in a gradually more infirm condition. Canadian men and women today have an average life expectancy of around 82.0 years, despite physical degeneration. This points to the continuing ability of pharmaceutical drugs and medical treatment to prolong life in the face of our natural decline.

Social determinants of health loom especially large in the first half of a person's life, when deaths from accidents, suicide, homicide, and infectious diseases are particularly common. Societies can do much more to prevent and limit accidents, suicides, homicides, and infections, all major causes of death in the first half of life. By contrast, they can do much less to prevent and limit cancers, heart disease, and stroke, all major causes of death in the second half of life.

Societies can also do a lot more about exogenous and communicable (i.e., infectious) diseases than they currently can do about endogenous diseases. Communicable diseases pass from one person to another. Examples include COVID-19, hepatitis, HIV/AIDS and tuberculosis. In Canada, communicable diseases are not generally among the five leading causes of death, although matters changed during the COVID-19 pandemic, with that disease accounting for more deaths than anything but heart disease and cancer.

Even in a "normal" year, however, communicable diseases account for a large fraction of Canada's healthcare spending. According to the Canadian Institute for Health Information, "In 2019, total health expenditure in Canada was expected to reach $265.5 billion, or $7064 per person. It is anticipated that, overall, health spending represented 11.5 percent of Canada's gross domestic product (GDP)." Of this, an estimated $8.3 billion went to control communicable diseases, even before COVID.

Among our seventeen countries, Canada falls in the middle of the pack for deaths from communicable and other exogenous diseases, as seen in Figure 5-2. Rates of death from exogenous diseases declined over the past century, in Canada and elsewhere, thanks largely to improved public health policies (such as vaccinations) and to the spread of economic prosperity.

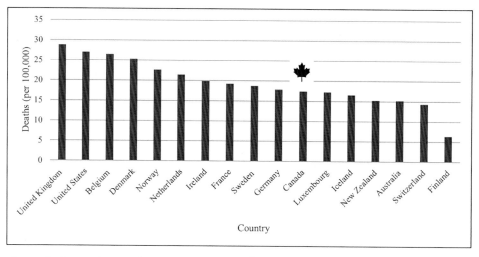

Figure 5-2. Death Rate (per 100,000 people) from Communicable, Maternal, Neonatal, and Nutritional Diseases, Canada and Comparison Countries, 2019.

As noted, most non-communicable diseases are endogenous, degenerative diseases. Examples, as noted earlier, include cancers and heart disease, but also diabetes and Alzheimer's disease. As Figure 5-3 shows, Canadians have a 9.6 percent chance from dying of one of these diseases. This risk grows rapidly after people reach their sixties. The risk of dying of one of these diseases in middle age—between 30 and 70—varies little from one comparison country to another. That said, the U.S. reports the highest risks, owing to far-from-universal healthcare

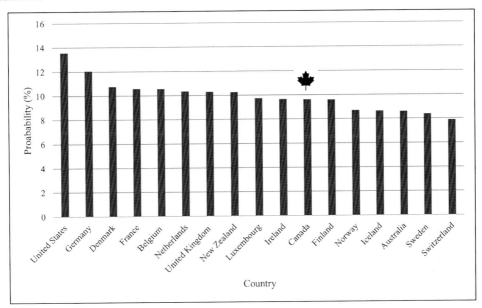

Figure 5-3. Probability of Dying from Any of Cardiovascular Disease, Cancer, Diabetes, Chronic Respiratory Disease between Ages 30-70, Canada and Comparison Countries, 2019.

Like accidents, which we discuss in the next chapter, noncommunicable diseases (including cancers) have many important social effects, such as time lost from work, school, and social engagements. Equally important, many of these diseases have social causes or predisposing conditions. We know, for example, that many types of cancer are associated with cigarette smoking, industrial pollution, or exposure to dangerous cancer-causing materials like asbestos. As we continue to pollute the natural environment with harmful substances, we will continue to increase the rates of death from cancer. This will occur even while we work hard to reduce cancers through various medical treatments.

People are less likely to die of noncommunicable diseases at a young age because our organs degrade slowly over time. Common experiences of stress increase the rate of this degeneration. Many people try to handle their stresses through self-medication with substances like alcohol or drugs. Often, however, doing so creates new and dangerous health problems, both for themselves and the people around them.

The first and most persuasive studies of the effects of social factors on noncommunicable disease were the Whitehall Studies, carried out in England by epidemiologist Michael Marmot. The first study focused on male civil servants aged 20–64 between 1967 and 1977. Then, researchers suspected a link between social inequality, work stress, and poor health but remained unsure (Marmot and Brunner, 2005; Marmot, 2004). The data gathered were revealing. As a civil servant's pay grade increased, his or her risk of death decreased dramatically. Over this ten-year period, people in the highest pay grade (and highest job status) had an annual mortality rate only one-third as high as people in the lowest pay grade.

Studies show that job status has a significant effect on workers' health. People in lower status jobs report less control over their work environment and a heavier workload. These and other factors result in higher levels of stress, which can increase the risk of cardiovascular disease. The sedentary nature of much modern work has also been shown to have adverse health effects.

The second Whitehall project, conducted between 1985 and 1988, focused on male and female civil servants between the ages of 35 and 55. This research studied the effect of psychosocial factors, such as stress and social support, on disease. Some of the health differences by pay grade, noted in the first Whitehall study, proved to be a result of lifestyle differences. For example, obesity and risky lifestyle habits were more common among people in lower status jobs. However, even controlling for lifestyle differences, the researchers found a significant effect of job status on health. People in lower status jobs reported having less social support and encouragement than people in higher status jobs. They also reported less control over their work, less use of their skills, and less variety at work.

Despite their lack of job control and underuse of skills, workers in the lower status jobs experienced a more demanding workload. They found their jobs more exhausting, draining, and depressing. For these reasons, they suffered more psychological stress and this excess stress led to increased risks of cardiovascular disease.

Disabilities and Chronic Illnesses

Disabling conditions and chronic illnesses also vary in prevalence from one country to another, and they too are influenced by social conditions such as economic inequality. In this section we consider a few chronic and disabling conditions.

Diabetes is a common chronic condition in Canada and around the world. Diabetes occurs when the pancreas cannot produce enough insulin (the hormone that regulates blood-sugar levels) or when the body cannot properly use that hormone. Type 1 diabetes is a rare condition that usually shows itself in childhood or adolescence. Type 2 diabetes is far more common, especially in industrialized societies, and usually occurs later in life. Research has shown that eating healthy foods, maintaining a healthy body weight, exercising regularly and avoiding smoking can help prevent Type 2 diabetes. According to the Public Health Agency of Canada (2017), in 2014 three million Canadians lived with diabetes. Every year, 200,000 Canadians are newly diagnosed with diabetes. As a result, one in 300 youths (1–19 years) and one in 10 adults (20+ years) is living with this condition. Further, the number living with diabetes continues to rise because people are leading longer lives, supported by medications.

Diabetes is worrisome because it can cause dangerous health complications such as kidney failure, blindness, and obesity. Diabetes is clearly linked to poverty: taking the world as a whole, four out of five people with diabetes live in low-income countries (IDF Diabetes Atlas, 2017). The number of people with diabetes is on the rise in low- and middle-income countries, largely due to a global increase in sedentary lifestyles and access to processed foods. In those countries, limited access to healthcare services and the high costs of necessary medication may hinder diabetics' chances of survival.

Diabetes clearly reflects the influence of social conditions, and we see a similar influence on other diseases. People in lower income groups are at a greater-than-average risk of experiencing many harmful conditions, which include poor air quality, unhealthy food choices, and harsh working conditions. It comes as no surprise that, in Canada, diabetes is most prevalent among low-income Canadians (Public Health Ontario, 2019).

Cross-national research by Wilkinson and Pickett (2013) and others reveals the more unequal a society is, the poorer health conditions will be. Turning this idea around, to improve people's health will mean making significant changes to the distribution of income and wealth in a society. Yet many people—mainly the wealthiest and even members of the middle class—resist efforts to redistribute income and wealth through taxation. They see no personal benefit or advantage in supporting this change.

Like diabetes, obesity is a global health issue that affects other diseases, such as cardiovascular disease. Figure 5-4 shows the percentage of the adult population that is considered obese across seventeen different countries, including Canada. Canada places in the top three, reporting a lower obesity rate than only the U.S. and New Zealand. Conversely, Sweden, Norway, and Switzerland report the lowest rates of obesity in this group of nations.

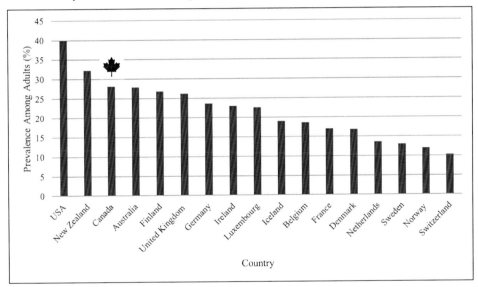

Figure 5-4. Prevalence of Obesity (ages 15+), Canada and Comparison Countries, 2016.

Scientists usually measure obesity by a person's body mass index (BMI). In turn, BMI is equal to a person's weight in kilograms divided by their height in meters squared. For adults, the World Health Organization defines being overweight as having a BMI greater than or equal to 25 and obesity as higher than or equal to 30. Findings from a World Obesity Federation study estimate that by 2025, 34 percent of Canada's population (over 10 million people) will be overweight or obese. The OECD estimates the world's overall obesity rate to be 19.5 percent. Overall, the worldwide prevalence of obesity nearly tripled between 1975 and 2016 (World Obesity Federation, 2017). This suggests that obesity today is a global problem, with globalized causes—diet and lifestyle.

In the Global North, a sedentary lifestyle is one important cause of this increasing obesity rate. A sedentary lifestyle, among several other influences, also leads to other major health problems, including an increased risk of heart disease and high blood pressure (American Heart Association, 2015). Another influence on the rate of obesity is the spread of fast-food outlets. Globalization has allowed fast food to spread around the world. This increase in availability contributes to the rise of obesity because fast-food is cheap and high in calories. Poor people, with less money to spend on food and less leisure time to spend on exercise, are therefore more likely to become overweight and obese than higher-income people.

An added problem, less often discussed, is the widespread stigmatization of obese and overweight people. Many assume that people become obese because they lack discipline or self-control. However, other cultural, social, psychological, and genetic conditions influence how much people eat, what they eat, how quickly they metabolize food, and therefore what they weigh. In addition, different cultural groups have different eating norms and develop eating habits according to these norms. We cannot assume that people who exceed the weight norms of a society are unhealthy, fail to eat well or do not exercise. For all these reasons, we should view both obesity and fat-shaming as social problems, and not personal failings.

Mental Illnesses and Suicide

Mental illness affects people from all walks of life. From a sociological perspective, mental illness is a culturally influenced way of viewing any behaviour the society judges unusual and undesirable. For that and other reasons, assessments of mental health and illness vary from one culture to another. However, medical doctors and psychologists diagnose patients with a mental illness when their symptoms result in significant distress or weakened functioning. There is some overlap between people with mental health disorders and substance use disorders. Often, those who cannot or will not access proper care turn to substances to self-medicate. Addictive substances can affect a person's brain and behavior, interfering with their ability to control their substance use. Therefore, we consider substance use disorders—colloquially referred to as drug addictions—to be diseases.

Figure 5-5 (opposite) shows the percentage of people with mental health or substance use disorders in each of our comparison countries. There is relatively little variation in mental health and substance abuse disorders among these high-income countries. To the extent they vary at all, New Zealand, Australia, and the U.S top the list, while Luxembourg, Denmark, and Iceland are found at the bottom. Canada, as usual, is in the middle of the pack, with just over 15 percent of the population identified as having a mental health or substance use disorder.

Mental health disorders and substance use disorders are common, hard to prevent and hard to cure. One in five Canadians can expect to experience a mental health problem during their lifetimes (Yourex-West, 2015). For example, one in ten Canadians will experience severe anxiety. Young adults are especially vulnerable to stress, anxiety, and depression. Sometimes, these disorders become so severe they lead to suicide, which we will discuss shortly.

Since mental illness is not always visible, it is hard to identify and treat. It is often stigmatized, so people try to hide their symptoms instead of seeking help. As well, different

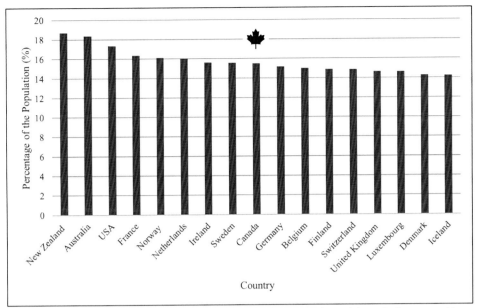

Figure 5-5. Percentage of the Population with a Mental Health or Substance Use Disorder, Canada and Comparison Countries, 2017.

countries devote different amounts of attention and funding to mental health. This means that people in different countries are more or less able to access affordable mental health-care. Because many people are afraid to talk about these problems, we cannot be confident about the available statistics on mental health in different countries. Nonetheless, some re-searchers, like Wikinson and Pickett (2015), have linked mental health problems to income inequality.

In Canada, people with the lowest incomes are more likely than people with the highest incomes to report that their mental health is poor or only fair. As well, cross-national data (Wilkinson and Pickett, 2015) show a strong correlation between mental illness and the Gini index of income inequality. This link does not prove that income inequality causes mental illness, only that the two are correlated. However, poverty and social inequality like-ly increase rates of mental illness by increasing levels of stress and reducing people's social support.

Depression is the most common mental illness in the world and the second leading cause of disability (Braam et al., 2014; World Health Organization, 2017). In 2012, 11.3 per-cent of Canadians reported symptoms defining a major depression (Pearson et al., 2013). Depression features prolonged and recurrent feelings of sadness and negativity. It often accompanies physical symptoms, such as fatigue and changes in eating and sleeping pat-terns. We find depression all over the world, but the ways people view depression vary from culture to culture. As a result, recorded depression rates, as well as interpretations of the disorder, vary around the world.

One significant cause of death related to mental illness is death by suicide. For sociol-ogists, the most relevant fact about suicide is that, though it is intensely personal, it is also socially patterned. The risk of suicide varies dramatically from one country to another, as well as from one group to another. People are almost twice as likely to commit suicide in Belgium as in Canada, for example (see Figure 5-6 on the next page). The cross-national variations in suicide are wide because there are significant social, cultural, and economic differences between countries.

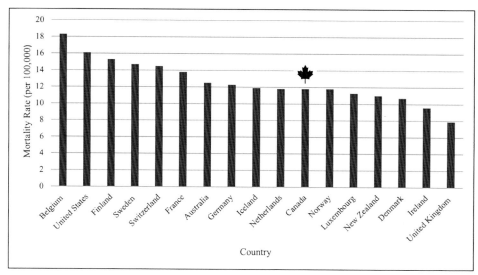

Figure 5-6. Suicide Mortality Rate (per 100,000 of the population), Canada and Comparison Countries, 2019.

As we see in Figure 5-6, Belgium, the United States, and Finland all have high rates of suicide. Views of suicide there may have made it difficult for people to seek help when dealing with their mental health issues. By comparison, Canada has more liberal views of suicide and recognizes good mental health as a national priority.

Denmark, with a suicide rate similar to Canada's, also promotes mental health, and with great success. Denmark has consistently ranked as one of the three happiest countries in the world (World Happiness Report 2018). In part, this may be due to Danish culture, which encourages sociability, intimacy, and close relations between people. Many Danish families schedule regular family time with one another. This builds a strong support network and high degree of social integration. Likely, this helps to explain Denmark's high happiness scores, low rates of depression, and low rates of death from suicide (Helweg-Larsen 2018).

In Canada, roughly eleven people commit suicide every day, totaling 4,000 every year (Government of Canada, 2019). In fact, suicide is the second leading cause of death among young people ages 15 to 34. We see a high rate of suicide among Canada's Indigenous people, especially Inuit in Nunavut (Oliver, Peters, and Cohen, 2012). In our society and many others (for example the United States, Finland, Australia, and New Zealand), Indigenous people suffer more disadvantages than any other group. This leads them to higher rates of depression and suicide in all of these societies.

However, one cannot discuss the suicide rates of Indigenous people without recognizing the impact of colonialism on Indigenous communities. No doubt, this colonial legacy plays a large part in the problems facing Indigenous youth today. Nor can we ignore the legacy of discrimination, poverty, high unemployment rates, high imprisonment rates, and family break-up that many researchers credit to government policies such as residential schools. Today, Indigenous communities also continue to have inadequate access to physical and mental health supports, good education, and housing.

Addictions

We often overlook the social nature of addiction. That's because when we think of people who are "addicted" to something, we think of it as their own problem: they lack self-control. So, we view addictions as we view obesity—a personal problem—and blame it on the victim. We do not realize that addictions are responses to a social context, not purely physiological or even psychological processes. In other words, they are the joint result of biological, psychological, and social conditions.

Today, experts prefer to use the term *substance abuse* to mean what we formerly called "addiction." The WHO defines substance abuse as "the harmful or hazardous use of psychoactive substances, including alcohol and illicit drugs." *Substance-use disorders* (SUDs) are described at length by the American Psychiatric Association in the updated *Diagnostic and Statistical Manual of Mental Disorders*, Fifth Edition. In the DSM-5, we find distinctive definitions for alcohol use disorder, opioid use disorder, and so on.

SUDs are identified by problematic social and personal behaviour. We can tell if someone has a SUD if they are not fulfilling their social duties—for example, missing school or work, or ignoring family responsibilities because of substance use. Typically, they are preoccupied with getting and using the needed substance. People with SUDs generally have a growing physiological tolerance to the effects of a substance. Over time, they need more of the substance (or, with gambling, more of the activity) to provide the same pleasure they got with a smaller amount previously.

People with SUDs crave the substance (or activity) in question, often unable to put it out of their minds. As a result, people suffering from SUDs have a hard time quitting and will usually try many times to do so. An addiction or SUD is a behaviour the individual cannot control, repeats often, and survives, despite massive personal and social costs.

> ### Box 5-1. The Defining Features of Addictions (or SUDs)
>
> • **Tolerance:** *Has your use of drugs or alcohol increased over time?*
> • **A desire to cut down:** *Have you sometimes thought about cutting down or controlling your use? Have you ever made unsuccessful attempts to cut down or control your use?*
> • **Withdrawal:** *When you stop using, have you ever experienced physical or emotional withdrawal? Have you had any of the following symptoms: irritability, anxiety, shakes, sweats, nausea, or vomiting?*
> • **Difficulty controlling your use:** *Do you sometimes use more or for a longer time than you would like? Do you sometimes drink to get drunk? Do you usually stop after a few drinks, or does one drink lead to more drinks?*
> • **Negative results:** *Have you continued to use even though there have been adverse effects to your mood, self-esteem, health, job, or family?*
> • **Putting off or neglecting activities:** *Have you ever put off or reduced social, recreational, work, or household activities because of your use?*
> • **Spending significant time or emotional energy:** *Have you spent a large amount of time getting, using, hiding, planning, or recovering from your use? Have you spent a lot of time thinking about using?*

For ease, from this point forward, we will use the terms addiction and SUD interchangeably, preferring addiction since it is better known. The defining features of addiction are set out in Box 5-1.

Of the various addictive behaviours, cigarette smoking, alcohol abuse, and drug abuse are the best-known. Addictions to gambling, shopping and sex are less widely understood but also hard to control.

Cigarette smoking is an addiction where we have made great strides. The smoking rate fell drastically in Canada in the last fifty years. Achieving this, however, took significant efforts to change social norms and ideas around smoking and its effects.

If we think back to the early twentieth century, World War I hugely benefited cigarette companies, which, as their contribution to the war effort, sent the soldiers abroad free cigarettes. At home, they advertised their product as patriotic, and sales went through the roof. In 1896, only 87 million cigarettes were sold in the U.S. By the early 1920s, after World War I, cigarette sales had risen to 2.4 billion, marking a 28-fold increase. The First World War also promoted a change in the role of women in Canadian society. In the first two decades of the twentieth century, women increased their presence in the workplace and won the right to vote. For women, the right to smoke cigarettes symbolized a new freedom and something like gender equality.

Increasingly, smoking became viewed as normal and, in some quarters, as a pleasant privilege. For a long time, Canadians and their legislators allowed and approved of smoking without considering the health effects. People smoked, and smoke today, because it gives them pleasure and lessens stress, though it (eventually) responds to dependency needs. Today, however, smoking has lost much of its earlier popularity. In Canada, there were 31.1 billion cigarettes sold in 2011 (Corsi et al., 2014). According to Statista, "In August 2020, over 1.8 billion cigarettes were sold in Canada, a slight increase from the previous month," suggesting an annual total of only 21.6 billion cigarettes that year. In 2016, 5.2 million Canadians (or roughly 16.9 percent) aged 12 and older smoked with some regularity and of those, only 3.7 million smoked cigarettes daily (Health Canada, 2016).

Despite this decline, cigarette smoking remains the leading cause of premature death in most high-income countries. An estimated 21 percent of all Canadian deaths over the past decade were related to smoking (Health Canada, 2016). This epidemic of tobacco addiction also poses one of the biggest threats to global health. Smoking kills over seven million people a year worldwide and is a leading global cause of death and illness (WHO, 2020).

For these reasons, in recent decades, governments have made efforts to reduce smoking. The Tobacco and Vaping Products Act, last amended in November 2018, requires tobacco product manufacturers to make their packaging plain and obey rules around color, size, shape, and warning information. All the Canadian provinces have banned smoking in the workplace and many ban smoking in public places such as parks, health institutions, and other locations. As a result, in Canada, smoking prevalence has declined by over 35 percent since 1965 for both men and women (Statistics Canada, 2017).

Men's smoking rates, which had been higher than women's, decreased the most. In 1965, the rate of smoking among men was 23 percentage points higher than among women. In 2018, the difference was less than six percentage points (Statistics Canada, 2019). A continued steady decline in smoking rates is occurring among both men and women. We see similar patterns in most of the world's high-income countries. For example, the smoking rates in Australia, New Zealand and the United Kingdom are 14.1 percent, 14.8 percent, and 19.2 percent respectively (WHO, 2020). Compared to the other 16 comparison countries, Canada's smoking rates are low.

Cigarette smoking grew enormously in popularity in North America during and after the First World War. Tobacco companies spent large amounts of money advertising cigarettes on radio and in mass-market magazines, as in the case of this advertisement for Camel cigarettes, which appeared in 1941. Ironically, in the light of what is now known about smoking's adverse health effects, the ads often tied the practice of smoking to good health and vitality. Here, iconic baseball star Joe DiMaggio promotes the popular Camel brand. DiMaggio died of lung cancer in 1999.

Figure 5-7 (next page) shows that European countries like France, Germany, and Switzerland have especially high rates of smoking compared to Canada. Nordic countries cover the middle range and Canada has the lowest rate of the comparison countries.

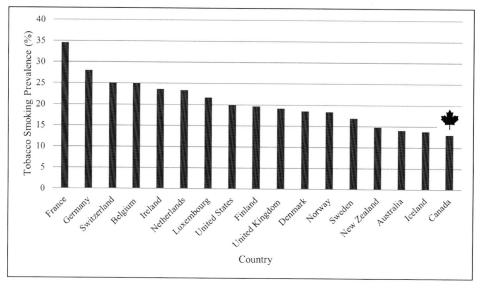

Figure 5-7. Tobacco Smoking Prevalence Rates (%), Canada and Comparison Countries, 2018.

Recently, e-cigarettes have increased teenagers' exposure to tobacco products. Youth wrongly see e-cigarettes as safer and less addictive than regular cigarettes. Many e-cigarettes come in "non-threatening" forms such as candy or breath strips and have enticing flavors such as bubble gum and vanilla. However, despite their safe-seeming appearance and taste, e-cigarettes deliver high amounts of nicotine and carry a high potential for nicotine addiction (CAMH, 2020). Researchers predict that 20.2 percent of youth ages 15 to 19 will soon be smoking e-cigarettes. This is worrisome, since e-cigarettes are as likely as other cigarettes to produce throat, ear, and nose cancer, gum disease, and bad breath (Grana et al., 2014; McNeill et al., 2015).

In the Nordic countries the relatively low rates of smoking and lung cancer have several causes. First, they reflect a steady increase in tobacco prices every year, the result of ever-higher taxes on the product. This rise in prices produces a 2 percent decrease in smoking each year. Second, smoking on work sites has been banned (Andersson et al., 2018). Third, governmental and non-governmental organizations have made vigorous efforts to reduce smoking and pollution from other sources. Iceland, to discourage cigarette smoking among adolescents, used national school-based antismoking initiatives and nation-wide media campaigns. Laws were also passed to decrease the availability and visibility of tobacco products (Kristjansson et al., 2016)

Like cigarette smoking, alcohol use is a national problem in many societies. In most cultures, people use alcohol to relax and improve recreational activities. Most people pace their alcohol intake and avoid getting drunk. However, some people cannot or do not want to do that. Often, we call them *binge drinkers*. Binge drinking is a pattern of occasional drinking that causes the blood alcohol concentration to rapidly rise to 0.08 percent of blood volume or higher. Achieving this takes around five drinks in the span of two hours for an average male and four drinks for an average female.

Binge drinking is especially common among college-age students. The National Survey on Drug Use and Health found that in the United States, 36.9 percent of college-aged people had binged on alcohol at least once in the last month.

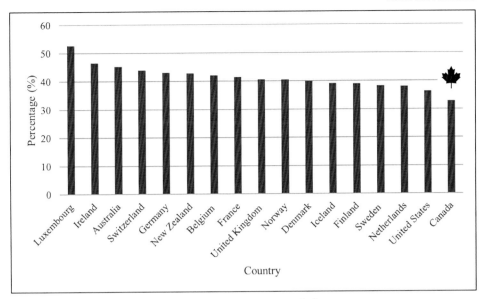

Figure 5-8. Prevalence of Heavy Episodic Drinking (%),* Canada and Comparison Countries, 2016.
*Percentage of people over 15 who drank 60 grams or more of pure alcohol on at least one occasion in the last 30 days.

As we can see from Figure 5-8, Canada has the lowest binge drinking rates among all the comparison countries. The high rate of binge drinking in the United Kingdom may reflect the low price of alcohol there (Plant et al., 2009). By comparison, the high rate in Denmark may reflect that country's high degree of tolerance of alcohol-related problems.

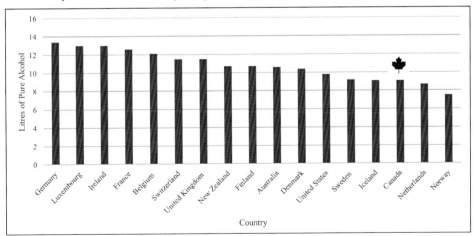

Figure 5-9. Alcohol Consumption per Capita (≥ age 15), Canada and Comparison Countries, 2016.

Canada's alcohol consumption rate per person is also a lot lower than in most comparison countries (Figure 5-9). Canada's lower rates of alcohol consumption reflect many factors, including the provincial management of liquor sales. In Canada, provincial governments manage liquor sales and set minimum prices for wines, beers and spirits, following local standards. Typically, provincial liquor outlets set higher prices to raise revenue and reduce dangerous alcohol consumption (Thomas, 2012).

Excessive drinking carries many social costs. For one thing, it increases the risk of domestic violence, assault, and homicide. For that reason, countries with the highest rates of drinking also have the highest rates of alcohol-related death. The World Health Organization says there are six alcohol-related deaths worldwide every minute of every day (WHO, 2018).

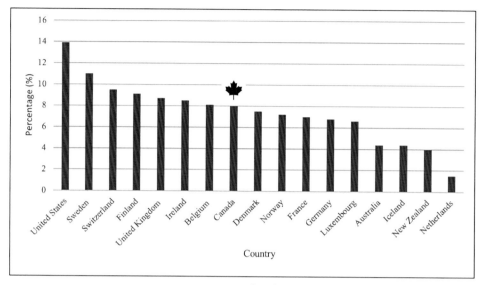

Figure 5-10. Percentage of the Population (15+) with Alcohol Use Disorders, Canada and Comparison Countries, 2016.

An estimated 4.9 percent of the world's population also suffers from *alcohol use disorder*, or alcohol addiction (WHO, 2018). A classification of alcohol use disorder requires having three or more symptoms of addiction for at least one month. In the figure above, which shows the rates of alcohol use disorders as percentages, Canada comes in around the middle of the comparison countries. Alcohol use disorders are highest in the United States and lowest in the Netherlands.

Alcohol and drug abuse are especially common among Canada's Indigenous population (Jiwa et al., 2008). As well as consuming alcohol, 62.5 percent of Indigenous people report having used illicit drugs, typically cannabis (prior to its legalization) and cocaine, during the past calendar year (Currie et al., 2013). As well, over the past fifty years, Indigenous people have started drinking at an ever-earlier age (Kunitz, 2008).

As with the high rates of suicide, the high levels of alcoholism among Indigenous people are largely due to the living conditions many Indigenous people must endure. On the reserves especially, we see the cycle of poverty, poor housing, trauma, and substance abuse being perpetuated in many of their lives.

Canada is also experiencing an opioid crisis, which continues to grow at an alarming rate. As Figure 5-11 shows, Canada has the second highest rate of deaths from opioid use in the comparison countries. Opioids—including codeine, fentanyl, or morphine—are all drugs that relieve pain. So, opioids also have the potential for dangerous use, as they dampen pain and induce euphoria. However, since opioids affect the region of your brain that controls breathing, it results in slower breathing. Taken to an extreme, such as with an overdose, this slowdown in breathing can lead to unconsciousness and even death.

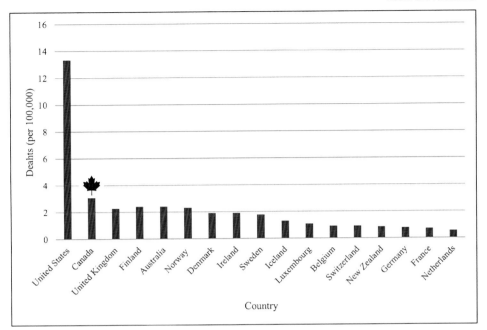

Figure 5-11. Deaths (per 100,000 population) from Opioid Use Disorders, Canada and Comparison Countries, 2017.

In 2017, there were nearly 4,000 opioid-related deaths in Canada, a number significantly higher than the 2,861 deaths in 2016 (Lisa and Jessica, 2018). Nearly three-quarters of opioid-related deaths involved fentanyl—a designer drug, specifically prepared in a laboratory—or fentanyl analogues (Lisa and Jessica, 2018). Fentanyl is produced mainly in China and transported to Canada through postal or commercial air delivery. Chinese companies make these drugs cheaply, at alarmingly fast rates, with some companies producing over one million pills each day (Battiloro, 2019).

Canadians consume the second-largest quantity of opioids in the world, second only to the United States. Many people who overdose on drugs do so using opioid drugs prescribed for someone else as a painkiller (Government of Canada, 2019). Unfortunately, doctors often prescribe more opioids than their patients need (Rieder 2018). Unused drugs may fall into the hands of family members or others if they are thrown away or remain at the back of a medicine chest. Therefore, Canadian doctors urge the parents of teens to keep their prescription drugs out of reach.

Canada, along with the United States, currently has some of the highest rates of prescription opioid use in the world (Fischer et al., 2018). By contrast, doctors in the Nordic countries prescribe less-addictive substitutes for opioids, to reduce harm and improve the quality of life for people who struggle with addiction (Selin et al., 2015). The opioid epidemic requires a national response, but in Canada, it has been hard to mobilize political support for the necessary programs.

Pandemics

In a world that is more tightly connected we will become used to epidemics and pandemics that involve many countries. Leaving aside the current COVID-19 outbreak, one serious pandemic of recent decades was the human immunodeficiency virus (HIV) and acquired immune deficiency syndrome (AIDS) pandemic. HIV-AIDS passes between people through the exchange of bodily fluids. This commonly occurs through unprotected sex, sharing needles, perinatal transmission, and the infusion of tainted blood. In the 1980s, despite rapidly rising infection rates, people often labeled and dismissed AIDS as a disease for "them" rather than "us." People viewed AIDS as an illness limited to three socially excluded populations: homosexuals, injection drug users, and Haitians. As a result, its emergence invited global prejudice, panic, and confusion.

Today, that has changed. By the end of 2017, an estimated 36.7 million people worldwide, including 17.8 million women and 2.1 million children under 15 years old, were living with HIV. Nearly 1.8 million people were infected in 2016 alone, 160,000 of whom were children under the age of 15. The number of global AIDS-related deaths is also huge: 35 million since the start of the epidemic, with nearly one million in 2017 alone. HIV-AIDS is still a leading cause of death in low-income countries such as South Africa (WHO, 2015). In Canada, there are over 68,000 people currently living with HIV, an estimated 14 percent of whom are unaware of their HIV status.

Finland has the lowest rate of new HIV infections per 100,000 among our 16 comparison countries (Figure 5-12 below). In 2018, roughly 4,000 people were living with HIV-AIDS in Finland, resulting in a prevalence rate of 0.1percent (UNAIDS, 2019). We can credit these low rates to Finland's successful HIV-AIDS treatment and care. This system is free under their Communicable Diseases Act and is integrated into the public healthcare system (European Center for Disease Control, 2012). Various factors depress the rate of HIV-AIDS transmission in a region. These include higher rates of contraception, more doctors, better education, and vigorous public health promotion (Mondal and Shitan, 2014).

One of the main modes of transmission in Finland is through drug injection (WHO, 2013). To combat this, Finland created 300 safe centres for injection drug users. Their goal was to safely treat those who are HIV/AIDS positive and provide methadone substitution therapy with the help of social workers. Further, a compulsory HIV/AIDS testing policy screens all pregnant mothers and all blood and organ donors and recommends screening for all refugees (WHO, 2013).

According to the Public Health Agency of Canada (PHAC)'s *HIV in Canada—Surveillance Report, 2018*, the number of new HIV cases in Canada jumped 25.3 percent between roughly 2010 and 2015. This occurred alongside, and because of, PHAC's funding cuts to community-based HIV organizations in Canada that received funding from their HIV and Hepatitis C Community Action Fund. Fully 40 percent of organizations that were previously supported by the Action Fund had lost their funding because they did not focus on the Conservative government's priorities of prevention-centered programming. Some of this policy-driven harm has since been corrected.

Figure 5-12 shows the rate of new diagnoses of HIV in the most recent data year across seventeen comparison countries, including Canada. As we see in the figure, Australia has much lower rates of new HIV infections than most of the comparison countries. Many factors have led Australia's success in dealing with HIV/AIDS cases. These include better condom education and the easy availability of condoms, more HIV awareness training at schools, and more education about safe sex practices for homosexual men. There has also been strong support from both the federal and state governments for various awareness campaigns. Australian governments viewed this as a social responsibility and thus focused

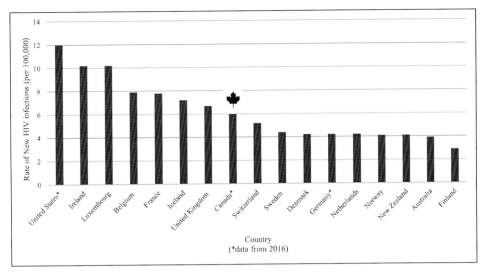

Figure 5-12. Rate of New HIV Infections (per 100,000 population), Canada and Comparison Countries, 2017 (or most recent data available).

on what structures could be altered or newly created to help prevent the spread of HIV (Aggleton and Kippax, 2014).

Like Australia, New Zealand also has a low rate of new infections. It achieved this by focusing on condom education and the promotion of condom use to prevent the spread of HIV, especially among young men who have sex with men (MSM) (Lachowsky et al., 2015). For example, the social marketing program "Get it On!" promotes the use of condoms among gay and bisexual men. Its goal is to educate people on why it is important to use a condom every time they engage in sexual activity. In a study to evaluate this campaign, people who heard the campaign message said they were persuaded by the program and understood the message clearly (Adams et al., 2017).

Another epidemic that originated elsewhere but afflicted people in the Global North was severe acute respiratory syndrome (SARS). Some rightly called this epidemic a product of globalization, because it rapidly spread to many countries in a short period. Scientists first recognized SARS as a global threat in February 2003, after it appeared in southern China during November 2002 (CDC, 2012).

The illness' impact was far-reaching. As the epidemic moved away from southern China, Hanoi, Hong Kong, Singapore, and Toronto became early "hot zones" (WHO, 2003). In hot zones, the number of cases increased rapidly, especially among health-care workers and their close contacts, as the primary means of transmission was through person-to-person contact. The rate of SARS deaths in Canada was among the highest in the world, with 251 cases and 43 deaths. Global economic costs because of lost trade and declining tourism numbered in the tens of billions of dollars, including a $1.5 billion loss for Canadian businesses (Conference Board of Canada, 2008).

Influenza typically causes fewer fatalities but is much more common. That said, major influenza outbreaks occur in human populations about three or four times per century, the most recent being the 1918 Spanish flu, the 1957 Asian flu, and the 1968 Hong Kong flu. The deadliest of these in the twentieth century, the Spanish flu, killed an estimated 30,000 to 50,000 people in Canada. It killed between 20 million and 50 million people worldwide, more than the number of combined military and civilian deaths during World War I.

The H1N1, or swine flu, pandemic of 2009 was the first significant influenza outbreak of the 21st century (Ma et al., 2020). Like SARS, this contagious respiratory virus, caused by type A influenza virus in pigs, spread rapidly across the globe. Again, it spread rapidly mainly because of the high modern-day rates of passenger travel. In 2009, the H1N1 virus was present in all the provinces and territories in Canada and 428 people died of it (a small fraction of the recent deaths from COVID-19). The pandemic cost Canada a staggering $2 billion to combat, mainly through vaccination.

The COVID-19 pandemic that began in early 2020 proved, however, to be the most consequential outbreak of disease since the Spanish flu when measured by its overall economic and social effects. Particularly vulnerable to the novel coronavirus were seniors and people with pre-existing health problems, especially respiratory problems. Direct effects aside, the pandemic brought many other problems to Canadian society. It has thrown people out of work and closed schools, while intensifying pre-existing problems such as domestic abuse, substance abuse, and mental illness.

Canada's homeless population suffered significantly over the course of this pandemic. Some of the supports that homeless people rely on, such as shelters, coffee shops, drop-in centres, and soup kitchens, closed for extended periods. Others turned people away because of overcrowding (CBC News, 2021).

The COVID-19 pandemic that began in 2020 caused enormous economic dislocation in Canada and around the world. Above, an almost empty car on Vancouver's normally busy Skytrain rapid transit system in June 2020.

For people with homes, compulsory social isolation caused latent family problems to surface. For example, evidence emerged of increased opioid use during the pandemic (Alexander, 2020). More people drank alcohol at times they normally would not, as the distinction blurred between work and the rest of the day. This increase in alcohol consumption had an especially undesirable effect on already-heavy drinkers and abusive partners, and evidence suggests that the occurrence and severity of domestic violence increased. UN Secretary-General Antonio Guterres called on world leaders to act to prevent domestic violence against wives and daughters (United Nations, 2020). For its part, the Canadian government provided up to $50 million to women's shelters and sexual assault centers to manage the expected increase in numbers of people seeking help.

The COVID-19 pandemic caused staggering economic effects. Millions of Canadians lost their jobs or had their work hours reduced. Younger workers were disproportionately affected, as were women. Small businesses, particularly those in the retail and service sectors, also suffered.

The federal and provincial governments launched a wide range of programs to assist individuals and businesses as the pandemic progressed. In doing so, the federal government incurred even larger budget shortfalls than at the height of the Second World War. Despite such government support, many Canadians reported experiencing troubling anxieties because of COVID-19, financial strain, and the fear of falling ill or losing a loved one. These findings match survey findings during earlier epidemics. For example, during the SARS epidemic, many people reported symptoms of depression and PTSD; and a correlation was found between longer periods of quarantine and increased symptoms of PTSD (Hawryluck et al., 2004). This study showed the potential risks to our mental health from long-term isolation. Humans need social interaction to lead healthy lives.

The COVID epidemic posed the worst challenge for people already dealing with mental health issues such as depression or addiction. Many people receiving psychotherapy could not visit their therapists. Despite efforts to deliver and receive therapy online, patients were often less motivated to follow set plans, giving way to potential relapses. Many organizations put resources online to give Canadians mental health support.

Concluding Remarks

This chapter has discussed the ways that social forces like poverty and inequality influence the physical, psychological, and social well-being of nations.

Traditionally, social scientists and political decision-makers focused on individuals who were sick and on their access to doctors, nurses, and hospitals. This traditional view of health responds to problems as they arise, often failing to prevent them. This view also focuses on the unique features of different patients and not their common or shared characteristics. In effect, it ignores the "big picture" and the reasons some communities, populations, or societies are healthier than others. This approach to illness is costly and does not produce as many person-years of health as we might wish.

By contrast, the *population health perspective*, a perspective adopted by sociologists and public health professionals, focuses on groups of sick people and the social and economic characteristics they have in common. In particular, population health researchers focus on the social and economic forces that produce illness, and the possible changes in society that would lessen these risks of illness. This approach to health, in the long run, saves many more lives, ensures more person-years of health, and costs less than the traditional medical model.

However, as we have seen, different societies have different priorities. They view the ideas of health and illness differently, so we must begin any evaluation of population health issues by considering cultural values and beliefs. People's health practices vary from one cultural group to another, and we must understand why. As a society, we want to ensure that as many people as possible are leading healthy lives, whatever their cultural values. Some countries, such as the Nordic countries, enjoy better overall health than other countries like Canada. We will consider the demographic, cultural, and institutional reasons for this in the final chapter of this book.

Having said that, where does Canada rank in comparison with the sixteen other countries we have considered in this chapter? Looking at the measures employed here to assess health and addiction issues, we would have to rank Canada in the middle of the countries we are studying. More precisely, Canada ranks on average seventh out of seventeen comparison countries when it comes to issues of health and addiction. Canada does well, comparatively, on measures of alcohol smoking, binge drinking, alcohol consumption per capita, life expectancy, suicide, and deaths from endogenous diseases. However, it does poorly on other measures of health such as opioid use disorder, obesity, and alcohol use disorders. Clearly, there is much yet to do in making Canada as healthy as some of its comparison countries.

CHAPTER SIX
Accidental Deaths and Injuries

As we saw in earlier chapters, Canada gets a mixed report card for the way it deals with its social problems. On the one hand, it deals with problems of poverty and economic inequality in a middling, ho-hum way, far behind the accomplishments of the Nordic countries. On the other hand, it is at the front of the pack on matters of social justice that affect immigrants and racialized minorities.

In this chapter, we will consider how well Canada is preventing and dealing with accidental deaths and injuries. Preventing accidental deaths and injuries is important for the human and economic well-being of a society. Accidents are also often a symptom of a poorly run society, which offers its citizens and workers little protection. Once again, we will see Canada coming in around the middle of the pack on this important domain of social problems.

Let's start this story by recalling an event that occurred far from Canada: an explosion in Beirut, Lebanon. On August 4, 2020, a massive explosion in Beirut shocked the world. In the end, it caused more than 200 deaths, thousands of injuries, and an estimated $15 billion (U.S.) in property damage.

We soon learned the ignition of ammonium nitrate in a storage plant near the harbour—mere minutes away from businesses, entertainment venues, and homes—had caused this explosion. The Lebanese prime minister, Hassan Diab, reported that about 2,750 metric tons of ammonium nitrate had sat in a port warehouse for the past six years "without preventive measures." It

The August 2020 blast in Beirut proved to be one of the largest man-made non-nuclear explosions ever recorded—the equivalent of a magnitude 3.3 earthquake. In this photograph taken in the explosion's aftermath you can see shattered grain elevators at the left and the crater caused by the explosion (which filled with water) to the right. The sound of the explosion was heard 240 kilometres away in Cyprus.

had arrived in Beirut on a Russian-owned ship in 2013. The ship, originally headed for Mozambique, had stopped in Beirut because of financial difficulties and unrest among the crew. Workers moved the ammonium nitrate off the ship into storage and there it remained, largely forgotten. No one had any idea who owned it, no one had any use for it, and no one was thinking about it.

How could the Beirut port authorities have lost track of this huge amount of dangerous material in a location so close to human habitation and office space? Some have speculated that, after Lebanon's lengthy civil war, local and national governments had largely fallen apart: they had become corrupt and indifferent. Government had suspended many of its normal roles, like building inspection and harbor security. Bribery may have also played a part. So widespread was the public dysfunction there wasn't even a particular individual or group to blame for this massive, life-destroying negligence. Happily, such a thing could never happen in a well-run country like Canada, where governments at every level ensure the safety of the population against accidental death and injury!

Or do they? Do you remember the massive train explosion in the town of Lac-Mégantic in Quebec in the early hours of July 6, 2013? On that occasion, an unattended 74-car freight train carrying crude oil rolled down a low hill, derailed, and exploded in the middle of town. Multiple tanker cars caught fire and exploded, resulting in forty-two deaths and five more people missing and presumed dead. The

This photograph of the vast fire that followed the train derailment and explosion in Lac-Mégantic was taken the next morning from a Sûreté du Québec helicopter.

blast destroyed roughly half of the downtown. Afterward, it was necessary to demolish most of the remaining buildings, because of petroleum contamination. The Transportation Safety Board of Canada (TSB), after studying the accident, reported in August 2014 that they had found eighteen direct and indirect (contributing) causes. These included leaving the train unattended on a main line, failing to set enough hand brakes, failing to have practiced backup safety procedures, failing to provide the locomotive with good maintenance, and inadequate training and oversight.

The United States-based Montreal, Maine and Atlantic (MMA) Railway ran this railroad. They had bought it from Canadian Pacific (CP). (It has become common in North America for smaller railways to buy less profitable routes from large ones.) CP had transferred the oil-carrying tank cars to the MMA train from one of its own trains.

The criminal trial of three MMA employees blamed for this disaster began on October 2, 2017. Prosecutors charged the locomotive engineer, rail traffic controller, and operations chief with forty-seven counts of criminal negligence causing death. However, on December

12, 2017 the defence announced that they would not call any witnesses, as they believed the Crown had not met the necessary burden of proof. The judge adjourned the trial until January 3, 2018. On January 19, jurors acquitted the three former MMA employees after nine days of deliberation.

The Quebec government considered suing MMA in a separate civil procedure. Their goal in this would be to recover the costs of aid given to victims. Hours after this information became public, MMA filed for bankruptcy protection in the U.S. and Canada, protecting the owners from any such suit. In January 2015, lawyers for the railroad agreed to distribute $200 million in settlement funds to families of the people who died, as well as other parties involved in the legal dispute. In May 2016, the federal government of Canada paid out $75 million to victims of the disaster. And in June 2016, Lac-Mégantic town council decided not to take legal action against Canadian Pacific either.

In the end, the citizens of Lac-Mégantic, Quebec, and Canada bore the costs of this disaster—financially and otherwise. Likely, the same will happen in Beirut. There, many charges have been laid, both against lower-level officials and more prominent figures, including the prime minister at the time of the blast. But skepticism remains about whether those ultimately responsible for the disaster will be appropriately punished. For the most part, local citizens bear the cost of mourning their dead and rebuilding their lives.

This pair of sad stories tell us nothing new. Disadvantaged populations offer suffer disproportionate harm from accidents involving dangerous conditions, including dangerous waste dumps (as in Beirut) and dangerous transport routes (as in Lac-Mégantic). This fact led researchers to coin the term *environmental racism* to describe the current state of affairs. By environmental racism, they mean the ways we burden neighbourhoods, districts, and countries populated mainly by people of low socioeconomic status—and who are often racialized—with dangerous hazards. These hazards may include toxic waste dumps, garbage dumps, and poisoned soil. Throughout the world, and especially in the Global South (like Lebanon), poor people and members of minority groups suffer disproportionately from these problems.

As the sociological expert on disasters Thomas Drabek (2017: 263) has noted, powerful people (like the owners of the MMA and CP railways) routinely impose risk on powerless people. The way we apportion risk is subject to human choice, though we often choose to ignore such choosing. "The consequences of social vulnerability are profound. Disasters have the greater impacts on the most socially vulnerable systems, be they individuals, families, communities, or entire societies." This has been as true of deaths from COVID-19 as it has been true of other disasters. It was true of the people who died in Beirut and the people who died in Lac-Mégantic. The heightened vulnerability of poor and powerless people is far from unknown. It is a certainty. So, in what sense are accidents accidental?

Some Classic Views about Accidents

As in earlier chapters, we can begin by looking for wisdom about accidents in past centuries. When we do so, we find the ancients scarcely understood accidents. Perhaps they viewed them as mishaps intended by fate or the gods. However, here are some thoughts to conjure with before we go forward sociologically.

The Roman emperor and Stoic philosopher Marcus Aurelius wrote, "The art of living is more like wrestling than like dancing, in so far as it stands ready against the accidental and the unforeseen and is not apt to fall." With this thought, Aurelius asserted that accidents and unforeseen events are not only accidental but unavoidable, and we must prepare for them. Or, as Confucius put it, "The superior person gathers his weapons together in order to provide against the unforeseen."

The most common thought expressed by powerful thinkers on this topic is that accidents and the unforeseen are orderly. Underneath the seeming randomness of an accidental event, there is order. Cause and effect prevail in the universe at all times. Along similar lines, the German poet and author Novalis claimed that "accident is simply unseen order." The historian H.A. L. Fisher felt there was "only one safe rule for the historian: that he should recognize in the development of human destinies the play of the contingent and the unforeseen." The scientist and science fiction writer Isaac Asimov, likewise, declared that "What is really amazing, and frustrating, is mankind's habit of refusing to see the obvious and inevitable until it is there, and then muttering about unforeseen catastrophes."

So, many scholars have urged us to see the forces hidden under a seemingly random set of events. Similarly, many artists have urged us to understand that the invention of new art means persuading the audience of the inevitability of the new. Thus, twentieth century composer Pierre Boulez wrote, "Creation exists only in the unforeseen made necessary." Expanding on this, novelist Philip Roth suggested that, "turned the wrong way around, the relentless unforeseen was what we schoolchildren studied in 'History,' harmless history, where everything accidental in its own time is chronicled on the page as inevitable. The terror of the unforeseen is what the science of history hides, turning a disaster into an epic."

In short, the notions of accident, chance, and the unforeseen are at once frightening and appealing. As long as we can imagine that something is inexplicable and without an obvious cause, we can feel like children again. We feel blameless, even if baffled and endangered. "The popularity of disaster movies," playwright David Mamet has said, "expresses a collective perception of a world threatened by irresistible and unforeseen forces which nevertheless are thwarted at the last moment. Their thinly veiled meaning might be translated thus: We are innocent of wrongdoing. We are attacked by unforeseeable forces come to harm us. We are, thus, innocent even of negligence. Though those forces are insuperable, chance will come to our aid and we shall emerge victorious."

But it may make the most sense to end this section with the words of Malala Yousafzai. She is the 15-year-old Pakistani woman whom Taliban zealots shot in the head, in hopes of ending her search for education and equal treatment. Unforeseeably, their effort backfired. Instead of silencing her, Malala became a global icon for women's rights and a winner of the Nobel peace prize. For Malala, the unforeseeable but unavoidable was all too real. She no doubt lived in fear of the unknown and unscheduled consequences of her self-assertion. All that she didn't know was exactly what would happen to her, and when it would happen. And in the end, the people with power—the politicians—were to blame. On this, Malala wrote, "A doctor can only treat patients. A doctor can only help the people who are shot or who are injured. But a politician can stop people from injuries. A politician can take a step so that no person is scared tomorrow."

As we will see again and again, accidental deaths and injury are understandable and, as a whole, we can prevent or reduce them if we mobilize the will to do so. High rates of accidental death and injury show a lack of will among political decision-makers and a deep failure to solve a major social problem. This failure is obvious in big accidents, such as the disasters at Beirut and Lac-Mégantic. It is obvious in the violence visited on Malala. It is also obvious in smaller accidents, such as workplace injuries and motor vehicle collisions that happen every day. To see the order in this seeming randomness, all we need to do is start looking for it.

Accidental deaths and injuries cause arguably more disruption to human life and prosperity than any other problem in our society: even more so than homicides and COVID-19, for example, which garner more public attention. Defining accidental, deaths and injuries can be tricky, however. For our present purposes, the term *accident* will not include deaths or injuries resulting from aggressive violence (such as the Taliban attack on Malala). Homicides and suicides, similarly, are not things we should confuse with accidental deaths. Accidents typical lack a clear motive or intent to harm. They are more often a result of negligence and neglect than of ill will.

Consider as an example occupational (or workplace) injuries and deaths, which are usually preventable. Workers who engage in physical labor, such as factory workers, miners, and mill workers, all know that inadequate or poorly enforced workplace safety procedures can easily produce accidental injuries on-the-job. In these cases, workers become "victims" of their dangerous workplaces. The production process may expose these workers to fumes, chemicals, or other harmful substances that cause health problems later. These health issues, including certain cancers and respiratory illnesses, are accidental or unforeseen injuries too.

The sociology of crime offers us a handy starting point for understanding accidents. That's because many types of victimization, including accidental victimization, have certain features in common. What sociologists call *routine activity theory* holds that our activity patterns affect our risk of injury and other victimization (Robson et al., 2012). These routine activities implicate the things we do, the places we do them, and the people around us at the time. In places we can call "hot spots," the risk of victimization is unusually high (Weisburd and Wire, 2018). To avoid harm—whether from criminals, accidents, or other sources of threat—we need to avoid such places. As we will see, the dangerousness of a hot spot and not the personal inadequacy of a victim predicts accidental deaths and injuries. For example, dangerous highways will have more collisions and deaths than safe highways. Dangerous factories will have more workplace deaths than other factories, and so on.

In this chapter, for reasons of space, we will pay special attention to only two kinds of accidents: injuries and deaths associated with workplaces, and injuries and deaths associated with road accidents. Workplace accidents are largely a result of governments failing to prevent employers from cutting corners at the expense of employee safety. Such accidental deaths and injuries can be prevented by adequate monitoring and enforcement of workplace rules. Similarly, road accidents largely result from governments failing to set and enforce reasonable speed limits. Both types of accident call for more and better rules; also, better policing of the rules. Preventing traffic accidents also requires a great deal of public education and health promotion. It means motivating people to drive safely, even if they do not want to think about doing so.

Smaller, more homogeneous countries may have an easier time carrying out both types of accident reduction. That's because reducing accident rates needs planning, which is easier when people want to cooperate. And, as we know from Esping-Andersen, social welfare regimes routinely use low-cost preventive measures to lessen higher remedial costs. Said more simply, in the long run it is cheaper to prevent accidents than fix the damage accidents do, and the Nordic countries know this.

Accident prevention begins with a wide-ranging, interdisciplinary study of accidents, with contributions from doctors, psychologists, safety engineers, social scientists, and legal experts. Sociologists, for their part, may be able to help uncover and interpret the social and cultural causes of accidental injuries. They are well-prepared to do so. Sociologists often work at the boundaries of different disciplines, seeing the points of contact, and searching for collaborative solutions. They also look for so-called group features that identify and help us understand the spread of accidental injuries among different kinds of people. In this way, a sociological study of accidental injuries may help us find the social practices that predict—and eventually prevent—accidental injuries.

Accidents, like the other topics we discuss in this book, are social problems. Accidents, like other social problems, have social effects: for example, they produce costly damage to property and injury to human victims. In doing so, they also affect social groups: families, workplaces, schools, and perhaps even entire communities. Also, as we will see, accidents have social causes. They are not purely random, nor are they merely the result of psychological or psychiatric forces: derangements, misjudgments, or momentary lapses in attention. There are social or "structural" determinants of accidents just as there are social determinants of health.

The Social and Economic Costs of Accidents

Accidental injuries and deaths are common and costly to Canadians. For example, accidental injuries were the eighth-leading cause of hospitalization for Canadians in 2018–2019, excluding pregnancy-related visits (Public Health Agency of Canada, 2019). The rate of car crash-related deaths in 2017 was 5 per 100,000 people, and there were 422 non-deadly injuries per 100,000 people (Government of Canada, 2019). Although the precise numbers change every year, accidental injury rates remain consistently high, compared with other health problems and sources of disability. Their degree of prevalence is also nearly constant from one year to another, meaning that some types of accident are especially common while others are quite rare.

Of course, Canada isn't the only country for which injuries and accidents are problems. The costs of illness, injury and healthcare are the largest public expenses in the Nordic countries. For instance, in Iceland and Norway, expenses associated with illness, injury, and health care represent the largest financial drain on the public budget. In Iceland, these costs amount to 36.6 percent of the social expenses, while in Norway they amount to 32.1 percent (Normann and Ronning, 2013). The costs of accidents and other health issues are high, when a country takes them seriously.

You may remember we discussed Gosta Esping-Andersen's theory of three "worlds of welfare" in chapter 1. There, Esping-Andersen notes the Nordic countries embrace a social welfare regime. This guarantees universal coverage to all who need public help, whether in the domain of employment, health, and education. One result of this is that the Nordic countries also do far more than liberal welfare regimes like Canada to fund public health research and promote public health initiatives. This is so they will have fewer social problems—less unemployment, less crime, less sickness, and fewer accidents—in the long run, and less to pay out of the public purse to fix these problems. They do more to prevent accidents than most other countries because they realize doing so is cheaper and better than paying the human and economic costs of accidents after they happen.

That's because *all* accidents come with both economic and social costs. The economic costs of accidents stem from many financial transactions that occur after an accident or injury. They include costs the individual or their family must bear, such as treatment-related costs and legal costs. They also come with the costs of lost productivity due to death, injury, and lengthy convalescence.

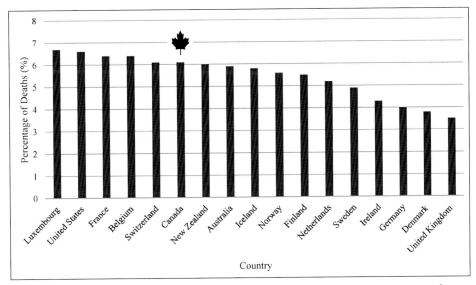

Figure 6-1. Deaths From Accidental Injury (as a Percentage of Total Deaths), Canada and Comparison Countries, 2019.

Figure 6-1 above shows the rate of deaths from all accidental injuries: that is, from road accidents, poisonings, falls, fires, drownings, and so on. On this dimension, Canada ranks sixth—near the middle of the pack. Comparison countries with the highest accidental death rates are Luxembourg, the United States, and France. According to these data, people are far less likely to die from an accidental injury in the United Kingdom, Denmark, and Germany, than they are in Canada or the United States.

The treatment-related costs of accidental injuries fall into three major categories: the cost of hospital treatment, the costs associated with temporary incapacitation, and the costs of permanent disability. The first cost is a result of immediate treatment: how much it costs to stay in hospital and receive medical attention there. Society also incurs extra costs if the injured person cannot work while hospitalized. This is the cost of lost productivity, and we will touch on it again soon.

The second category—the cost of temporary incapacitation—refers to the cost of continuing to pay employed people a portion of their salary while they are in the hospital. Then, not only is society paying the cost of their lost productivity, it is also paying people while they cannot work. Of course, some people are so severely injured that they are never be able to work again. Accidents throw these victims and their families into new and challenging economic circumstances. In the Nordic states, society also provides an income for people whose physical disabilities prevent them from earning an income.

In Canada, workers who are hurt on-the-job and no longer able to work receive an income—typically, a fraction of their normal income—in the form of workers' compensation payments. Workers' compensation is the oldest social program in Canada, first introduced in Ontario in 1914, then in Manitoba in 1916. In Canada, workers' compensation is organized and paid at the provincial level. In Ontario, for example, we pay injured workers (or their families) for their loss of retirement income, noneconomic losses, and death benefits as well as payments for lost earnings. We also compensate the worker who is unable to work ever again (AllOntario.ca). Canada's other provinces have similar workers' compensation policies.

However, payouts from workers' compensation do not equal the income a fully able person could earn by working throughout his or her adult life. A severe accidental injury typically means a drop in the victim's standard of living. As well, the injured person may have to take on costs of medical and home care they would not have needed had they remained healthy. Sometimes, these expenses are lifelong.

There are legal rules that aim to protect victims of accidental injury from financial ruin. However, administrative and legal processes increase the societal cost of unforeseen injuries. Besides being complicated and often flawed, these administrative processes are expensive. The costs include assessing damages, collecting funds from the liable individual, and watching the victim to ensure he or she is using the claimed funds properly. These costs add up. One study found that for every dollar an injury victim receives, the public incurs a dollar or more in administrative and legal costs (Friehe, 2008).

Physical and emotional suffering are also serious (though hard to measure) costs that result from injuries (De Castro Ribas et al., 2006). Sometimes, these emotional costs grow out of financial ones. For example, severely injured people can become depressed because they are economically and socially dependent on others. This may undermine their sense of autonomy or make them feel that they are failing to pull their own weight as productive members of society (Hoofien et al., 2001)

Like the economic costs of injury, the social costs of injury fall into several different categories. As we noted, injured workers typically receive a mere fraction of their previous salary. This can have huge impacts on their standard of living, as mentioned earlier. Many families of injured workers report having to disrupt their children's education plans and even sell their personal belongings, like cars and homes, to meet expenses (Khanzode, 2012). Second, reduced physical abilities carry social costs, such as limiting school attendance or sports participation (Chan, Paramenter, and Stancliffe, 2009). Third, dire injuries may limit people's relations with their friends, resulting in social isolation (Hoofien et al., 2001). This may make it harder for them to meet new people, go on dates, or marry, for example. For those who are already married, it may increase the risk of divorce or separation (Hoofien et al., 2001).

Depending on the severity of the injury, physical problems (such as paralysis) can affect people's mobility, making them dependent on others to transport and care for them. Deprived of independence, these people cannot lead the same lifestyle they once enjoyed. As a result, it can also affect their mental health, increasing the risk of depression and anxiety.

So, accidental injuries carry many important consequences, and these can lead to huge private and public expenses. The total cost of public spending on accidental injuries varies widely from one country to another. These differences in cost reflect variations in the extent and kinds of injury in these different countries. However, they also reflect the willingness of each country to spend public funds on financial and medical help for people disabled by an accidental injury.

"Public spending on incapacity" is an OECD measure of such social protection. It measures the extent of financial responsibility that each country assumes for its economically incapacitated members. Spending on incapacity includes paid leave, disability payments, and special allowances (OECD, 2019). It also includes the cost of social services for disabled people, such as "day care and rehabilitation services, home-help services and other benefits in kind." As we see in Figure 6-2, Canada ranks the lowest of all our seventeen comparison countries, meaning that we spend the smallest percentage of our GDP on providing public and cash benefits for incapacitated people. By contrast, three Nordic countries—Denmark, Norway, and Sweden—are the most generous in their spending on disabled citizens.

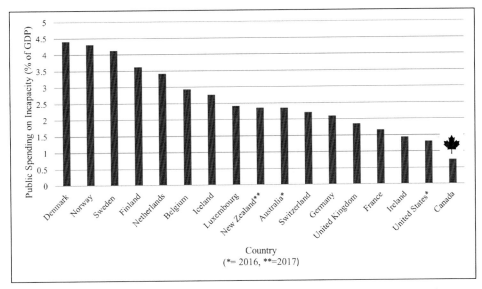

Figure 6-2. Public Spending on Incapacity (% of GDP), Canada and Comparison Countries, 2015 (or most recent data available).

We cannot assess all of the costs of accidental death and injury in dollars and cents. However, to the extent we can calculate costs, in 2010, accidental injuries cost Canadians $22.1 billion (Parachute, 2015). We can break this figure down into direct and indirect costs. Direct costs are payouts for medical treatment, while indirect costs reflect the economic consequences of lessened productivity in the workforce (Chan, Paramenter, and Stancliffe, 2009). Other indirect costs of accidental injury include insurance payments for extended disability. Harder to measure are the costs incurred when family members must take time off from work or school to look after the injured person.

According to the U.S. National Safety Council, "every 7 seconds a worker is injured on the job. That means 510 people are injured an hour, 12,600 a day, 88,500 a week, and a shocking 4,600,000 workers are injured every year." Not surprisingly, these many injuries carry huge costs for families and for society as a whole, and this is true in every country we might study. A study by the European Commission calculated the costs of work-related injuries in fifteen member states of the European Union. They found that in 2000, workplace injuries cost these countries an estimated 55 billion euros—around $80 billion in Canadian dollars. No less than 88 percent of these costs were due to lost productivity: a result of the time injured employees had to take off work to recover. Some people were so severely injured in accidents they became permanently unable to work. By calculating the costs of their "early retirement" from the workforce, the study found that such permanent disability cost an estimated 29 billion euros in lost productivity. Accidental deaths on the job resulted in a further 3.8 billion euros in lost productivity.

Like the statistics on injury rates, these data on the costs of injury likely underestimate the true extent of the problem. For example, it is hard to find out the full cost of hospitalization and rehabilitation services. The full cost of treatment—be it medical, pharmaceutical, nursing, physiotherapeutic, or home care—is usually much higher than the injured person and his insurance company pays, for example. Society pays some of these costs in merely managing the provision of public healthcare. And because health care varies so widely across countries, it is hard to gather comparable data on the full costs of injury of different kinds.

Internationally, many of the same kinds of "accidents" lead to similarly high rates of injury, hospitalization, and death rates in comparison to Canada. The World Health Organization estimates that globally, 1.35 million people die every year from automobile accidents. Further, between 20 and 50 million suffer injuries in automobile accidents every year (WHO, 2020). This makes automobile accidents the eighth-leading cause of death overall, accounting for 2.5 percent of all deaths worldwide. Auto accidents are also the number one cause of death for children and young adults. In short, automobile accidents are the deadliest form of accidental injury in the world.

Occupational Risks and Workplace Accidents

Much of the available data about injuries is about workplace injuries. Employers and governments want to track injuries and lessen them, as they affect productivity and profit. The risk of injury at work depends on the nature of the job, with some types of work being more inherently dangerous than others. Manual workers, such as construction workers or miners, are at a higher risk of work-related injuries than clerical workers, for example (European Agency for Safety and Health at Work, n.d.; Nenonen, 2011).

Construction workers account for 6.6 percent of the industrial workforce, yet people in this line of work account for over 20 percent of workplace deaths. However, we would be wrong to ignore the danger of factory work. Mechanized work—in factories and elsewhere—is both tiring and boring, so injury-inducing problems like exhaustion and boredom are built into the work itself. Assembly lines divide the production into small, monotonous, repetitive tasks, making it hard for workers to keep a steady focus, hour after hour (Attwood et al., 2006). Unfortunately, small mistakes with heavy machinery can have enormous effects.

Employers have an incentive to create and enforce safety procedures, owing to the costs of failing to do so. They try to reduce injury rates by enforcing safety standards and even hiring accident investigators of their own. However, much work remains dangerous, even today. And because work remains dangerous, the early-industrial period debate about workers' compensation continues.

Some critics think that workers' compensation encourages workers to take unnecessary risks and ignore precautions. They fear we will see more workplace injuries if injury benefits are made more generous (Kaestner and Grossman, 1998; Fortin and Lanoie, 2000). By contrast, other observers think that well-paid workers will be more cautious and take fewer chances than poorly paid workers, owing to the opportunity costs of an accident. Well-paid mine workers, for example, are usually more cautious than poorly paid colleagues, even though they get more work done in less time. Workers who are paid better wages are more aware of the costs of injury, both to themselves and the company.

Non-fatal workplace injuries are common, though the severity of these injuries varies greatly. Some injuries need limited or no time off work while others result in lifelong disability or disfigurement. Many think that the risk of injuries is increasing with the decline of full-time, stable employment and the rise of short-term contractual work. More and more workers do part-time, contractual, or freelance work, or they are self-employed, and few of them are protected by unions. No one is looking out for these people to make sure they are working in safe spaces and following safety procedures (Quinlan et al., 2001; Gallagher and Underhill, 2012). In fact, few rules or policies protect these workers.

As we see from Figure 6-3, workers are least likely to suffer a workplace injury in Norway, the UK, and Sweden. Among our comparison societies, people are most likely to suffer a workplace injury in France, Finland, and Luxembourg. As before, Canada is in the middle of this distribution. As usual, this suggests that countries vary in their concern about social problems and their willingness to invest money in solving them.

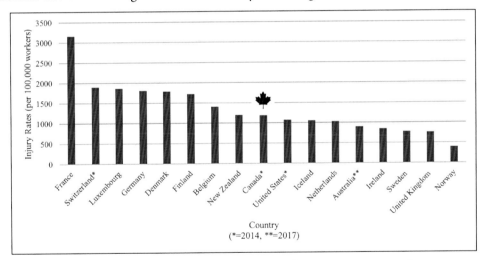

Figure 6-3. Non-Fatal Occupational Injury Rates (per 100,000 workers), Canada and Comparison Countries, 2015 (or most recent data available).

Many factors affect the rates of fatal occupational injury. These include health and safety procedures, workers' experience, and the proportion of workers who work in dangerous sectors of employment. As we see in Figure 6-4 (overleaf), deaths from workplace injuries are especially common in the U.S., Luxembourg, and France, and least likely in the Netherlands, the UK, and Sweden. Again, Canada ranks in the middle of the distribution.

Over the past hundred years, work and workplaces have changed a great deal. Fewer people in the Global North now work on assembly lines, having been replaced by smart machines. More often, they work in offices, service institutions (such as schools and hospitals), and retail stores. This doesn't mean, however, that workplace injuries have disap-

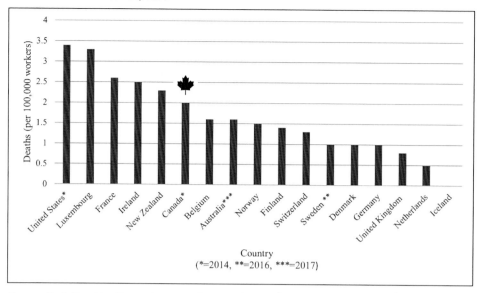

Figure 6-4. Deaths From Occupational Injuries (per 100,000 workers), Canada and Comparison Countries, 2015 (or most recent data available).

peared. Given our globalized world, employers compete fiercely to cut their costs through outsourcing and subcontracting (Nenonen, 2011), and this leads them to adopt a so-called "lean production" model.

In this model, employers hire only a few permanent employees to perform the most necessary local tasks. Other work is done elsewhere, for lower wages and often by less skilled workers (European Agency for Safety and Health at Work, 2002; Gallagher and Underhill, 2012). At home and abroad, this results in a growing population of *precarious workers*: people who lack stable employment and hold temporary, subcontracted, short-term, or freelance positions instead. Observers estimate that more than one in five Canadian workers hold precarious jobs, most of them women (Hennessy and Tranjan, 2018).

Precarious work can quickly become dangerous too, and often leads to injury (Guadalupe, 2003; Gallagher & Underhill, 2012). One study found that, despite precautions, 40 percent of the deaths every year in Finland's manufacturing sector involve outsourced workers (Nenonen, 2011). Outsourced workers are more likely to "slip through the cracks" of existing safety measures and rules (European Agency for Safety and Health at Work, n.d.). Employers often want to avoid paying for costly training, given the high turnover rates of poorly skilled workers. They may provide workers with initial instructions or guidance, but supervision on outsourced manufacturing sites is limited.

Authorities are often unclear about who is responsible for protecting outsourced workers. This leaves the workers themselves vulnerable to a poor enforcement of safety rules and procedures (Mayhew and Quinlan, 1997; Gallagher and Underhill, 2012). Often, the workers are obliged to use old, poorly kept machinery and work in unsafe environments (Katsakiori et al., 2010). Given their preoccupation with efficiency and cost cutting, many companies forgo safety equipment that would cost them money to buy and keep up. As well, employers want to keep labour costs down, so they can quote low, competitive prices to customers. However, such low-cost budgeting often means unsafe conditions for precarious workers (Mayhew and Quinlan, 1997).

Time and familiarity play a role in workplace accidents too. Outsourced, subcontracted workers often have to do more work in less time, often in an unfamiliar workspace (European Agency for Safety and Health at Work, n.d.). When under pressure to finish the work quickly, workers may try to cut corners. For example, they may ignore using safety equipment, such as safety harnesses, that takes time to put on and take off (Mayhew and Quinlan, 1997). Compared to other industries, construction work is one of the most dangerous kinds of work. The number of deaths in construction is typically high and has a large effect on the total number of workplace deaths in a country as a whole.

The data in Figure 6-5 show that deaths in construction work are especially common in the U.S., Iceland, and France and much less common in Sweden, the Netherlands, and the UK. We have no statistics for Canada as a whole, only statistics for Ontario. Therefore, Ontario here represents Canada and falls in the middle of the distribution.

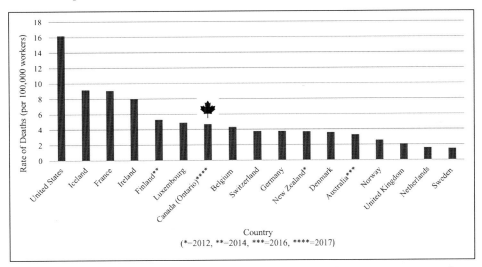

Figure 6-5. Rate of Deaths From Injuries in Construction (per 100,000 workers), Canada and Comparison Countries, 2015 (or most recent data available).

Driving and Traffic Related Accidents

Worldwide, driving and traffic related accidents cause many deaths and injuries. Car crashes injured about 154,886 Canadians in 2017, and killed 1,841 (Transport Canada, 2017).

One major cause of traffic accidents is risky driving. All types of risky driving can impact judgment and reaction time, often leading to crashes. Everyone knows that alcohol hinders our ability to assess risks, make good decisions quickly, and avoid hazards. Yet one study found that almost 12 percent of licenced drivers in Canada admit to driving after having consumed alcohol (Beirness and Davis, 2007). In fact, in 2013, alcohol was reportedly a factor in about 36 percent of car crash-related deaths (Brown et al., 2015).

The likelihood of driving while drunk, like many other risk-taking behaviours, has a demographic aspect. Drunk drivers—more generally, people who drive after drinking—are disproportionately likely to be young and male. Young men in our culture tend to pride themselves on taking risks, and display other risky health behaviours such as smoking and driving without a seat belt. We know that all of these behaviours are associated with the risk of injury (Karjalainen et al., 2012; Palk et al., 2011).

Another risky behaviour associated with car accidents is driving while under the influence of drugs. According to research, 28 percent of Canadians have driven under the influence of cannabis (Public Safety and Emergency Preparedness Canada). Those who do so often think the effects of cannabis on driving are less dangerous than the effects of alcohol. However, driving under the influence of drugs can be just as risky as drunk driving, or even riskier. Fully 40 percent of drivers who are killed in accidents test positive for drugs, compared to only 33 percent who test positive for alcohol (Government of Canada, 2019).

A third risky behaviour is distracted driving, caused by the use of a phone or handheld device while driving. People who text while driving are twenty-three times more likely to crash (or almost crash) than drivers who give their full attention to the road (VTTI, 2013). Talking on the phone while driving is slightly less dangerous than texting, but still risky. Yet more than one-quarter of all drivers admit they use their phone while driving (Perreault, 2016). Even using a hands-free device is dangerous, because concentrating on the phone conversation takes people's attention away from the road.

There have been many, varied efforts to combat risky and distracted driving practices. One of the best is making and enforcing rules. In 2010, to address drinking and driving among teens, Ontario passed a law that bans drivers 21 years old and younger from having any alcohol whatever before they drive. Penalties for breaking these rules typically include fines, imprisonment, or license suspension for any driver whose blood-alcohol content is above the legal limit.

However, many of these efforts have only a brief effect on DUI (drinking under influence) rates—if any effect at all (Hilton, 1984; Blais, et al., 2015). That said, legal blood alcohol limits do have a proven effect on the number of accident deaths, if not the drunk driving rate (Blais et al., 2015; Lovenheim and Slemrod, 2010). The drivers most affected by these rules are mainly social drinkers—people who typically drive and drink safely. But social drinkers are not the biggest cause of motor vehicle deaths and injuries. Repeat drunk drivers pose a more significant threat and cause more damaging, deadly car crashes. These most dangerous drivers are rarely deterred by increased surveillance and harsher penalties.

It is hard to catch people who drink and drive unless their impaired driving results in a crash that brings police to the accident site (Bertelli and Richardson, 2007). Laws against drinking and driving remain ineffective mainly because we have insufficient resources to enforce them consistently. Police tend to focus their prevention efforts on holiday seasons and major roadways. But plenty of drinking and driving happens at other times, in other places.

Just like drunk driving, driving while high on drugs or distracted by texting are both punishable in Canada with fines, license suspensions and jail terms of up to six months. However, as with laws about drinking and driving, laws against distracted driving are less effective than we have hoped. Many of the most common distractions are outside a person's car: people, objects, and events that compete for a driver's attention. So, apart from banning cell phone use while driving, there are few reliable ways to target distracted driving.

Rates of deadly accidents are significantly affected by how far people travel in cars, and this in turn depends on the size of the country itself. By calculating deaths per unit of distance traveled, we remove some of the differences in rates between large countries (like Canada) and smaller ones. Nonetheless, as we see below, the U.S.—a large country—stands near the top of comparison countries in the number of traffic deaths per kilometre traveled, along with Belgium and New Zealand. By contrast, Sweden, Switzerland, and Norway have the lowest number of deaths per kilometer traveled. Again, Canada is in the middle of the distribution.

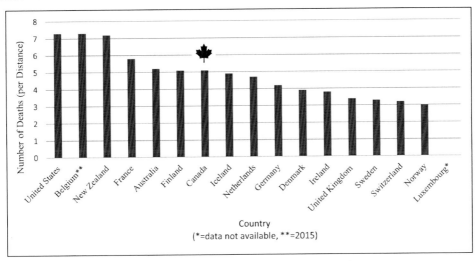

Figure 6-6. Number of Road Deaths (per distance travelled), Canada and Comparison Countries, 2016 (or most recent data available).

Concluding Remarks

Accident risks are, almost entirely, a product of locations, lifestyles, and situations. That's why it's best for your health to avoid dangerous workplaces, highways, homes, and neighbourhoods. However, accidents are also more likely to befall vulnerable and disadvantaged people than anyone else. This is especially true of workplace accidents, home accidents, and even environmental disasters. That's because vulnerable people are more likely than other people to hold dangerous jobs, inhabit dangerous neighbourhoods, and live in unsafe homes.

It seems likely the same explanation applies to people who are, reputedly, "accident prone." Some have tried to explain accident proneness as a personality trait. However, it is equally likely that so-called accident-prone people are people just like us but live in high-risk neighbourhoods and hold jobs that carry a high risk of accidents. Accident researchers have concluded that, despite the widespread appeal of this concept, accident-proneness is almost impossible to prove using rigorous experimental methods.

On a macro level, we seem almost doomed to high rates of accidents. Our hectic, profit-driven society is, in a sense, "programmed" to create accidents, and individual people suffer the results. Some are victimized more often than others because they have more need to visit accident-prone locations, lead accident-prone lifestyles, and spend time in accident-prone situations. So we have accidents because we live in an accident-prone society. No one in such a society can avoid every accidental injury and its unavoidable cost. All we can hope to do is reduce the number of total accidents and steer clear of risky situations, if possible.

All our actions involve calculated risk-taking, weighing expected benefits against expected costs. We learn to expect risks in almost everything we do, but the information we receive about these risks may often be wrong or distorted. Some features of our culture—for example, advertising and gambling—promote risk-taking with money. And some features—for example, notions about masculinity—promote risk-taking with our time and our bodies, for recreation or just to prove we are fearless.

As we've seen, accidents and accidental injuries are social problems, like crime, poverty, and illness. They range from small, common events that irritate individuals but are not life threatening to huge disasters that endanger millions of people for extended periods.

We often know how to prevent accidents, and even huge disasters. Doing so means taking proper stock of the uncertainties associated with technology (e.g., automobiles) we use. It also means anticipating the range of possible human errors and thinking of ways to reduce their likelihood. A failure to do so may result in life-threatening events like the nuclear meltdowns as Chernobyl, Fukushima, and Three Mile Island. Or it may result in environment-destroying events like the BP Deepwater Horizon oil spill in April 2010. Unfortunately, there is always a danger we will fail to imagine, consider, and plan for failures in system design, and the ways they combine with simple human errors.

We have noted that accidents, like crimes and illnesses, tend to seek out the weakest and most vulnerable members of society. That's why, for example, the poorest people and poorest countries have the highest risks of auto injuries and work-related deaths. Within every society, the poorest people are most likely to be victimized, by accidents as in other ways. Beyond that, other demographic groups run especially high risks of injury and death, such as young men in a wide variety of work and leisure activities. To a large degree, these heightened risks are self-inflicted, a result of testosterone and hazardous cultural notions about masculinity.

As we have also seen, researchers today are making great efforts to develop ways of predicting, measuring, and preventing accidental deaths and injuries. For example, with compulsory breath analysis, new technology can reduce the risk of auto accidents by preventing a car from starting. Self-driving cars may also prove to be safer than cars driven by humans. On the other hand, new technology often causes new and unimagined social problems, or goes only a short way to solving the original problem. At this point, it would be unreasonable to suppose that technological innovations will solve all of the accident problems we discussed in this chapter.

Finally, many links and likenesses exist between simple accidents and major, complex accidents. What we learn from one kind of accident we can usefully apply to another, if we have the ingenuity to do so. We will never be free of accidental injuries. But we always have choices and calculations to make about relative costs and benefits of any course of action. And we can never ignore the role of situational factors in the injuries we suffer.

We can use our knowledge of accidents to prevent and minimize accidental injuries and deaths in the future. To some degree, this will mean demanding that other people and organizations make changes to reduce the danger they are causing us. The first step in this involves carefully examining past accidental injuries in search of their underlying causes. By examining previous "accidents" we can learn from our mistakes, but only if we can reduce those complicating issues outlined above. And by studying countries that are more successful than Canada—typically, countries in northern Europe—we can learn ways to reduce accidental deaths and injuries in Canada.

Having said that, where does Canada rank in comparison with the sixteen other countries we have considered here? Looking at the measures employed to assess the prevention and handling of accidents, we have to rank Canada either at the bottom of the middle one-third of comparison countries or the top of the lowest one-third. Canada does well in its public spending on people disabled by accidents. However, in deaths and injuries per capita—whether on the road, at work, or elsewhere—Canada is below the median performance of comparison nations, ranking tenth to twelfth out of seventeen countries. We have a long way to go to solve this problem.

CHAPTER SEVEN
Environmental Issues

In the earlier chapter on health issues, we mentioned the results of a recent Environics Institute study. Not surprisingly, Canadians surveyed there placed the greatest possible importance on dealing effectively with the COVID pandemic. Many social issues that attracted popular concern in past surveys—problems like crime, poverty, or racial discrimination—received a lower priority. The environment was one such problem. Fewer people expressed concern about the environment than in earlier surveys.

That said, when respondents were asked to comment on the statement that "Protecting the environment is more important than protecting jobs," 46 percent of the sample agreed or strongly agreed with this statement. Only one respondent in seven strongly disagreed with this statement, thinking that jobs were much more important. This suggests that Canadians feel strongly about protecting the environment, even when confronting COVID and the resulting economic crisis.

Attitudes on this issue varied from province to province, with a majority of Albertans (56 percent) disagreeing with this statement—that is, favouring jobs over environmental protection. By contrast, only 39 percent of respondents in neighbouring British Columbia disagreed with the statement and, similarly, only 37 percent of respondents in Nova Scotia and 36 percent in the three northern territories (Nunavut, Yukon, and the Northwest Territories) disagreed. They were much more likely to take a pro-environment stance.

It has taken a long time for humanity to come to grips with this issue of environmental protection. As a species, we humans are consuming the world's resources at an unprecedented rate. In doing so, we continually demand more of the natural environment on which we depend. For example, we cut down trees for lumber and use whole forests to build cities. We extract vast amounts of oil and other fossil fuels to keep up with an increasing demand for energy. We obey the rules of "more and bigger," forgetting that Earth has finite limits even if our wishes do not.

Humanity has anticipated yet ignored our present problem for more than two hundred years, since Thomas Malthus first introduced us to an inescapable fact of mathematics. In 1798, Malthus published an essay theorizing the human population would soon outstrip its food supply. That's because populations tend to increase exponentially. By doing so, they outpace the ability of agriculture to produce enough food, unless humans take action to prevent this. You can blame mathematics: every exponential (or geometric) series of numbers grows faster than every arithmetic (or additive) series of numbers. Said another way, the geometric series (x^y) will, always, in the end, exceed the arithmetic series ($x+y$). This will happen invariably, no matter what positive values we assign to x and y or how long we run the test.

This fact is important, Malthus said, because land availability controls the food supply and, in the end, can only grow by small increments, as an arithmetic series. By contrast, if not controlled, the supply of people grows exponentially, as a geometric series. If humanity is to survive, the food supply must grow as fast, or faster, than the number of people who need to eat. However, Malthus reminds us, for mathematical reasons this cannot happen. In the long run, freely reproducing people will run out of food—if they don't die first from disease or violence. Their one chance of survival is by limiting childbearing. Specifically, said Malthus, they must avoid bearing children until married and avoid marrying until financially able to supply food for the family.

Now, history has proven many of Malthus's assumptions wrong. Present-day contraceptive technology means people can marry and have sex without producing babies. Modern agricultural techniques and adapted food stocks are yielding much more food per acre than Malthus ever imagined. As a result, many billions of people live on Earth today—far more than Malthus thought possible. However, there is a certain logic to Malthus's reasoning that we cannot escape. In the future, no matter how innovative we are, humanity will exhaust limited resources that are non-renewable. Then there will be too many humans for the world to support.

The question today is, how soon will our population size and rate of population growth, combined with our destructive habits, make Earth uninhabitable, and will the end come through famine, disease, violence, or pollution? How and when will the world's population overwhelm the natural environment, creating global problems of scarcity: for example, a shortage of clean water, clean air, and non-renewable natural materials? We will touch on just a few of these issues in this chapter.

Population aging complicates these issues. Said another way, because of declining fertility and increased longevity, populations are aging all over the globe. The number of people aged 65 and older is increasing at a faster rate than any other age group. Researchers do not see this trend ending and project that a quarter of the population in Europe and North American may be aged 65 and older by 2050 (United Nations, 2019).

With rapid population growth and population aging, a third population problem with environmental causes and outcomes is large-scale population migration. Because of the uneven distribution of resources, many people from more impoverished parts of the world are becoming refugees and economic migrants. Changes in the local environment undermine many people's livelihoods and well-being, forcing them to leave their homes and seek shelter elsewhere. For example, as rain and snow lessen in parts of the world, crops are more likely to fail. People who depend on agriculture for a living have to seek economic opportunities elsewhere. Natural disasters, like floods, forest fires, and droughts, which are increasing because of climate change, may also force people to uproot their lives.

These environmental disasters pose problems not only for the people directly affected but also for the global community. A sudden influx of refugees into any country poses dangers that range from security to resource availability. Some countries simply lack the capital or organization to face a dramatic increase in the population. Other countries, where people are unwilling to admit large numbers of immigrants, may also face political challenges

Dhaka, the capital of Bangladesh, is one of the world's fastest growing cities. Bangladesh itself is the world's most densely populated country of substantial geographical size. Its population of about 170 million people occupies an area only slightly larger than Southern Ontario, which despite being the most densely populated region of Canada has a total population only 1/14th that of Bangladesh. Although Bangladesh's fertility rate has dropped to roughly replacement levels, the high proportion of young people in the population means the total population is expected to grow by another 80 million people before levelling out in the 2100s. Complicating matters still further is the fact that most of Bangladesh is less than 12 metres above sea level. Much of the country could find itself underwater if sea levels continue to rise because of climate change.

in addressing the crisis. In some parts of the world, authorities turn back thousands of people at national borders. They must return to their country of origin or advance to a refugee camp.

Under conditions of extreme climate change, massive crop losses displace entire families and communities (Hanna and Oliva, 2016). Such displaced families often end up makeshift camps with poor living conditions. Such displacement worsens people's access to food, health care, sanitation, and education. So, it's hard to know whether overall family well-being will improve or worsen, at least in the short run. The effects on children, in particular, would depend on whether they move to cities with their parents or stay behind with other family members. If sudden increases in urban populations aren't matched by increases in social services, children's health and education may suffer.

Canada currently runs the world's second-largest refugee resettlement program. Historically, this program has been able to help refugees seeking protection from political instability or human rights violations, especially those migrating from war-torn countries. The Canadian government supports this program, thanks to the Immigration Act of 1978 which allows for admissions based on humanitarian grounds (Boyd and Vickers, 2000). As the climate crisis worsens and the number of climate refugees increases, the notion of humanitarian grounds may expand to include people displaced by climate change.

A rapidly increasing, aging, and mobile population poses huge problems for humanity. When compounded with climate change, the population problem becomes a global crisis.

Climate displacement is just one example of how the issues of population and environment may intersect. But it is helpful to remember that climate change is not just a source of population problems; it is also a problem caused by humanity's extreme behavior.

Global Warming and Climate Change

Today, everyone has heard of climate change and global warming, and many know that they are caused by what scientists call the *greenhouse effect*. Gases such as carbon dioxide, methane, water vapour, nitrous oxide, ozone, and so-called fluorinated gases collect in the atmosphere. Sunlight can easily pass through them to reach the surface of the earth. However, these gases are to varying degrees opaque to the infrared radiation the earth emits after being heated by the sun. As a result, the atmosphere traps heat, and average global temperatures rise.

Even though climate change sets off a general warming of the global climate, it also produces volatility and unpredictability in our weather patterns. For example, some regions experience extreme bouts of uncharacteristically cold temperatures. Similarly, some regions experience extreme drought and wildfires, while others suffer from floods and disastrous storms. Climate change presents a wide range of extreme problems.

Earth's climate has changed throughout the planet's history, but in the last three hundred years humans drastically sped up these changes. The concentration of carbon dioxide in the atmosphere increased by about 50 percent between 1750 and 2021. Researchers estimate current atmospheric levels of carbon dioxide are the highest in 14 million years.

Climate change means volatility, confusion, and unpredictability. Natural disasters become more frequent and more severe. The weather patterns we have relied on—such as snow in British Columbia which, once melted, powers the hydroelectric plants the province depends on—become unpredictable.

As we see in Figure 7-1, Canada produces little in the way of total greenhouse gas emissions, but the amount is high if we consider our production per person (Figure 7-2).

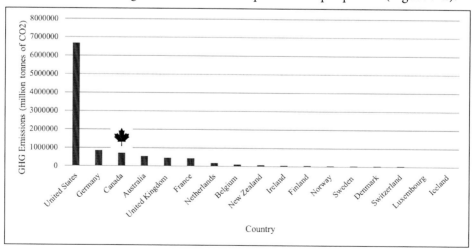

Figure 7-1. Total Greenhouse Gas Emissions, Canada and Comparison Countries, 2018.

With climate change, the world is now breaking records for warmest years, months, and days. Ice sheets and glaciers, especially in Antarctica and Greenland, are melting, causing

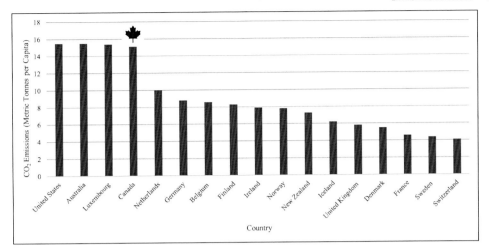

Figure 7-2. CO_2 Emissions per Capita, Canada and Comparison Countries, 2016.

ocean levels to rise. This change threatens both the natural ecosystems of those frozen landscapes and densely populated coastal cities located on every continent. By now, it is already too late to prevent climate change, since irreversible damage has already been done. If we are to survive, we must find ways to slow this change down or adapt to it.

Even a small increase in global temperatures can lead to higher sea levels and devastating changes in rain and snowfall patterns. These climate changes, in turn, harm the natural vegetation and wildlife of local ecosystems, alter the crop yields of agricultural regions, and cause deserts to replace fertile areas. As well, rising sea levels, like many other natural disasters, come with enormous costs in terms of both lives and money.

In recent decades, there have been international efforts to solve and prevent these problems. However, international talks—even agreements—have often fallen short of the action necessary to address these issues. Consider the Kyoto Protocol, which many nations adopted in 1997. By July 2006, 164 of 168 countries had signed and approved the protocol to lessen the global emission of greenhouse gases. However, the United States called the Kyoto Protocol irresponsible, since lessening the use of fossil fuels would hinder American oil and coal industries and U.S. economic growth.

Canada finally approved the protocol in December 2002 and then withdrew from it in December 2011, under the leadership of the Conservative Party, despite massive opposition from environmentalists. When Justin Trudeau became prime minister, Canada once again joined the international effort to reduce greenhouse gases. Canada has declared it will reduce greenhouse gas emissions by 30 percent by 2030 (UNFCC, 2018).

You will recall that many nations signed the Paris Agreement as part of the United Nations Framework Convention on Climate Change. Coming into effect in 2016, this treaty dealt with greenhouse-gas-emissions mitigation, adaptation, and finance, and aimed to prevent temperatures from rising because of global greenhouse emissions. In both of these matters, we have seen positive developments already. First, new investments in renewable energies now surpass new investments in fossil fuels. Second, there has been a slowing of the rate of increase of oil petroleum consumption, and third, a drop in the global consumption of coal, though this may be short-lived. Fourth, there has been a gradual phasing-out of fossil fuel subsidies and fifth, an increase in energy-efficient technologies (for example, a drop in the price of LED lighting).

Of course, countries vary in their progress toward these milestones. Canada is doing better than the U.S. but not as well as France, Germany, and the UK.

For various reasons, some countries have made other multilateral agreements to improve the environment. In late 2005, for example, the United States, Australia, China, India, Japan, and South Korea signed an agreement known as the Asia-Pacific Partnership on Clean Development and Climate (AP6). Unlike the Paris Accord, it allows member nations to set individual targets for reducing emissions without a compulsory enforcement scheme. Canada became the AP6's seventh member in 2007.

Environmental Degradation, Pollution, and Waste

Climate change is not the only environmental problem facing us. Many environmental problems stem from our treatment of natural resources. We often both overuse and misuse these resources, while producing an enormous amount of waste.

For example, industrial agriculture strains the ecosystem by both consuming vast amounts of water and degrading the fertility of the soil. Often, the food that agriculture produces is shared unequally, so food waste collects in some places while people in other places starve. Something similar happens in the industrial manufacturing sector, where many producers waste raw materials, rather than converting them into usable products or recovering them for later use. The resulting by-products are a form of pollution that may poison the soil or water on which we rely.

Resource extraction and processing industries in Canada are major sources not only of pollution but of high-paying jobs, leading to politicians' struggles to reconcile economic development with adequate environmental protections. Above, the Stelco steelmaking facilities in Hamilton, Ontario.

People with the most wealth and power often cause the greatest environmental damage through their harmful industrial practices and wasteful personal lifestyles. Meanwhile, people who lack such wealth and power often suffer declines in their health and well-being (Comim et al., 2009). The problem we face is not just an over-consumption of natural resources, but also a reckless exploitation of these resources for short-term gains by a small group of people at the expense of others.

Water scarcity is a prime example of the reckless use of a resource by a privileged few at the expense of many others. Water scarcity occurs when the demand exceeds the supply of water available in a region. According to the United Nations Department of Economic and Social Affairs, by 2025, an estimated 1.8 billion people will live in countries or regions without any water by 2025. By then, fully two-thirds of the world's population may experience *water stress.* Such stress occurs whenever the supply of freshwater cannot meet the demand, or when the water's poor quality limits its use (UN, 2014).

Water shortages caused by climate change can even result in conflict between nations. Countries may fight for control over the water supply, use water control as political leverage, and destroy water supplies to gain military victories. For example, water shortages in Syria caused by climate variability and mismanagement intensified the country's disastrous civil war. The results were a failed agricultural economy, food shortages, poverty, and massive population displacement (Gleick, 2014).

Global water use has increased significantly in the past fifty years. It has risen because of population growth and agricultural growth, especially in arid regions such as the U.S. Southwest. Excessive use further strains the supply of clean and drinkable water, and Canada has been among the worst of water abusers. Among the twenty-nine high-income industrial nations that make up the Organization for Economic Co-operation and Development (OECD), only Americans use more water than Canadians.

As Figure 7-3 shows, we enjoy our high levels of water use, at least in part, because of the amount renewable freshwater resources available in Canada. Only Iceland has more freshwater available per person than Canada.

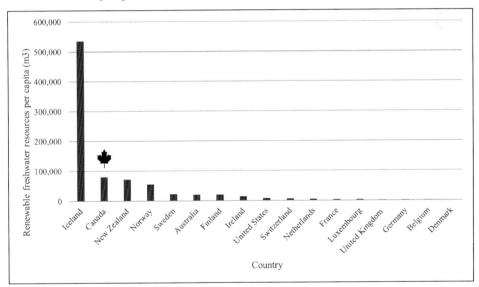

Figure 7-3. Renewable Freshwater Resources per Capita (m³), Canada and Comparison Countries, 2015.

When people do not value water properly, they abuse the resource by buying it in volume at a low price—for example, to bottle and export it for sale elsewhere. At the same time, there are populations in Canada with far too little access to safe and affordable water. For example, many Indigenous communities lack access to safe, clean water. After decades of discussion, there are still boil-water advisories in Indigenous reserves across the country. British Columbia and the Xeni Gwet'in First Nation recently made the news as government finally lifted the last long-term boil-advisory in the province, after almost twenty years. However, several shorter-term advisories are still in effect (FNHA).

Even the rainy coastal city of Vancouver may soon face water shortages, because of population growth and climate change. In 2015, for example, the city experienced little snowfall, followed by an unusually dry summer. This resulted in severe water rationing, including a total ban on lawn watering and car washing (Chung, 2018). Even before the drought, the Vancouver region had to ration water every summer. A new water conservation plan enforces yearly lawn watering controls.

However. Vancouver's already limited water supply may come under even more pressure as the city's population grows by an estimated 35,000 people a year over the next few decades (Chung, 2018). Climate disturbances, such as an increase in the severity of extreme weather events, could further strain water these supplies.

Researchers from the Netherlands have quantified and mapped our global "water footprint." Doing so has highlighted how patterns in international commerce create inequalities in water access and, therefore, in water use. Water scarcity is a global issue that affects different regions to differing degrees. As with other goods and resources, poor people are the first to feel the effects of scarcity, leading many to migrate or flee their homeland.

Loss of Food Diversity

The loss or pollution of water, air, and soil all decrease the diversity of food available, while increasing health hazards and the risk of natural disasters (Lampert, 2019). Over-exploitation of the natural environment is obvious in the global disappearance of fish stocks, for example. Fish and other sea creatures—shrimps, scallops, clams, lobsters, and so on—are important sources of protein and nutrients for humans. Many people today are concerned that we are consuming the Earth's stock of fish faster than it can renew itself. If this continues, entire species of fish and other sea creatures may die out.

Though fishing is an important Canadian industry, Canada catches few fish compared with the United States. In 2017, the United States harvested over five million tonnes of seafood, compared with Canada's catch of less than one million tonnes. One city in Alaska, Dutch Harbor, landed close to half Canada's total annual catch in 2018 (National Marine Fisheries Service, 2020).

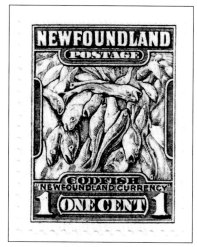

This 1932 postage stamp issued by the Dominion of Newfoundland (at that time still independent of Canada) epitomizes the historical importance of the cod fishery.

As the fishing industry grows in response to rising consumption, the extinction of marine life becomes ever more likely. Consider, for example, the near disappearance of cod from Canada's east coast fisheries. This issue is especially significant because of the long and celebrated history of cod fishing in Canada. The political economist Harold Innis (1894–1952) made cod fishing an important part of Canadian and British imperial history by developing a theory called the *staples thesis*. This thesis proposes that the exploitation and export of staple products (or basic commodities) shaped Canada's culture, economy, and political history (Watkins, 2013).

Innis notes that technology played an important role in developing the cod fishery. The English developed a method of curing the fish that allowed it to be easily shipped back to Europe. This led European investors to develop an interest in Canada, which had easy access to huge codfish stocks. Europeans began to fish here and then settle here, to access the cod in the surrounding waters. In this way, cod played a key role in expanding the British Empire and developing Canada as a nation.

Yet today, this historic cod fishery is nearing extinction. According to the Department of Fisheries and Oceans (DFO), one main cause of this steep decline in cod populations was a large increase in their natural mortality rate. This increase in mortality occurred because of warmer water temperatures and decreases in the cods' food supply. Another main cause has been the over-fishing of waters off the coast of Canada.

Some countries have done well in their management of fish stocks, helping fish populations to recover from such overfishing. Norway offers a good example of this success. In the late 1960s, Norway experienced a collapse in its herring stock, which hurt a national economy that was largely dependent on fishing (Mikalsen and Jentoft, 2003). In 1972, Norway put into place the Limited Entry Act, which allowed the Norwegian government to restrict herring fishing in its coastal waters (Mikalsen and Jentoft, 2003). Norway's successful management strategy allowed the herring population to recover.

The story is similar for salmon. Atlantic salmon have long been a favorite target of both recreational and commercial fishermen. Currently, people fear that Atlantic salmon stocks will suffer a devastating collapse similar to that of the cod in Canada and the herring in Norway. Both overfishing and global warming have significantly decreased the salmon stock (Bissett, 2018). In 2016, the Atlantic Salmon Federation reported the number of wild salmon returning to rivers in Atlantic Canada and Quebec had dropped by 27 percent from 2015, the year before.

Water and Air Pollution

Pollution represents a significant threat to the natural environment and human health. The Great Lakes, a major source of freshwater in North America, have experienced much pollution (Driedger et al., 2017; Sherman et al., 2015). Pollutants from surrounding areas—heavily farmed rural regions and populous industrial centres—find their way into the lakes. Once there, they poison the water, promoting extreme algae growth and killing aquatic life (Brooks et al., 2016). Recent interventions improved the quality of water in the Great Lakes, but the World Wildlife Foundation still rates it only as "fair" (WWF, 2017).

Equally troubling is the increase in air pollution. This is a global concern, especially for large cities where automobiles and industrial plants contribute significantly to poor air quality. Air pollution has been linked to higher rates of stroke, lung cancer, and respiratory and heart diseases among humans. The World Health Organization reported that bad outdoor air caused around 4.2 million premature deaths in 2016, many of them in less economically developed countries (2018).

One ingredient of air pollution is fine particulate matter, abbreviated "PM2.5." Globally, PM2.5 poses the greatest threat to human health, specifically through respiratory and cardiovascular diseases. According to the WHO, the annual mean concentration of PM2.5 should remain below 10 micrograms per cubic metre to keep the risk of negative health impacts low (2020). Currently, however, 91 percent of the world's population lives in regions that exceed this guideline (WHO, 2020). Of the OECD countries examined, almost half surpass the guideline, with Belgium showing the highest exposure to air pollution at 12.73 micrograms per cubic metre. Canada fares better than this, remaining on the lower end of the range with 7.09 micrograms per cubic metre.

Of course, the concentration of air pollutants is greatly affected by population density. The more densely populated a region, the more likely it will have significant air pollution. With a moderate population size and a vast amount of territory, Canada's population density is only 4 people per square kilometre. Compare this to Belgium, which has around one-third of Canada's population but a density of 376 people per square kilometre. Canada's problem is less pressing than Belgium's, but far from trivial.

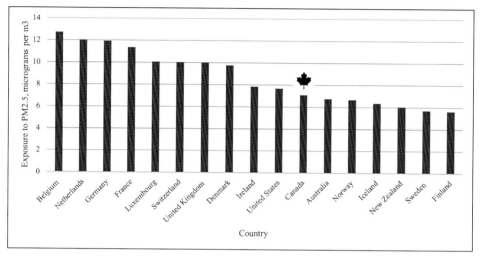

Figure 7-4. Air Pollution Exposure (to PM2.5, micrograms per m³), Canada and Comparison Countries, 2019.

PM2.5 is also a significant contributor to smog. Daily exposure to air pollution has become part of the normal metropolitan experience in most parts of the world. In principle, nature can repair itself and recover from air pollution. However, when pollutants exceed what nature can remove, they build up in the atmosphere.

Equally menacing is the rapid buildup of waste, both on land and in the oceans. Mass production creates vast amounts of by-products that need disposal. In the course of their daily lives, individuals also produce huge quantities of leftover paper, clothing, food, metals, plastics, and other synthetics. Canada is one of the developed world's leaders in per capita production of garbage. Among the OECD countries, only Denmark produces more municipal garbage than Canada. In fact, Canada produces almost twice as much municipal waste per capita as Belgium.

According to Statistics Canada (2018), the total amount of waste produced by Canadian households increased from 9.3 million tonnes in 2008 to 10.2 million tonnes in 2016. A report by the Conference Board of Canada (2013) also found that in 2008, Canada produced 777 kilograms of garbage per person. This achievement once again put Canada in second place after only Denmark. Typically, in absolute terms, wealthier countries produce more municipal waste per person. However, Canada's waste production is high even compared to other wealthy nations, such as the UK and Australia.

Currently, the world is experiencing a major rise in waste production, not all of it due to Canada. As a country—any country—becomes richer, its waste typically changes. More packaging, more imports, more electronic waste, and more broken toys or appliances all add to the waste (Hoornweg, Bhada-Tata and Kennedy, 2013). People in high-income countries prefer to buy new items, rather than fix and re-use old products. High-income

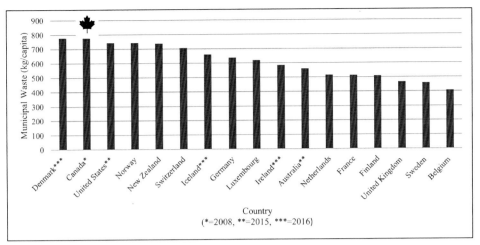

Figure 7-5. Municipal Waste Production (kg/capita), Canada and Comparison Countries, 2017 (or most recent data available).

countries, as a result, produce about 34 percent of the whole world's waste (The World Bank Group, 2019).

Researchers expect that, by 2050, the waste produced in urban regions will double. To decrease waste production, some countries in North America and Europe have tried pay-as-you-throw schemes, which have met with some success. Under these programs, as fees for disposal increase, the volume of waste decreases. A Belgian study found that such schemes can decrease household waste generation by 9.1 percent over ten years.

Another pressing issue facing urban regions is electronic waste. Electronic waste includes electrical and electronic equipment (EEE) and their discarded parts (Balde et al., 2017). In 2010, an estimated 224,000 tonnes of e-waste were produced across Canada (VanderPol, 2014). Yet despite this large and growing amount, Canada produces less e-waste than its comparison countries. This is because Canada started to manage its e-waste twenty years ago, taking local action to control the problem.

However, the collection and disposal of electronic waste carries risks. Items like cellphones or laptops may contain sensitive data. Waste collection must properly dispose of both the physical product and the data it carries. E-waste also poses health risks, as humans may come into contact with harmful materials when handling it. Further, certain populations who live close to waste disposal sites are at greater risk than others. Depending on how collectors dispose of it, the e-waste may produce a build-up of harmful chemicals in soil, water, and food, which can sicken human populations (Orisakwe et al, 2019).

Currently, cities use three main waste disposal methods: landfills, incineration, and recovery and recycling. In a landfill, organic materials decay naturally over a short period. However, plastics take hundreds or even thousands of years to decay in a landfill site. An alternative method is to use incinerators to burn the plastics alongside other forms of waste. However, this releases potentially harmful chemicals into the air (Verma et al., 2016; Rochman and Browne, 2013; Ngaza et al., 2018). Both dumping and burning are unsustainable practices, as the world is quickly running out of places to dump its trash. They are also damaging to the environment and human health.

China was once the world's dumping ground, as half of the world sent its recyclables there for processing (Hounsell, 2018). However, to reduce its waste build-up, the Chinese government set limits on foreign recyclables. China now also demands a higher standard of cleanliness from the waste it accepts. This has left Canadian cities struggling to find places to ship their recyclables.

Oil Politics, Health, and Indigenous Communities

Canada currently faces three especially pressing environmental concerns: oil politics, human health, and both as they apply to Indigenous communities. Let's begin with the explosive topic of oil production and shipping.

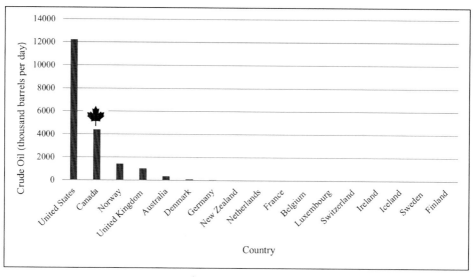

Figure 7-6. Crude Oil Production (thousand barrels per day), Canada and Comparison Countries, 2019.

Canada has the world's third-largest oil reserves, mostly in the form of oil sands found in western Canada It is also the world's fourth-largest crude oil producer, contributing 4.6 million barrels each day in 2018 (Natural Resources Canada, 2020). When compared with our sixteen other countries, Canada comes second only to the United States, the world's largest oil producer. Canada produces more than twice as much oil as Norway, the next largest producer in this group of countries.

Oil is a vital commodity that contributes trillions of dollars to the GDP of countries all around the world. Yet only a few nations control large oil reserves. The global inequality in access to oil results in political tension. Oil-producing countries (and corporations) try to leverage the price of this resource for economic and political gain. In the hands of wealthy or powerful countries (and corporations), oil represents control—control in the global competition for fossil fuels that supply nearly 85 percent of the world's energy needs.

Even today, despite growing calls for green energy, oil remains a defining part of the Canadian economy. Hundreds of thousands of jobs depend on this industry. As the world's fourth-largest exporter of crude oil, the country earns tens of billions of dollars from this natural resource (Natural Resources Canada, 2020). No province is more dependent on this industry than Alberta, which produces more than 80 percent of Canada's oil.

However, despite bringing great economic benefits to Canada, oil comes with great environmental costs. Oil-sand extraction and processing result in significant greenhouse gas emissions, which contribute to global warming (Hanania et al., 2019). The same production process also contributes to the global water shortage, as extracting petroleum from the oil sands needs vast amounts of water. Little of this water returns to the natural water system for future use. Further, oil sand extraction releases dangerous pollutants into the air that threaten our health. Two of these pollutants are nitrogen oxides (NOx) and sulfur oxides (SOx). Both increase the number of fine particles into the air and raise the risk of respiratory illnesses.

Extracting and refining oil also produces waste by-products consisting of hydrocarbons and other contaminants that harm surrounding ecosystems. And finally, when an oil-extraction site shuts down, it is difficult—even impossible—to return the land to its natural state, because of residual chemicals that have been released into the environment. The region effectively becomes uninhabitable by living creatures, human and otherwise. So, in these ways, oil production threatens the climate, water, air, and land.

As the world grapples with climate change, there are increasing calls for a transition to clean energy. Specifically, there is a wish to move away from oil, natural gas, and fossil fuels to wind, solar, and hydropower. However, where oil flows, oil politics follow. Environmental issues attached to oil are especially difficult to address because they are heavily politicized. Some oil-rich countries have banded together in an organization called the Organization of the Petroleum Exporting Countries (OPEC) to try and control the price of oil to their advantage. When the price is too low, they cut oil production across all the participant countries, reducing supply against a fixed demand to raise the price. This gives these countries significant power in manipulating the global economy.

One of the most controversial issues surrounding oil production in Canada is the building of pipelines. This form of technology transports oil to various domestic and U.S. refineries. It is an essential part of oil exportation, which helped contribute $108 billion to Canada's gross domestic product in 2018 (Canada's Oil & Natural Gas Producers, 2019). To many, these pipelines are an essential part of the Canadian economy, providing both jobs and a guarantee for future production. Since infrastructure is an expensive long-term investment, the country continues to produce and export oil to maximize the value of the pipelines.

However, many oppose building pipelines, as well as oil extraction in general. That's because pipelines cut through undeveloped natural regions, run the risk of leaks, and further contribute to an industry already under criticism for its negative environmental impacts. Various Indigenous groups have been especially vocal against pipelines. The pipelines often cut through their traditional lands, threatening both the sanctity of these regions and the well-being of those who live there. As well, the American government and various states (e.g., Michigan) oppose pipelines that carry oil from Canada to U.S. refineries.

The danger that oil pipelines will burst and pollute the water is especially stressful for many Indigenous communities. They already live with unsafe drinking water and pipeline construction increases their already great risks. Some Indigenous communities have agreed with companies proposing pipelines while others have withheld consent.

Oil politics often pits economic gain (and jobs) against environmental protection, making it hard for opposing sides to reach a compromise on this polarizing issue. Even an unexpected epidemic like COVID-19 can disturb the oil economy. When millions of people stayed home, people drove their cars less, the demand for oil dropped, and prices fell. Similarly, as the effects of the pandemic began to show signs of receding in mid-2021, oil prices (and consumption) moved back toward pre-pandemic levels.

Environmental Issues and Health

We cannot separate environmental issues from matters of health. Consider another example: the dumping of harmful chemicals into the air, sea, and soil. This practice has allowed organic pollutants such as pesticides to build up in the soil. Eventually, these chemicals enter the human food supply. Chronic exposure results in an alarming buildup of harmful synthetic chemicals and heavy metals in our bodies. Researchers have called this buildup *body burden* (Gennings, Ellis, and Ritter, 2012).

Children prove especially vulnerable to chemical, physical, and biological pollutants in the environment, since their immune systems are only partly developed. Among children under five years old, indoor air pollution caused by fossil-fuel combustion for cooking and heating is responsible for respiratory infections that cause 600,000 deaths per year worldwide (Perera, 2018). Ailing and elderly members of society also run a higher-than-average risk of this, because of their fragile health.

Pollution and climate change affect Canada's regions differently, with disastrous health effects on particular demographics, such as low-income people. In response to rising health concerns, an environmental justice movement has emerged. *Environmental justice* refers to the fair distribution of environmental burdens and benefits among different demographic groups. It wants to ensure that no group of people is unduly and unfairly affected by negative environmental impacts.

Like accidents and other health issues, environmental issues often worsen existing social inequalities by threatening the health of already marginalized people. Consider, once again, the problems facing Indigenous people. In northern Canada, Inuit peoples have higher levels of exposure to toxins than the general Canadian population.

This exposure is likely a result of pollutants like mercury that build up in traditional Inuit foods, which come directly from the polluted environment (Laird et al., 2013). In southern Ontario, mercury in the waterways has contaminated drinking water for many First Nations communities. For example, the Aamjiwnaang First Nation lives surrounded by chemical plants and oil refineries in an area known as "Chemical Valley." Beyond creating unsafe breathing conditions for residents, these plants sometimes also release benzene, a cancer-causing chemical used in some industrial processes (Luginaah et al., 2010).

The effects of such pollution are spread unevenly across Canada, often along class and racial lines. Some industries even locate factories near Indigenous reserves because they know Indigenous populations have little power to prevent it. This environmental racism can occur even without direct intent. Though environmental issues arise in every country, some of them, such as those around oil and Indigenous communities, are especially relevant to Canada. Solving environmental issues often means addressing long-standing social issues such as racial inequality and discrimination.

The Role of Public Belief and Political Will

Research reveals three main reasons global cooperation on environmental issues is so hard to achieve. First, it is costly to reduce greenhouse gases. Both supervision and enforcement are also difficult. Second, short-term interests drive many political and corporate decisions.

Protests against government inaction on climate change, like this one held in Toronto in March 2019, have grown in size and number in recent years. Although such protests have had some effect on public opinion, most environmental scientists believe that if the pace of moving toward a carbon-neutral economy does not speed up, irrevocable changes to the Earth's climate will occur by the end of the twenty-first century. The consequences for civilization might well be dire.

This makes it hard for politicians and businesspeople to accept the immediate costs of environmental action in return for delayed future benefits. Third, it is hard to get consensus on the key issues, since the effects of climate change vary around the world. Besides, many voters are unwilling or unable to see the link between industrial activity and environmental destruction. As a result, they are unwilling to support government spending on this matter. They may also reason that other countries are not honouring their commitments either.

There can be no effective response to environmental issues without strong political support for such actions and the costs they will entail. This, in turn, means that a majority of voters must support costly change, and to do this they must understand the need for such change. However, research has often shown wide and deep ignorance of environmental issues and widespread skepticism about the reported research findings.

Public attitudes towards climate change have changed very slowly. For example, climate skepticism was not yet widespread in Britain by 2011, only ten years ago, but some were already expressing doubt about scientific claims (Poortinga et al., 2015). Climate skepticism was especially common among older people with low incomes, little education, and traditional, conservative values. Skepticism was less common among younger, better-off and better-educated people.

In 2015, more than half the American public accepted the scientific consensus that climate change is happening because of human actions. However, a large minority—about 30 percent to 40 percent—continued to think the causes of climate change were mainly natural

(Hamilton et al., 2015). A smaller minority—about 10 to 15 percent—think the climate is not changing at all or express no opinion.

By the mid-2010s, a sharp political divide on climate change existed among Americans, with liberals and Democrats expressing greater belief in and concern about climate change than conservatives and Republicans (McRight et al., 2015). A Eurobarometer survey of twenty-five EU countries revealed a similar "belief gap" between liberals and conservatives. In fourteen Western European countries, citizens on the left consistently reported a stronger belief in climate change (and stronger desire to mitigate it) than citizens on the right.

For climate change deniers, factual information is largely irrelevant. Human values and political orientation, on the other hand, serve as important predictors of climate change beliefs and concern, as are the demographics of gender, age, and education (Poortinga et al., 2019). Level of education also consistently influences people's climate change opinions.

Not just values and demographics influence people's views of climate change. So do their views of science. Scientists overwhelmingly agree that climate change exists and is caused by human activity. However, non-scientists hold different models of, or ideas about, science, and these ideas affect their interpretation of this scientific consensus. Using survey data from the UK, France, Germany, and Norway, Bertoldo et al. (2019) found that people who perceive a high degree of scientific consensus are more likely to believe in manmade climate change. However, this link is strongest among people who view science as a "search for truth," and not merely a debate.

Overall, scientific information about climate change does not appear to exert a significant effect on public concern (Brulle et al., 2012). But media coverage, which may or may not reflect the scientific consensus, directly affects the degree of public concern about climate change. More coverage creates more concern. And time and again, political ideology emerges as the factor that strongly predicts a belief in climate change.

For example, Zanocco et al. (2018) studied public responses to four cases of extreme weather events (tornadoes and wildfires) in four U.S. communities. They asked respondents whether they thought these events were connected to climate change. Without fail, political ideology predicted these respondents' answers. Those who connected extreme weather events with climate change mainly lived in communities where a belief in climate change was already high, or where elites framed the event as a sign of climate change.

Elites often play a prominent role in shaping public views of climate change, and *elite cues* are critical in shaping public opinion. Elite cues shape media coverage and, in that way, shape public opinion. Members of the public use media coverage to learn the positions of political elites they trust and identify with (Carmichael and Brulle, 2016). And because the media depend on elite and/or official sources for information, the framing of a particular issue usually follows the opinions expressed in official circles. Said simply, media coverage largely reflects the statements of political elites. Conversely, the media have little effect on elite opinions.

As suggested earlier, right-wing populist (RWP) parties and their supporters are more strongly inclined to express climate skepticism; also, to be hostile to carbon taxation and the use of renewable sources (Lockwood, 2018). One explanation of this is that, in all postindustrial states, the rise of populism is driven by technological change and globalization. By this reckoning, hostility to climate change policy is a result of job losses in high-carbon industries. It also draws on hostility to any new form of taxation.

However, this approach has trouble explaining why right-wing populism appeals to far more people than just the economically "left behind." The way nationalism and authoritarianism combine with anti-elitism provides a more compelling explanation. Together, these elements produce a world view in which "the people" are seen to be ruled by a corrupt and illegitimate liberal, cosmopolitan elite. The ideological nature of RWP also creates an attraction to conspiracy theories, which are a consistent feature of climate skepticism.

The EU's eco-friendly policies have been a breeding ground for populist protest for over a decade (Stegemann and Ossewaarde, 2018). In particular, right-wing populists have favoured traditional modes of energy production that are freed from the control of foreign providers, science, and EU legislation. These right-wing movements also question scientific notions of causation, where environmental issues are concerned. However, such tactics are not the sole preserve of anti-EU right-wing populists. Proponents of green policies are not above stretching the truth either, in ways that suit their viewpoints.

In Britain, it is rare to find total skepticism about the existence of climate change (Fisher et al., 2018). However, most Britons doubt that climate change is mainly caused by humans or that its results will be harmful. Most Britons worry less about climate change than about energy becoming too expensive. So, they are conflicted about taxing energy from fossil fuels, which could impose a cost on them.

Globally, one of the main hindrances to moving ahead on environmental issues is that doing so demands a feeling of international camaraderie and common concern that is lacking. On this matter, we even see differences between Canada and the U.S. Lachapelle et al. (2012) note there is a greater appetite in Canada than in the U.S. for an aggressive climate policy.

Variations in the Approach to Sustainability

Despite this absence of a shared environmental concern, scientists have recommended various strategies to reduce carbon emissions and slow climate change. Many of these have now been tried, with varying results.

The climate debate in Canada has focused mostly on organizational and institutional steps to tackling climate change. Less attention has been given to changing individual behaviour, beyond the promotion of recycling (Wynes and Nicholas, 2017). However, a study at Lund University in Sweden found four main ways an individual can help to reduce climate change. These include bearing and raising one fewer child, living without a car, avoiding air travel, and eating a plant-based diet. The authors state that these four personal strategies are much more effective than enhanced recycling programs or the replacement of incandescent light bulbs by low-wattage alternatives like LEDs.

Few people are aware of this research and its recommendations. Most think they can make the greatest impact through recycling or driving a hybrid car. Yet the Lund researchers are right: living without a car saves 2.4 tonnes of equivalent CO_2 per year. Similarly, eating a plant-based diet saves 0.8 tonnes of CO_2 equivalent per year. Combining these strategies could have a major impact on reducing climate change, if everyone took part. Through studies like these, scientists can educate people on how to make choices that have a positive impact on climate change.

However, most citizens rely on government and industry to lead the way with new ideas and environment-saving innovations. So far, renewable energy accounts for only 16 percent of total energy consumption in Canada. The rest mainly comes from fossil fuels. By contrast, Iceland leads in green energy usage. Some estimate that 80 percent of Iceland's energy consumption comes from renewable sources.

There are many reasons that some countries, like Iceland, use more renewable energy than others. It may be because of the ready availability of power produced by water, wind, or sunlight. Iceland, for example, relies almost exclusively on hydropower and geothermal energy. However, much of this potential may be wasted if there is a technical inability to store such energy. As well, the use of some renewable energy sources (like hydroelectricity) leads to reliance on weather patterns beyond human control—patterns that, with climate change, are increasingly unpredictable.

Canada and many other resource-rich countries may also be reluctant to switch to renewable energy. That's because much of their economy relies on extracting fossil fuels—specifically oil and natural gas. A sudden and drastic switch to renewable energy sources would create political hostility among voters in the West—especially Alberta—who depend on the oil industry for jobs and revenue.

Again, though understandable, this proves to be short-run thinking. Research shows renewable energy is eventually more cost-effective than energy from fossil fuels, despite the early costs of switching. Advances in technology also give us hope that we will soon have the capacity to produce and save this energy cheaply. Australia, one of the largest emitters of CO_2 per capita, now has the technical capacity "to safely run a power grid in which 75 percent of the electricity comes from wind and solar," and could reach such a target, at least occasionally, by the mid-2020s (Morton, 2020). Expanding the contribution made by renewable energy is often as much a matter of political will as technological know-how.

Another way to reduce emissions is to encourage people to use green transport: notably, cycling, walking, and taking public transit. The transport sector is one of the world's largest contributors to greenhouse gas emissions. Canada has the second-largest amount of transport-related CO_2 emissions per capita, as we see in Figure 7-7 below.

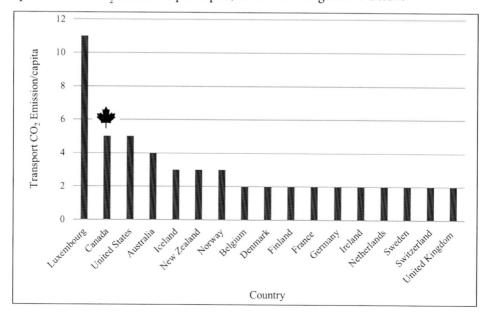

Figure 7-7. Transportation CO_2 Emissions per Capita, Canada and Comparison Countries, 2016.

In 2016, Clean Energy Canada, the David Suzuki Foundation, Environmental Defense, Equiterre, and the Pembina Institute called for more federal investment in public transit to reduce greenhouse gas emissions in the transportation sector. They also recommended auto-sharing, increasing the market share of zero-emission cars and buses sold, and reducing the carbon reliance of all vehicles in Canada. Yet many governments ignore the dangers of global warming, often because of the influence of private corporations that profit from oil extraction and lenient environmental policies.

On the other hand, many lower-income countries that suffer the extreme effects of climate change lack the money, technology, political stability, or political will to change. Often, only rich, powerful states can afford the technology needed to control the worst effects of climate change, like flooding, drought, and forest fires. This means that climate change causes the most harm to the most impoverished populations of the world. They simply lack the financial means to deal with environmental disasters. However, as we have seen, in many high-income countries, the public will to make environmental changes is crippled by political ideology, environmental skepticism, and a deep distrust of science.

Concluding Remarks

In this chapter, we discussed environmental degradation and the contributors to climate change. We compared Canada with countries known for being leaders against climate change—Sweden, Switzerland, and Denmark—and noted the importance of strong environmental policies. In 2021, Canada still did not have a comprehensive national policy on climate change, though our climate is warming at twice the rate as the global average (see Dangerfield, 2018; Bush and Lemmen, 2019).

Having said that, where does Canada rank in comparison with the sixteen other countries we have considered in this chapter? Looking at the measures employed here to assess the handling of environmental issues, we have to rank Canada at the bottom of the middle one-third of the nations that we are studying. Canada does comparatively well on such matters as pollution per capita, its handling of e-waste, and access to freshwater. However, it scores poorly on greenhouse gas emissions (in large part due to oil production) and municipal waste per capita. Canada ranks eleventh out of the cohort of seventeen comparison countries.

That said, Canada's efforts—great or small—have relatively little impact on the world situation. Environmental destruction occurs on a global level. Everyone is affected by what happens everywhere. An epidemic in China, a famine in Sudan, a drought in the Sahara, or forest fires in the Amazon basin all affect Canada one way or another. Environmental destruction, like excessive population growth, human trafficking, and cybercrime, requires global cooperation to be addressed. Eventually, our choices—as states and as individuals—will determine the future of the environment and of humanity.

CHAPTER EIGHT
The Many Worlds of Canada

It's important to pause at this point and note that Canada is not homogeneous nation. It's a collection of social worlds or semi-nations. For some social problems, almost as much variation exists among the Canadian provinces and territories as among the seventeen countries (including Canada) discussed in this book.

As well, some of the countries to which we are comparing Canada have populations smaller than some Canadian provinces. Even the largest of the Nordic countries, Sweden, has a population much smaller than that of Ontario. Denmark, Finland, and Norway *combined* have a population only slightly larger than that of Ontario. Considered individually, each is only a bit bigger than British Columbia, Canada's third-most-populous province. For its part, Iceland has a smaller population than such midsized Canadian cities as Halifax, Nova Scotia, and London, Ontario. From this standpoint, the Nordic countries are more aptly compared to provinces than to Canada as a whole. Indeed, of the sixteen countries to which we have compared Canada throughout this book, only the United States, Germany, France and the United Kingdom have larger populations.

Table 8-1 indicates the populations in 2016 of all seventeen of our comparison countries, as well as the thirteen Canadian provinces and territories, ranked from largest to smallest. Interestingly, were Ontario an independent country, it would be the eighth largest on the list, tucked in between the slightly bigger Netherlands and slightly smaller Belgium. Quebec is almost as large as Switzerland, and Ireland, New Zealand, and British Columbia are all virtually the same size.

Table 8-1. Comparative Populations

United States	323,015,955
Germany	82,193,768
United Kingdom	66,297,944
France	64,667,596
Canada	35,171,728
Australia	24,262,712
Netherlands	16,981,295
Ontario	13,242,160
Belgium	11,354,411
Sweden	9,836,007
Switzerland	8,379,917
Quebec	7,965,450
Denmark	5,711,350
Finland	5,497,713
Norway	5,213,000
Ireland	4,695,779
New Zealand	4,659,265
British Columbia	4,560,235
Alberta	3,978,145
Manitoba	1,240,700
Saskatchewan	1,070,560
Nova Scotia	1,070,560
New Brunswick	730,705
Luxembourg	579,264
Nfld. and Labrador	512,250
Iceland	332,206
Prince Edward Island	139,685
Northwest Territories	41,135
Nunavut	35,580
Yukon	35,110

Canada's provinces differ not only in population size and geographical area but in many other ways. As we saw in the last chapter, for example, Canadians disagree widely about the need to protect the environment as opposed to the need to protect jobs. There are good reasons for this wide variation among provinces. First, they vary culturally and ecologically, from east to west, the same way as the American states. This variation largely reflects the history of settlement in North America: when people settled different parts of the continent and where they came from. The settlement was gradual, from east to west (for the most part). It also reflects vast continental differences in climate and topography, with importance for staples extraction and, eventually, industrial development.

Second, the populations of the provinces (and the three territories) vary compositionally from north to south. Generally, Canadians closest to the border with the U.S. are the most urban and prosperous. That's largely why most immigrants head for southern Canadian locales. As you travel north in Canada, the settlements you find are more rural and less prosperous. They also tend to house a higher proportion of Indigenous people who, as a group, are more rural and less prosperous than other Canadians. These urban-rural, southern-northern differences play a large part in producing Canada's widely different rates of social problems from south to north (also, east to west, since many Indigenous people live in northwestern Canada).

Since Confederation in 1867, Canada has been a federation of provinces, large and small. The British North America Act gave some of the most important powers to the provinces, not the federal government. These include legislative control over education, welfare, and certain aspects of healthcare. In turn, this meant that rates of, say, poverty—and the results of poverty—could vary from one province to another. And although criminal law was reserved to the federal government, criminal law *enforcement* fell mainly to provinces and municipalities. As a result, arrest rates, prosecution rates, and imprisonment rates can vary widely from one province to another.

With all this in mind, is "the Canadian nation" a useful unit of analysis? Or is Canada so divided that we cannot usefully compare it with other smaller, more homogeneous countries and draw lessons from these countries? We hope to answer that question in this chapter. We will see that, despite likenesses among the provinces, when it comes to social problem measures, there are distinct and important variations. This means it is problematic to speak about Canada (and its problems) as a whole. We always need to examine regional and provincial variations. In this chapter, we will make a small start in that direction, mainly to remind the reader that everything in this book needs to be read with an appreciation of interprovincial variation.

With that in mind, we will quickly review some of the same social problems we examined in earlier chapters, focusing on differences among the provinces and territories—and the reasons for those differences.

Poverty and Economic Inequality

As we see in Figure 8-1, Nova Scotia is now the province with the most poverty—the highest proportion of low-income people. By contrast, Alberta has the least poverty. We lack complete data on the territories. However, we learn from the *Yukon Poverty Report Card 2020* (Yukon Anti-poverty Coalition, 2021) that Statistics Canada calculated a low-income measure for Yukon in 2018. At that time, 10.9 percent of Yukoners were found to live in poverty. The Yukoners most likely to be considered low income, based on this measure, include lone-parent families (22.1 percent), persons not in census families (23 percent), and households living outside of Whitehorse (14.5 percent).

Data from the Northwest Territories show that, in 2018, 16.3 percent of all families were deemed low income families after taxes. This number, however, ranged widely, with the percentage of low-income families numbering only 8.8 percent in Yellowknife but 28.5 percent in non-urban communities. In some small non-urban communities, the proportion of low-income families varied between 20 percent and 60 percent of the population.

We could find no comparable statistics for Nunavut. However, in December 2020, the Borgen Project, a U.S. not-for-profit organization formed to fight poverty, reported that "Nunavut's child poverty rate of 31.2 percent [was] well above the Canadian average of 18.6 percent."

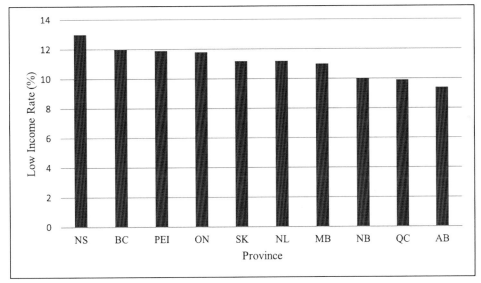

Figure 8-1. Percentage of People with Low Income, by Province, 2018.

We see similar interprovincial variation in Gini indices of income inequality (Figure 8-2, overleaf). Income inequality is highest in Ontario, followed by Newfoundland and Labrador, Alberta, and B.C. Quebec, New Brunswick, and Prince Edward Island post the lowest Gini Indices of income inequality.

Sharp and Capeluck (2012), in an outline of regional trends in income inequality between 1981 and 2010, explore the impact of redistributive policies—namely, taxes and transfers—on these trends. Here, they measure income inequality using both pre-tax and after-tax income. Doing so, they find that Canada's national Gini index *after* taxes and transfers was 0.395 in 2010. This was 23.7 percent lower than the "market" (i.e., *before* taxes and transfers) Gini coefficient. Of this reduction, roughly 71 percent was a result of transfers and 29 percent a result of taxes.

Using the same methods, these researchers found much variation across the provinces. First, they found that the market (or pretax-and-transfer) Gini coefficient increased by 19.4 percent between 1981 and 2010. About 44 percent of this growth in inequality was offset by both taxes and transfers. Second, they found significant differences among the provinces in both levels of inequality and the offsetting of inequality by taxes and transfers.

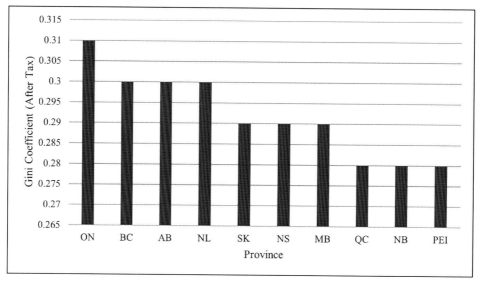

Figure 8.2. Gini Indices of Income Inequality (after tax), by Province, 2017.

The province with the greatest market income inequality in 2010 was Newfoundland and Labrador, with a Gini coefficient of 0.560. Second highest were Ontario and British Columbia. The province with the least market income inequality was Manitoba, with a Gini coefficient of 0.483, followed by Prince Edward Island and Alberta. In short, the market income inequality was 15.9 per cent higher in Newfoundland and Labrador than in Manitoba.

In 2010, the inequality-reducing effect of taxes and transfers was largest in Newfoundland and Labrador, followed by Nova Scotia, Prince Edward Island and Quebec. British Columbia and Alberta did the least to offset market income inequality with taxes and transfers. The Gini coefficient for income calculated after taxes for British Columbia in 2010 was 0.414, the highest of any province. In short, the income redistribution effort was greatest in the five most eastern provinces (Quebec and the four Atlantic provinces). It was least in the four western provinces, with Ontario in the middle, at a level almost identical to the national average.

Between 1981 and 2010, the after-tax Gini index grew most in Newfoundland and Labrador, British Columbia, Ontario, and Alberta. These increases were driven by increases in the market income Gini coefficient. Income inequality barely grew in Manitoba and Saskatchewan over this period, and it did not change at all in Prince Edward Island. The rank ordering of provinces by after-tax inequality changed (only) slightly between 2010 and 2017. The take-away message here is that, though the statistics and rank ordering changed somewhat over time, the range of inequality was preserved. As well, the same factors that influenced income inequality in 2010 also influenced them in 2017.

Other factors besides taxes and redistribution policies influence income inequality. For example, Breau (2007) cites increases in international trade, technological change, educational diversity, and the unemployment rate as contributing to greater inequality between provinces. These increases have been larger in some regions than in others. Deindustrialization and declining government transfer payments also explain varying rises in inequality.

By contrast, demographic factors, like immigration and population aging, are only secondary effects of the trends reported above. They are not and were not themselves responsible for these changes in inequality. On this, Breau reports (2007: 85):

The evidence suggests that globalization has affected income inequality. Trade openness is clearly an important factor behind the rise in inequality across Canadian provinces. Recent cutbacks to government spending on social programs also contributed to the rise in inequality.

Thus, government taxing and spending aside, provinces and regions vary dramatically in the ways they are affected by globalized trade. In large part, this is why some Canadian provinces are much richer and also more unequal than others, with Ontario and British Columbia in the lead.

Recent surges in populist sentiment in many countries, such as the U.S., have focused our attention on the political consequences of such regional inequality. Marchand et al. (2020) note that the continuing rise in inequality at the national level has accompanied increases in inequality within and across regions. In turn, these regional differences reflect differences in economic development, working conditions, unionization, and other socio-economic factors. Typically, regions with high concentrations of manufacturing have lower-than-average levels of inequality, especially if they are unionized.

By contrast, regions with high concentrations of arts and entertainment workers, as well as knowledge-intensive business services, have higher-than-average levels of inequality. Regions with high concentrations of tertiary and quaternary sector activities—in particular finance, insurance and real estate, arts and entertainment and knowledge-intensive business services—have highly unequal income distributions. In short, as some regions move more quickly than others towards tertiary and quaternary work, they move more quickly toward high income inequality.

In the short run, more inequality reflects regional economic growth. That is, more growth, marked by movement into knowledge-intensive and financial services, means more inequality. Persisting high levels of inequality may also prompt government policies to reduce inequality and promote further growth. The provinces often vary in their response to these problems.

Provinces also vary dramatically in the opportunities they provide for upward mobility. Research in Canada and elsewhere shows that people in the lowest income deciles remain stuck in those deciles. Another way of saying this is that poor people tend to remain mired in poverty. And as we see in Figure 8-3 on the next page, in Canada the rates of social immobility vary from one province to another.

Provinces with the greatest economic growth typically have the lowest rates of poverty immobility. As a result, poor people are more likely to be upwardly mobile in Alberta, Ontario, and British Columbia than in any other provinces. For the same reason, there is the least low-income mobility (or most immobility) in the Maritimes, Manitoba, and Saskatchewan. However, such provincial variations in mobility are relatively small. This means that all over Canada, the poorest people are similarly stuck, socially and often geographically. It also means that rapid and significant economic growth does not do much to improve conditions for the poor.

As a result, poor Canadians must rely on government support, popularly known as welfare programs. However, Canadian provinces vary widely in this area (see Figure 8-4 on the next page). The provinces do not coordinate their welfare legislation or legislative reforms to respond similarly to increases in inequality and poverty. Nor do they all respond similar-

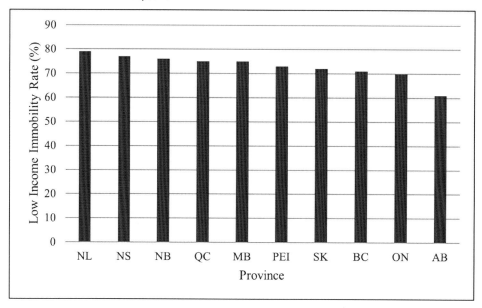

Figure 8-3. Low Income Immobility, by Province, 2017–18.

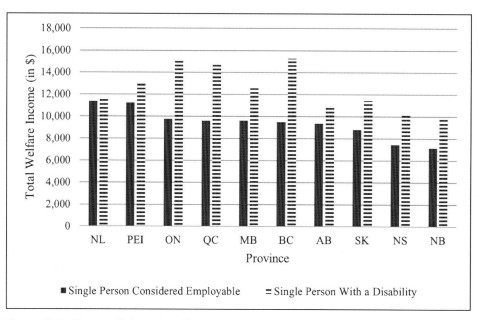

Figure 8-4. Change in Total Welfare Income, by Province, 2017 to 2018.

ly to similar problems, such as the economic need of people with disabilities that limit their employability and employment income.

Social Justice Issues

Social justice also varies from one province to another. For example, Figure 8-5 shows the gender wage gap—the difference in average earnings between men and women—in different provinces.

As we see, this gap looms far wider in Newfoundland and Labrador—almost three times wider—than in Prince Edward Island. Between 1997 and 2014, women in all provinces narrowed the gender wage gap, but made less progress in Alberta and in Newfoundland and Labrador than elsewhere (Schirle, 2015). Much of this variation across provinces disappears, however, once we account for the gender differences in jobs. Said another way, much of the gendered wage gap in each province is explained by gender differences from one industry or occupation to another. However, important unexplained differences remain.

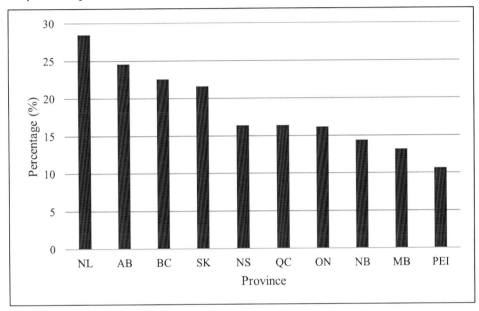

Figure 8–5. Gender Wage Gap (as a Percentage), by Province, 2016.

On this matter, Schirle and Vickers (2015) note that a large part of the male-female gap in average wages was once explained by differences in the average skills or job characteristics of men and women respectively. These would include, for example, which occupation or industry men and women typically worked in, and their educational attainments. However, today, this is no longer the case and a larger fraction of the gendered gap remains unexplained. This portion may represent gender differences in job characteristics that researchers cannot measure. Equally, it may reflect systemic discriminatory practices that result in women receiving less than male counterparts who are doing the same job.

We see in Figure 8-6 (next page) that intimate partner violence (IPV), mainly by men against women, is much more common in the territories, and especially in Nunavut, than in the provinces. It is especially common in the territories when compared with Ontario, British Columbia, or Prince Edward Island, where the rates of victimization are low.

We also find dramatic regional variations in crime. Sinha (2013: 13) notes that Saskatchewan and Manitoba consistently record the highest provincial rates of police-reported violent crime. In 2011 they had rates of violence against women roughly double the national rate. Ontario and Quebec had the lowest rates of police-reported violence against women. As with violent crime overall, the territories have consistently recorded the country's highest rates of police-reported violence against women. In 2011, the rate of violent crime against women in Nunavut was nearly thirteen times the rate for Canada as a whole. Similarly, the rate in the Northwest Territories was nine times the national average. Yukon's rate, although the lowest among the territories, was still four times the national average.

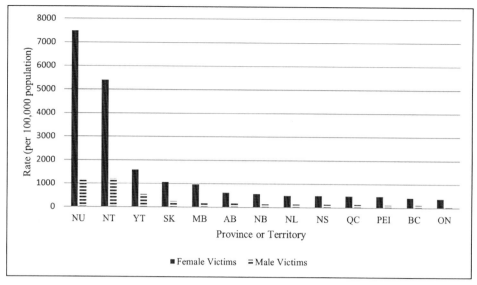

Figure 8-6.Victims of Police-Reported Intimate Partner Violence, by Sex and Region, 2018.

Earlier research suggested that differences in the demographic characteristics of territorial residents may help explain women's high risker of violence there (Brzozowski et al., 2006). According to the 2011 census, the population of the territories was significantly younger than the national population on average, a consistent risk factor for victimization. Further, people living in the territories are more likely to have other socio-demographic factors associated with victimization. These include identifying as Indigenous, being single, and having less than a high school education.

What we have said about violence against women can also be said about violence against girls under 12. Here, Sinha (2013: 15) notes that police-reported rates of violence against girls under 12 were highest in Saskatchewan and Manitoba and lowest in Ontario and Prince Edward Island. This, as noted, is in keeping with regional variations in violence against adult women.

Continuing with issues of social justice, provinces also vary both in the absolute numbers and in the percentages of racialized people they contain. As you can see in Figure 8-7a, Ontario's population includes the largest number of racialized persons in absolute terms. This is not particularly surprising. Ontario is by far the largest province, with a population nearly 75 percent larger than Quebec's.

When we turn to racialized minorities as a percentage of population, Ontario yields top spot—barely—to British Columbia. B.C. has been a major destination for immigration in recent decades, particularly from Asia. Ontario also attracts large numbers of racialized immigrants. They tend to concentrate in the province's urban areas, especially the Greater Toronto Area, now the sixth-largest metropolitan area in Canada and the U.S.

Although Quebec's population includes a large absolute number of members of racialized minorities, they make up a much smaller fraction of the total population than in B.C., Ontario, Alberta, and even Nova Scotia and Manitoba. Many factors account for this. Some immigrants fear settling in a province whose sole official language is French will limit their economic prospects. The Quebec economy also suffered during the heyday of the sovereigntist movement in the 1970s, '80s, and '90s. As a result, Quebec's population grew by

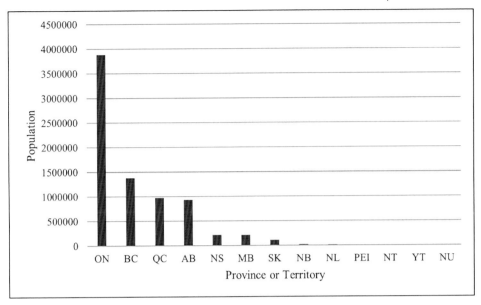

Figure 8-7a.Total Visible Minority Population, by Region, 2016 Census.

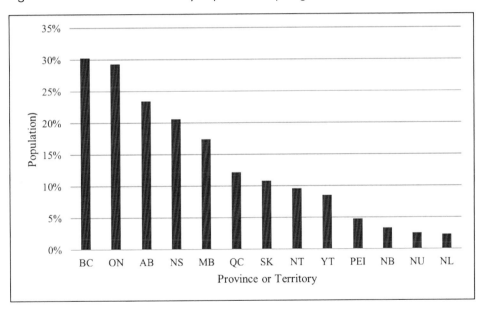

Figure 8-7b. Percentage of Visible Minorities in Population, by Region, 2016 Census.

only about a million people between 1971 and 2016, while Ontario added more six million people to its population—many of them racialized immigrants.

For the most part, the Prairie provinces (especially Manitoba and Saskatchewan) and the Atlantic provinces (Nova Scotia aside) are less demographically diverse than B.C. and Ontario. It should be noted, however, that these regions, as well as the territories, include large Indigenous populations, as we shall see later in this chapter.

Using Canada's Survey of Labour and Income Dynamics data, Lightman and Gingrich (2018) examined patterns of economic exclusion in Canada's labor market in 2000 and 2010. Doing so, the authors find evidence of persistent disadvantage tied to immigrant status, race, and gender in Canada's labour market. Specifically, people identified as Black,

South Asian, and Arab, as well as recent immigrants and women, fare worst in the labour market. About geographic location, the authors (2018: 15-16) note that:

> Individuals in rural areas faced significantly more economic exclusion than urban individuals in both years, as did people residing in all geographic regions other than Ontario in 2000. Demonstrating the shifting economic landscape across Canada, individuals in Eastern Canada, Quebec, and Western Canada were significantly less economically excluded in 2010 than in 2000, with individuals in the latter case faring better than equivalent individuals in Ontario in 2010.

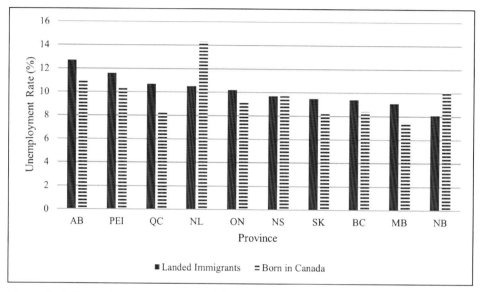

Figure 8-8. Rate of Unemployment (%) for Landed Immigrants and Native-Born Individuals by Province, 2020.

Along similar lines, we see in Figure 8-8 the widely varying rates of unemployment among landed immigrants. They are higher in many provinces than the rates of unemployment among people born in Canada. Many of these immigrants are racialized people, while many of the native-born people are not. The only two exceptions to this rule are New Brunswick and Newfoundland and Labrador, where the rates of unemployment are higher for people born in Canada than for people born elsewhere.

Given these statistics, Bilodeau et al. (2012: 579) not surprisingly note that "Canadian provinces have long been considered as 'small worlds,' each with its own cultural distinctiveness and province-building.... The ten Canadian provinces have different orientations to political life, different levels of attachments and loyalties to the federal and provincial governments and distinct policy preferences."

These authors recognize there are many reasons for regional variations in immigration and racial diversity, and why therefore we ought to study provincial public opinion on those matters. Everywhere in Canada, public opinion towards immigration has evolved over time. As immigration became more central to economic development, provinces gradually became important actors in making policy related to immigration. For example, since 1991, the Quebec government has been solely responsible for selecting economic immigrants settling in the province. In 1996, the federal government adopted a Provincial Nominee

Program to facilitate this. It allowed provinces and territories "to identify a limited number of economic immigrants to meet specific regional needs or to receive priority attention for immigration processing."

Since then, all provinces except Quebec have agreed to follow this program. Many provinces have also adopted programs to ease the integration of immigrants. These include language training programs and measures to promote the recognition of foreign credentials. As well, all provinces except Newfoundland and Labrador have adopted multicultural or intercultural policies to improve interracial relations. Thus, immigrant arrivals and the number of visible minorities vary greatly across Canadian provinces. What's more, these issues matter for all of the provinces, even for those that receive a relatively small number of immigrants.

Crime and Victimization

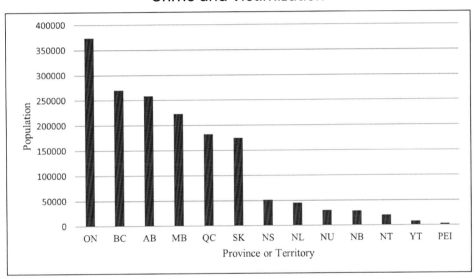

Figure 8-9a. Total Indigenous Population by Region, 2016 Census.

Indigenous people in Canada face a disproportionate number of problems, including disproportionate victimization and incarceration. As well, Indigenous people are much more numerous in certain parts of Canada than in others. For example, we see in Figure 8-9a (above) that large numbers of Indigenous people live in Ontario, British Columbia, and Alberta. However, as Figure 8-9b on the next page demonstrates, they form a higher proportion of the total population in the territories, the Prairie provinces, and Newfoundland and Labrador.

Given the disadvantages and discrimination facing Indigenous peoples, social problems are most common in regions where there are more Indigenous communities. These problems include high rates of crime, victimization, and violence, as well as those of ill health and poverty,

For instance, in 2014–15, Indigenous Canadians represented a much higher-than-average number of admissions to provincial, territorial and federal custody, and that remains true today. They make up only about 5 percent of the general population. Yet Indigenous people account for almost 30 percent of all sentenced admissions to custody (federal and

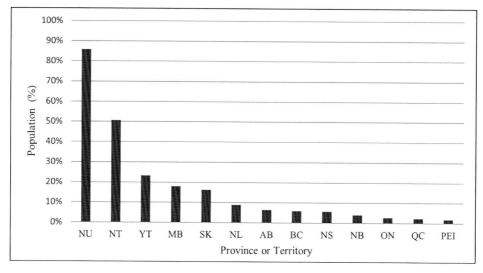

Figure 8–9b. Percentage of Indigenous Population by Region, 2016 Census.

provincial/territorial combined) (Roberts and Reid, 2017). This percentage is significantly higher than in 1978, when the first reliable statistics on corrections are available.

Trend data show the problem of Indigenous imprisonment is getting worse, not better. Finally, and most relevant to the discussion in this chapter, the trends vary across jurisdictions. In some provinces, Indigenous rates of admission to prison are strikingly higher than non-Indigenous rates. Among the provinces, Indigenous adults make up the largest part of admissions to custody in Manitoba (74 percent) and Saskatchewan (76 percent). These two provinces also have the highest proportions of Indigenous adults in their provincial populations, at 15 percent for Manitoba, and 14 percent for Saskatchewan (Malakieh 2018). As Roberts and Reid (2017) write, despite some variations from one jurisdiction to another, "every picture tells the same story." No matter where they live in Canada, Indigenous people are over-represented in prisons.

Accordingly, we could say that Indigenous peoples in Canada are both under- and over-policed. They are over-policed in the sense that they are more likely to be arrested for crimes than non-Indigenous Canadians, regardless of overall crime rates. They are under-policed in that they are more likely than non-Indigenous Canadians to be the victims of crime, and less likely to feel protected by the police.

Figure 8-10 (opposite) shows the rates of self-reported physical and sexual assaults for Indigenous victims. The data are rates of self-reported victimization among Indigenous people for the crimes of sexual and physical assault in the different provinces and territories in 2018. One possible explanation for the high rates of victimization rates is the poverty and economic inequality that Indigenous people face. People of lower-than-average socioeconomic status are more likely than other Canadians to be the victims of violent crime, and this certainly is true of Indigenous Canadians.

As with other social problems we have examined, we find great variation among the provinces and territories when we examine crime and victimization statistics. Overall rates of violent crime in Canada, including homicide, are higher in rural areas than urban areas (Roy and Marcellus, 2019). As well, higher rates of rural crime are mainly found in the northern areas of the provinces.

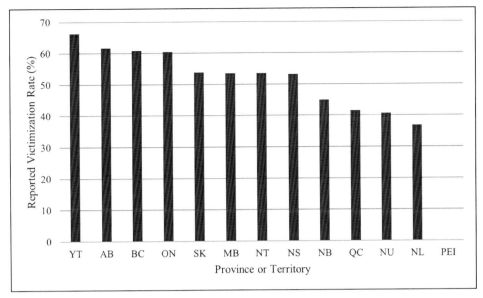

Figure 8-10. Self-Reported Violent Victimization of Physical or Sexual Assault among Indigenous People in Canada, 2018.

In 2018, homicide rates were three times higher in the northern regions of Canada than in the southern regions. The greatest differences were seen in Manitoba and Saskatchewan where rates for the northern region of these provinces were seven and six times higher respectively than for the southern regions. Nationally, the homicide rate was highest in the rural areas of the North (7.30 victims per 100,000 population). The lowest rate of homicide was found in rural areas of the South at 1.42 homicides per 100,000 population. These trends have been consistent since 2009, the earliest year for which data for these geographic breakdowns are available. Figure 8-11 shows provincial and territorial homicide rates for the year 2018.

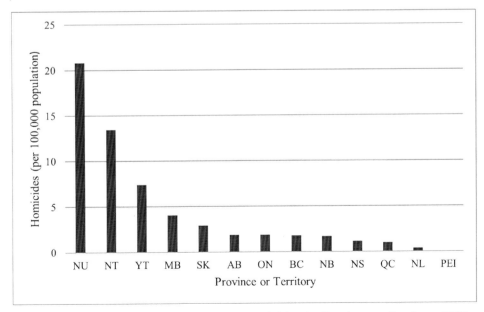

Figure 8-11. Number of Police-Reported Homicides by Province or Territory, 2018.

As we see, the territories and Prairie provinces have the highest homicide rates in the country. One possible explanation for these differences in homicide rates between provinces and territories is firearm ownership. Higher rates of firearm ownership contribute to higher homicide rates, because one in three homicides are connected to the use of firearms. Firearms are smuggled into Canada at different entry points, varying their availability to different populations.

As mentioned earlier, not only are rates of crime different in the north and south of Canada; they also vary between men and women. Rates of criminal victimization peak in the Prairie provinces and territories. Disturbingly, Indigenous people are much more likely than non-Indigenous people to be the victims of violent crime (Figure 8-12). Nunavut, the Northwest Territories, and Yukon report far higher rates of criminal victimization than, say, the Maritime provinces, where very few Indigenous people live. Young women (ages 0–24) are especially likely to be victims of violent crime in the northern territories. Indeed, Indigenous women and girls are at especially high risk of violence nationwide, with the federal Inquiry into the Missing and Murdered Indigenous Women and Girls (MMIWG) declaring the crisis of violence a genocide.

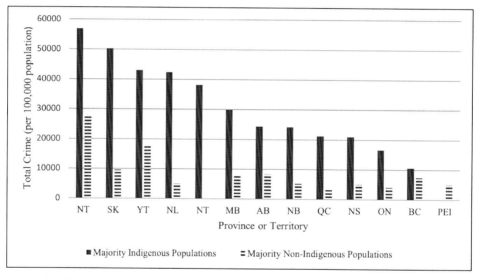

Figure 8-12. Police-Reported Crime Rate for Majority Indigenous and Majority Non-Indigenous Populations, by Province and Territory, 2018.

Health and Addictions

Wide regional variations exist in the statistics on health and addictions. For example, we see in Figure 8-13a that life expectancy at birth in Canada varies by a surprisingly amount. Averaging across the sexes, it ranges from roughly 79.4 years in Newfoundland and Labrador to 82.5 years in Ontario and British Columbia.

Figure 8-13b presents life expectancy figures for women and men in each province. In British Columbia, a baby girl born in the mid-2010s could expect to live 84.8 years. By contrast, a baby boy born in Newfoundland and Labrador could expect on average to live 77.2 years. In short, a girl born on Canada's West Coast could expect to live 10 percent longer than a boy born on Canada's East Coast. That's roughly the same gap as exists between Japan (the world's longest-lived nation) and Iran (country #49 in overall life expectancy).

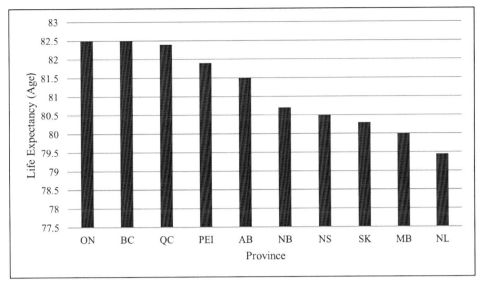

Figure 8-13a. Life Expectancy at Birth (Age) by Province, 2014–16.

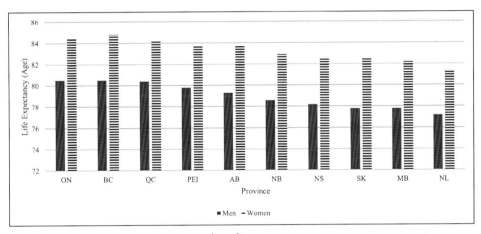

Figure 13b. Life Expectancy at Birth (Age), Women and Men Compared, by Province, 2014–16.

We also find wide provincial variations in mortality rates, from one province to another. The mortality rates are highest in the Maritime provinces and lowest in Ontario and Alberta, as we see in Figure 8-14 (overleaf). This is largely because young people, including young immigrants, come to Ontario and Alberta for work. Conversely, mortality rates are generally higher in the Maritime provinces, where the populations are much older on average, because more young people are leaving these regions than are entering them.

The provinces and territories also vary in their levels of morbidity, or poor health. Nationally, Colin et al. (2017) note that people in Newfoundland and Labrador and Prince Edward Island spend significantly more of their lives in poor health. Why this is so remains unclear, though it likely reflects differences in age and income we discussed earlier.

Because of provincial differences in average age, mortality rates from heart disease and stroke—which are age-related—are much higher in most Maritime and Prairie provinces than in Quebec, British Columbia, and Ontario. We see this in Figure 8-15 (overleaf). Variations in economic well-being may also explain some of these interprovincial differences.

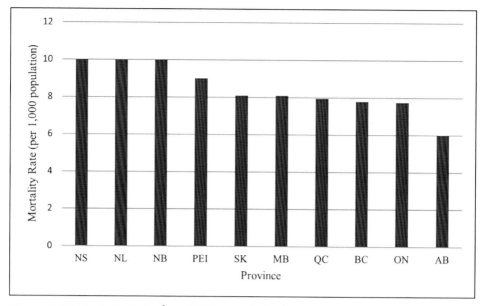

Figure 8-14. Mortality Rate (per 1,000 population) by Province, 2019.

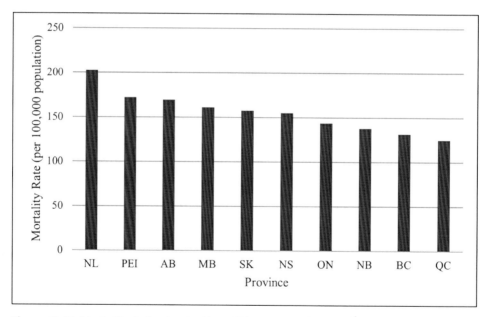

Figure 8-15. Mortality Rate due to Heart Disease and Stroke (per 100,000 population) by Province, 2009–11.

Filate et al. (2003) report significant regional variations in deaths from cardiovascular disease (CVD) per 100,000 population. Specifically, Newfoundland and Labrador has the highest CVD mortality rates, while Nunavut and the Northwest Territories have the lowest ones. Regional variations in smoking and unemployment are the most important factors associated with CVD mortality at the regional level.

That said, Kreatsoulas and Anand (2010) note that CVD health among Indigenous people is especially poor. They report that Indigenous people have an even higher prevalence of CVD than Canadians of European ancestry. Not surprisingly, they also have a higher

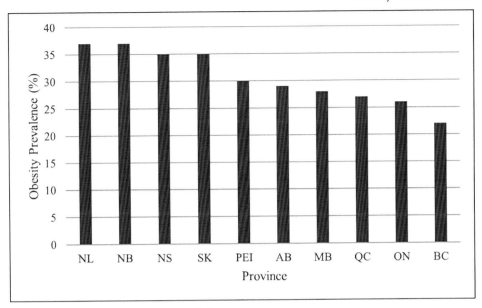

Figure 8-16. Obesity Prevalence (%) by Province, 2017.

prevalence of risks, including higher rates of smoking, diabetes, obesity, abdominal obesity, hypertension, cholesterol and family history. As well, Indigenous people have an excess of social disparities including poverty and *environmental dispossession*—a term referring to the processes by which Indigenous peoples lost control of their traditional environments.

Obesity rates also vary dramatically from one province to another, with the highest obesity rates in the Maritimes and the Prairies, as Figure 8-16 shows. In large part, this variation is due to differences in age, immigration status, and social class within each provincial population. Younger people, recent immigrants, and higher income people are less likely to be obese, and they are more numerous in British Columbia, Ontario, and Quebec.

Vanasse et al. (2006) note the rates of obesity vary substantially among the 106 Canadian health regions: from 6.2 percent in Vancouver to 47.5 percent in Indigenous population areas. At the regional level, a lack of leisure-time physical activity and low fruit and vegetable consumption are both good predictors of obesity. Vanasse et al. remark (2006: 679) that

> Nearly half (49.7%) of Canadians aged 20 years and older had a low level of physical activity during their leisure time … in 2003 with regional rates varying from 33.5% in British Columbia to 71.0% in Newfoundland, while 55.8% ate fruits and vegetables less than five times per day. Once again, these [fruit and vegetable eating] rates varied substantially between health regions: from 46.3% in British Columbia to 79.8% in Newfoundland. It is interesting to note that two regions famous for their fruit production like Niagara in Ontario and Okanagan in British Columbia exhibit higher rates of low fruit and vegetable consumption than the national overall rate of 55.8%.

A high proportion of children aged 3–5 years in Newfoundland and Labrador are reportedly overweight or obese. This leads Canning et al. (2004) to conclude that prevention measures should begin before the age of three years. Their conclusion agrees closely with the finding that the prevalence of obesity among children and adolescents is high in the Atlantic provinces (Shields and Tjepkema, 2006). The fraction of children and adolescents under 17 who are obese or overweight is above the national level (i.e., 26 percent) in Newfoundland and Labrador, New Brunswick, Nova Scotia, and Manitoba. By contrast, children and adolescents in Alberta and Quebec are less likely to be obese or overweight.

As we see in Figure 8-17, the provinces also vary dramatically in their rates of mental disorder and suicidal ideation. Once again, with a few exceptions, the rates of both are much higher in the Maritime and Prairie provinces than they are in Ontario, Quebec, and British Columbia. However, the pattern here is more mixed, for two reasons. On the one hand, the provinces vary widely in age, income, and other conditions that influence mental health. On the other hand, the provinces also vary in the availability of mental health professionals who would diagnose, record, and treat mental disorders.

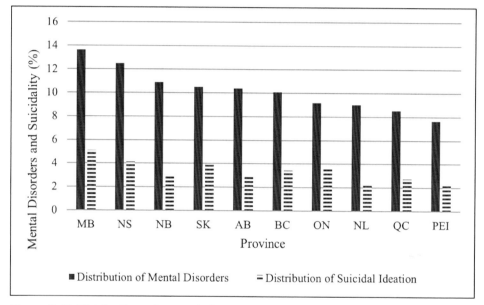

Figure 8-17. Distribution of Mental Disorders and Suicidal Ideation by Province, 2012.

Similarly, as we see in Figure 8-18 (opposite), the provinces vary widely in alcohol and substance use disorders. The Prairie provinces tend to have the highest rates and the Maritimes the lowest. Exceptions to these patterns exist because of the same competing influences (of diagnosis and treatment) we discussed in respect to Figure 8-17 above.

As noted, the annual prevalence of measured mental disorders and suicidality show significant interprovincial differences. Palay et al. (2019) report that Manitoba displays the highest prevalence of alcohol use disorder compared to the other provinces, and that Nova Scotia shows the highest prevalence of substance use disorders. Manitoba also exhibits the highest prevalence of suicidal ideation. British Columbia and Ontario exhibit the highest prevalence of suicidal planning, and Ontario alone exhibits the highest prevalence of suicide attempts. By contrast, Quebec and Prince Edward Island display the lowest prevalence of any substance use or mental disorders.

Palay et al. (2019) note that these variations in provincial prevalence are not attributable to sociodemographic differences. Other possible contributing factors may include

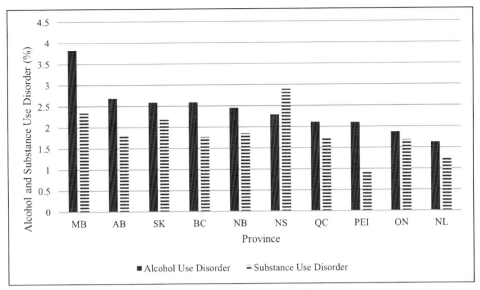

Figure 8-18. Alcohol and Substance Use Disorder (%) by Province, 2012.

support systems, job losses, trends in financial mobility, or migration between provinces. Provinces may also differ in their per capita mental health funding and may invest their health funds in different geographic or clinical areas, such as addiction treatment centers, youth interventions, or crisis services.

Similarly, as we see in Figure 8-19, the provinces vary considerably in their prevalence of cigarette smoking. The rate of cigarette smoking is nearly twice as high in Newfoundland, for example, as it is in British Columbia. Typically, cigarette smoking, like obesity, correlates with age and income. Older and lower-income people are more likely to smoke cigarettes than younger people with higher incomes and more education.

Between 1950 and 2011, rates of smoking for both women and men were higher in the Atlantic provinces and Quebec than in other parts of Canada, although for men these

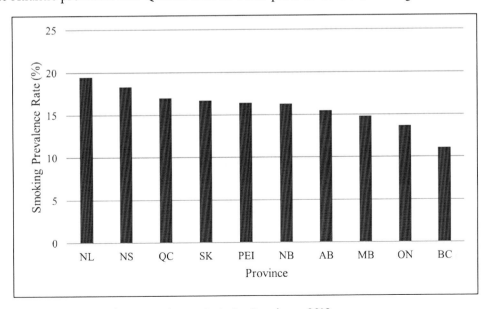

Figure 8-19. Smoking Prevalence Rate by Province, 2019.

differences declined after the 1990s. Research by Corsi et al. (2013) shows that people with lower-than-average levels of education have higher levels of smoking initiation and lower levels of cessation. Some of the regional variation in cigarette smoking may reflect this variation in the average educational levels in different parts of Canada.

Accidental Injuries and Deaths

We see similarly large variations when we compare provinces and territories on accidental deaths and injuries. In Figure 8-20, we also see a regional variation in workplace insurance coverage against on-the-job injuries, though this variation is only moderate. In all parts of the country, insurance coverage rates exceed 70 percent and, at the top end, are nearly 100 percent.

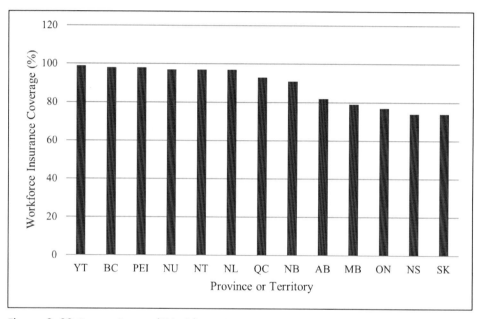

Figure 8-20. Percentage of Workforce Insurance Coverage, by Region, 2020.

The provinces also vary in workplace injuries among Canadians aged 15–24 years. Even taking into account differences in occupation, Saskatchewan youth were about twice as likely as Ontario youth to be injured at work (Breslin et al., 2006). Two notable patterns are obvious in the provincial data on accidents. First, Quebec, Alberta, and British Columbia have high percentages of injuries caused by contact with sharp objects. And compared with Ontario, Saskatchewan has proportionally more overexertion injuries, and injuries classified as "other." Not surprisingly, type of job is a major correlate of injury risk, with manual jobs showing higher risk of injury than non-manual (administrative or clerical) jobs. However, even controlling for the type of job, visible minorities, students, and 15–17 -year-olds have a lower likelihood of workplace injury than other young workers.

In comparing deaths from injuries (Figure 8-21), we see even wider regional variations. The percentage of workplace injuries that results in deaths is far higher in the northern territories than in Prince Edward Island, Ontario, and Quebec, where it is lowest. This variation reflects, on the one hand, the fact that work is more dangerous in the northern territories and, on the other, that access to safety equipment and good healthcare is poorer.

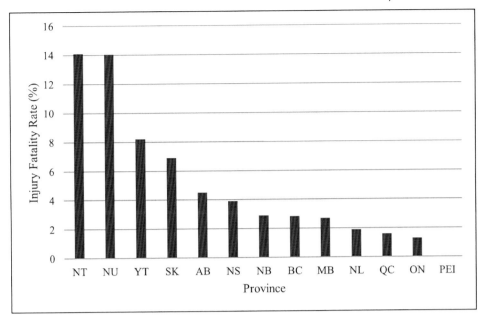

Figure 8-21. Injury Fatality Rate (%) per 100,000 workers, by Region, 2018.

Excluding the territories and Prince Edward Island, none of which have more than 100,000 workers in total, Saskatchewan's five-year average injury death rate ranks highest, followed by Alberta and Newfoundland and Labrador (Tucker and Keefe, 2018). From 2011 on, death rates due to injuries declined in most jurisdictions. However, a comparison of the average 2011–13 rate to the average 2014–16 rate revealed an 83 percent increase in New Brunswick and a 32 percent increase in Newfoundland and Labrador.

Among jurisdictions with more than 100,000 workers, Newfoundland and Labrador also has the highest five-year average death rate from occupational diseases, followed by Nova Scotia, Alberta and British Columbia. Injury-related death rates show a general downward trend in Canada. However, some jurisdictions show increasing rates, others declining rates. A comparison of the 2011–13 rate to the 2014–16 rate shows Nova Scotia with the greatest increase, followed by New Brunswick and British Columbia.

Likely, these variations reflect differences in the work people do in these provinces—for example, office work as opposed to manufacturing as opposed to farming or resource extraction. They may also reflect differences in the efforts each province makes to prevent such injuries. As a result, Tucker and Keefe (2018: 33) recommend the following steps to reduce workplace deaths throughout Canada:

- Targeting high risk industries and occupations.
- Ensuring compliance with existing occupational health and safety regulatory frameworks.
- Improving enforcement activities (e.g., focussed inspections, targeted programs and initiatives).
- Creating multipronged primary prevention initiatives that combine consultation, education and enforcement activities.
- Developing public awareness campaigns, partnerships and community outreach.

Traffic accidents cause a great many injuries and deaths in Canada. Many traffic accidents involve driving under the influence or distracted driving. In Figure 8-22, we once again see wide regional differences in deaths and bodily harm connected to Criminal Code traffic violations. Again, the northern territories have by far the highest rates, while Ontario has the lowest. These results reflect a variety of factors, including the quality and extent of law enforcement, local driving "cultures," excessive alcohol consumption among drivers, and more.

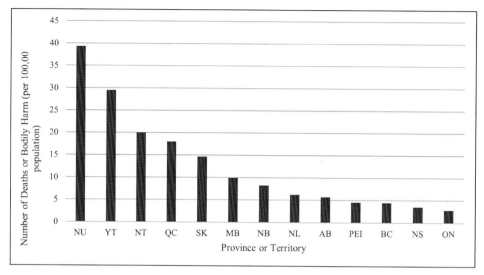

Figure 8-22. Victims of Police-Reported Criminal Code Traffic Violations Causing Death or Bodily Harm (per 100,000 population) by Region, 2018.

From 2000 through 2004, there were 14,082 motor car accident deaths in Canada, for an average annual average death rate of 9.0 per 100,000 population (Ramage-Morin, 2008). Rates varied widely across the country, with the highest rates being in the Yukon. Prince Edward Island, New Brunswick, Manitoba, Saskatchewan, Alberta and British Columbia also had rates above the national average. Only Ontario and Newfoundland and Labrador had rates below the Canada average, then. As we see from the figure above, Ontario continues to have the lowest rates of automobile deaths, while the northern territories continue to have the highest ones.

Ramage-Morin (2008) suggests two approaches to lessening the rates of traffic accidents causing death. The first is to focus on preventing distractions by cell phones and other devices, and minimizing the amount of driving by people under the influence of alcohol and drugs. The second is to enforce the use of adult seat belts and age- and size-appropriate restraints for young people. These same strategies may also benefit other vulnerable, high-risk road users such as pedestrians, cyclists, children and seniors.

Figure 8-23 (opposite) shows that consolidated government spending for hospital outpatient services also varies a lot from one region to another. The territories have the highest rates of outpatient hospital spending, for several reasons. First, since the populations are small, there are no economies of scale in providing the needed services. Second, as doctors are scarce in northern Canada, compared with southern Canada, hospital outpatient services must handle more injuries and sicknesses of all kinds. Third, the higher rates of

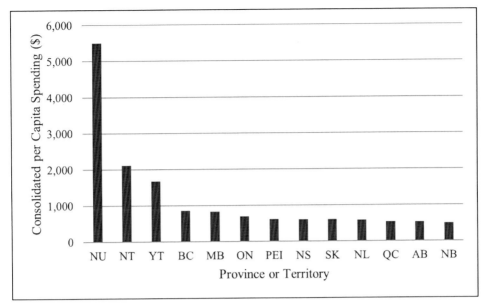

Figure 8-23. Consolidated Government Spending for Hospital Outpatient Services (per Capita) in Canada, 2019.

workplace accidents and traffic accidents reported in earlier figures may also increase the need for outpatient services.

Environmental Issues

As we see in Figure 8-24, regions vary dramatically in their effect on the natural environment. Provinces most heavily engaged in resource extraction (especially fossil fuel extraction and logging) produce the most air pollution. Alberta, B.C., Manitoba, and New Brunswick score highest on this metric, the territories, Saskatchewan, and Quebec lowest.

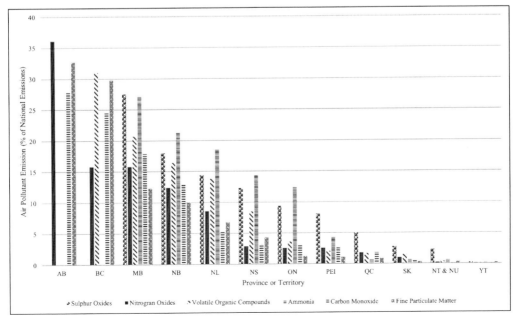

Figure 8-24. Canada's Distribution of Air Pollutant Emission by Region, 2018.

Figure 8-25 below focuses on oil extraction, and here Alberta is far ahead of all the other provinces, followed by Saskatchewan, Newfoundland and Labrador, and British Columbia. As we know, oil production is a controversial issue in Canada; it brings to Canadian communities both economic growth and environmental degradation. Oil production has become a contentious issue in Canadian politics. A recent example of this is the dispute between British Columbia and Alberta over the Trans Mountain pipeline expansion in 2018 and 2019. The dispute escalated into a trade war between the two provinces, with Alberta banning B.C. wine and threatening to cut oil supplies to the other province.

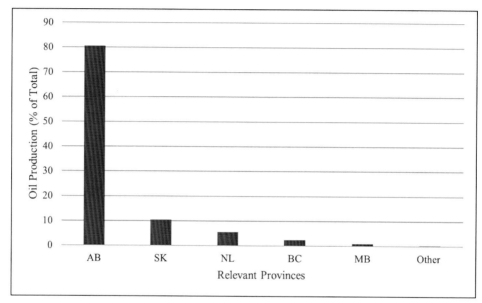

Figure 8-25. Oil Production in Canada by Province, 2019.

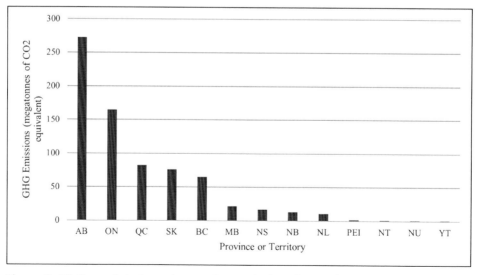

Figure 8-26. Canada's Greenhouse Gas Emissions by Region, 2018.

While only some provinces are engaged in oil production, other kinds of industry also produce significant pollution. Measuring greenhouse gas emissions provides a different picture. As before, Alberta is in the lead because of oil extraction, with the other oil-extracting provinces also scoring highly. However, Ontario and Quebec also score highly here, because of their high levels of industrial production and automobile traffic.

Canada's greenhouse gas (GHG) emissions currently represent about 1.6 percent of the global total. Indeed, Canada is among the top 10 global emitters of greenhouse gases and one of the largest emitters in the Global North. Within Canada, GHG emissions vary widely across provinces, ranging from 267 megatonnes (Mt) in Alberta to 1.8 Mt in Prince Edward Island in 2013 (Booth and Boudreault, 2016). In per capita terms, Saskatchewan and Alberta are among the developed world's largest emitters at 68 and 67 tonnes respectively. By contrast, per capita emissions in British Columbia, Ontario and Quebec are much less, in the 10 to 14 tonne range and therefore comparable to the best performers in Western Europe. Provinces also vary widely in their stated GHG emission targets. In 2016, Alberta proposed to increase emissions towards a 2020 peak, then come back down to 2016 levels by 2030. Ontario, Quebec, and Manitoba planned to reduce their emissions by 56, 27 and 8 Mt respectively. None of these goals has been met.

In Figure 8-27, we see that the provinces and territories vary widely in their access to freshwater, with Quebec, Ontario, the Northwest Territories, and Nunavut in the lead. Access to freshwater is an important resource. It will become even more important, and more valuable, with climate change and global warming in the future.

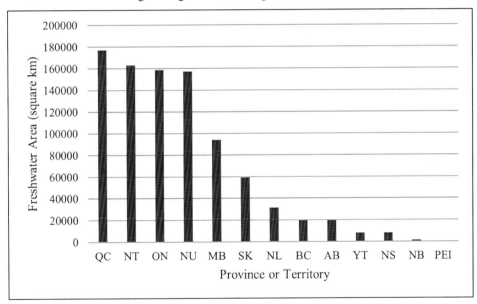

Figure 8-27. Canada's Freshwater Area by Region, 2016.

Access to freshwater has also been an important contributor to the industrialization of Ontario and Quebec, which consume a great deal of water for both residential and industrial purposes. So far, the availability of water has not contributed much to settlement and industrialization in the northern territories. There, both a harsh climate and great distance from main population centres have kept the population down, making the availability of water much less valuable.

The provinces show some variation in their industrial, commercial, and institutional use of potable water. Here, Ontario and Quebec lead the pack, consuming 426.1 million cubic metres and 382.5 million cubic metres of water, respectively, in 2013 (Statistics Canada

2013). Similarly, as we see in Figure 8-28, the provinces and territories vary widely in their per capita residential use of water. There we see Newfoundland and Labrador using about four times as much water, per capita, as Nunavut, Alberta, and Manitoba.

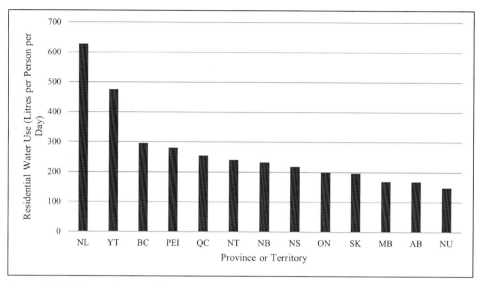

Figure 8-28. Canada's Residential Water Use per Person, by Region, 2013.

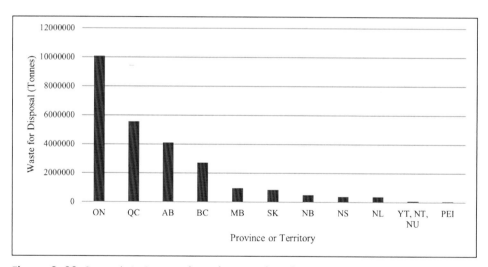

Figure 8-29. Canada's Generation of Waste for Disposal by Region, 2018.

Schindler and Donahue (2006) predict dire water shortages will soon occur in the Canadian West. Though Canada as a whole boasts plentiful freshwater, freshwater is scarce in the Prairie provinces. Happily, the twentieth century was likely the wettest century of the past two thousand years. The frequent, long periods of drought that characterized most of the past two millennia were largely absent. However, climate change and human changes to the environment have already reduced the flows of major rivers on the Prairies during the summer months, when human demand is greatest. Schindler and Donahue (2006) predict that climate change will continue to melt glaciers and snowpacks and evaporate the available water. Given continued cyclic drought and rapidly increasing human activity on the Prairies, we can anticipate a crisis in water quantity and quality in the present century.

Finally, the provinces also vary dramatically in the waste they produce, with Canada's most populated provinces—Ontario, Quebec, Alberta, and British Columbia—far in the lead (Figure 8-29). The territories and Prince Edward Island trail far behind in waste production, a fact explained by their smaller populations.

Concluding Remarks

In this comparison of Canada's provinces and territories, we have seen marked and often dramatic variations in the distribution of Canada's social, economic, and environmental problems. Clearly, less variation exists for some problems than others. As a prime example, the rate of movement out of, or escape from, poverty is low in all Canadian provinces, despite some variation. For most issues we have examined, the range of variation is wide.

Note, too, that there are patterns to these provincial variations. Typically, the Maritime provinces resemble each other. The same is true of the Prairie provinces and of Ontario and Quebec. Sometimes, the largest provincial differences are between Quebec on the one hand and Alberta on the other. This suggests that Quebec may be a version of the social welfare state—a Canadian version of Sweden, say—while Alberta is a version of the liberal state—a Canadian version of Texas.

Likely, the range of variation among Canadian provinces and territories is wide for the same reasons we find a wide range of variation between countries. Some provinces, like some of our comparison countries, are more industrialized than others. Some are more rural or have a smaller share of Indigenous people. Some receive a higher proportion of immigrants and have a higher proportion of racialized residents than others. Some have a younger population. All of these factors, and others, affect the incidence of social problems and the ways provinces deal with them.

That said, provinces and territories do differ significantly in their incidence of problems, and the ways they deal with these problems. This variation may be greater in Canada than we would find in other large modern countries like France or Germany (for example). There, we may see marked variations from one part of the country to another—for example, between the former West Germany and East Germany, or between northern and southern France. Nonetheless, we will find less variation in social problems and their solution in those countries. That is either because they are not federated nations like Canada and thus lack the same degree of regional or provincial independence as we find in Canada or the U.S., or, if they are federal states, the differences between the regions tend to be smaller, perhaps for historical reasons or because of smaller geographical area.

Our goal here is not to deny that Canada is a genuine country, or that Canada can learn important things by comparing itself with other countries. On the contrary, we can learn a great deal, especially from the Nordic countries, even though they are much smaller and more homogeneous than Canada. But what we learn must be tempered by an understanding that Canada cannot easily adopt the policies and programs that have worked so well in other countries. There are many reasons for this, constitutional as well as geographic, demographic, and cultural. Adopting practices that work well in other countries would take an enormous, though perhaps justifiable, effort of will and political skill to overcome regional differences.

In the next chapter, we will discuss more thoroughly what we have learned from our comparisons and try to imagine a path forward for Canada.

CHAPTER NINE
The Path Ahead

In this book, we assessed Canada's place in a world shrunken by widespread, fast-changing information, global travel, and a broad sharing of ideas, goods, and services. After comparing Canada with sixteen similar countries, we have come to several conclusions.

First, it is difficult to compare performances on different social problems, across countries (and across provinces too!). But if we assign the same weight to all the problems we have examined in this book, Canada stands tenth out of seventeen comparison countries. Clearly, Canada's not the worst of the pack but neither is it the best. Canada has a way to go to improve its rankings in a wide variety of domains.

As we have seen, Canada has not handled poverty, crime, illness, or addiction as effectively as its best comparison countries. In fact, poverty, crime, disease, and addiction continue to afflict some parts of Canadian society to a destructive, soul-crushing degree. One often-mentioned example of this concentration of social problems is the rural and remote on-reserve Indigenous population.

Given what we have found out about other similar countries, we must conclude that Canada can do more and do better. We know this because other, similar societies have done better in reducing the incidence of these problems and the harm they bring. In some domains, Canada stands in the forefront: for example, in its response to immigration. However, it has fallen behind leading comparison nations on other issues, such as dealing with homelessness or the country's drug addiction and overdose crisis. By studying these comparison nations, we can learn *how* Canada might do better in the future in these areas, too.

From studying social problems in a comparative perspective, we can also conclude that Canada is not immune to problems that begin elsewhere. Specifically, many of the social problems facing Canadian society are global in their origins and scale, affecting many countries at the same time. This is especially true of refugee, environmental, disinformation, disease, and crime issues. Canada cannot solve these problems alone. They need global solutions and call for international discussion and cooperation. Canada must act to promote such cooperation and, meanwhile, try to reduce the harm done within Canadian borders.

Understanding Canada's place in the world reminds us we still have important problems to solve. We can learn how to solve them by examining the strategies and policies other, similar, countries use, and by cooperating with other countries that hold similar interests. And we can share our knowledge and experience with other countries tackling problems we deal with more successfully.

In this final chapter, we try to answer the following questions:

Is Canada's place in the world desirable and admirable, or shocking and disturbing?

How should Canadians feel about Canada and its approach to social problems?

What can we learn from other countries about dealing with social problems?

Comprehensive Measures of Well-Being

First, however, we will consider several comprehensive measures of well-being, showing how Canada is doing overall. Our purpose here is to verify the conclusion, stated above, that Canada is doing a middling job in solving its social problems.

First is the Human Development Index, created for the United Nations to offer a comprehensive measure of societal functioning. Researchers recognized that traditional measures of national wealth—for example, GDP per capita—fail to capture the overall well-being of a nation's population. That is because, in all societies and increasingly in the world's wealthiest societies, wealth is unequally divided. Therefore, researchers have included two other measures of well-being: a measure of education and literacy and a measure of longevity and health. Both of these added measures help to capture how widely a society has shared its prosperity.

In Figure 9-1, we see Human Development Index scores for Canada and sixteen comparison nations in 2019. Here, Canada occupies eleventh place, just ahead of New Zealand and the United Kingdom. At the top of the list is Norway, followed by Switzerland and Ireland. The differences are slight: essentially all seventeen countries are doing almost equally well, and that is very well indeed. However, as usual Canada is in the midde of the pack, neither best nor worst of the nations we consider.

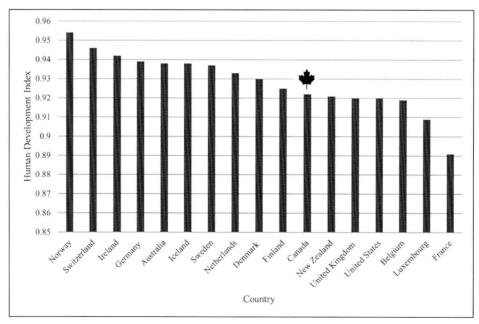

Figure 9-1. Human Development Index (HDI), Canada and Comparison Countries, 2019.

Data from a second comprehensive measure of societal well-being—the State Strength Index—are provided in Figure 9-2. This index is an inverted form of the Fragile State (formerly, the Failed State) Index. The Fragile State Index (FSI) has been published annually since 2005 by the United States Fund for Peace and the American magazine *Foreign Policy*. It shows which nation-states of the world are the most and least fragile. The least-fragile states have the most secure borders, the most stable governments and legal systems, and the most reliable public institutions. They are also most predictable in delivering needed resources—food, housing, and jobs, among others—to their citizens.

In other words, the State Strength Index measures the provision of "peace, order, and good government," to which Canada has dedicated its political system. The data in Figure 9-2 show that Canada stands in seventh place in its group of comparison nations. This puts it just ahead of New Zealand and Sweden but well ahead of the United Kingdom and the United States. At the top is Finland, followed by Norway and Switzerland. Once again, Canada is in the middle of the pack, neither the best or worst of seventeen comparison nations. All six countries ranking ahead of Canada have smaller populations.

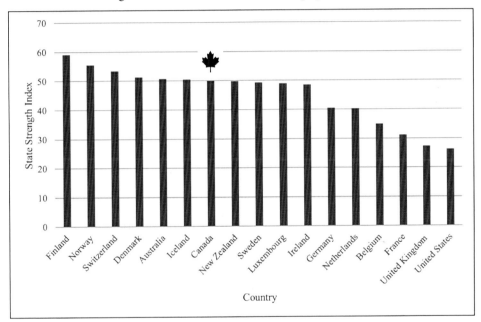

Figure 9-2. State Strength Index, Canada and Comparison Countries, 2019.

A third comprehensive measure of societal well-being is the State Integrity Index, for which we see data in Figure 9-3 (overleaf). This chart is based on the Perceived Corruption Index, compiled and published each year since 1995 by the non-governmental organization Transparency International. Nations judged to be high on state integrity are, conversely, judged low on perceived state corruption. These data show Canada to be in twelfth place on this measure, tied with Australia and the United Kingdom, and just ahead of Belgium. At the top of the list is New Zealand, followed closely by Denmark, Finland, and Sweden. Again, Canada is in the middle, not a top or bottom country among its comparison nations.

A fourth comprehensive measure of societal well-being is the Social Progress Index, compiled by Deloitte (Porter, Stern and Green, 2017). This index measures a country's performance on various political and social metrics. The three dimensions of interest include, first, the fulfillment of basic human needs such as housing, safety, sanitation, and health. Second, they include the foundations of well-being such as environmental quality, access

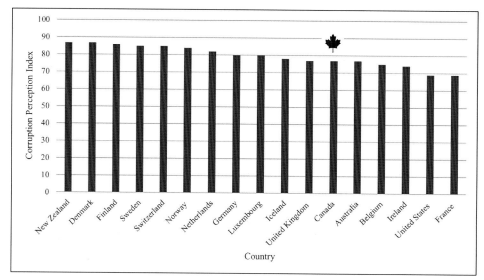

Figure 9-3. State Integrity Index, Canada and Comparison Countries, 2019.

to knowledge and information, and wellness. Third and finally, they include inclusion and tolerance, personal rights and freedoms, and access to advanced education. The stated aim of this composite index is to provide a non-economic measurement of social progress and well-being around the world (Porter et al., 2017).

Figure 9-4 (below), shows that, once again, Canada sits around the middle of our seventeen comparison countries. While not scoring as high as Norway and Denmark, Canada does better than Luxembourg, Belgium, or the United States. As usual, the United States does badly on this measure.

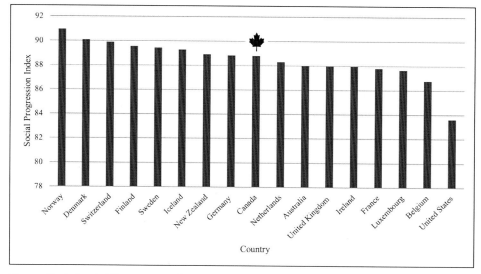

Figure 9-4. Social Progress Index, Canada and Comparison Countries, 2019.

A fifth and final comprehensive measure is the self-rated life satisfaction scale. This OECD index of life satisfaction measures people's evaluation of their life as a whole. It uses response categories based on people's ratings of their current life compared to the best and worst lives they can imagine, on a scale of 0 to 10 (OECD Stats, 2017).

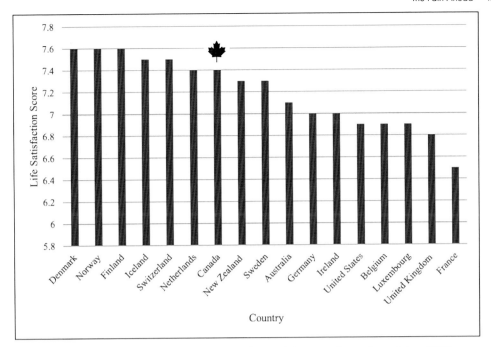

Figure 9-5. Life Satisfaction Score, Canada and Comparison Countries, 2019.

These data show dramatic differences in life satisfaction among our seventeen comparison countries. Canada ranks seventh, with Norway, Denmark, and Finland tying for the high overall life satisfaction scores. The UK, Luxembourg, and France report the lowest life satisfaction scores, with France especially low.

Interestingly, in these five indices we have just reviewed, no country with a larger population than Canada's *consistently* ranks higher than Canada. Germany ranks higher than Canada in two out of these five measures and Canada ranks higher than Germany in two, with one measure a virtual tie. Of the other large countries, only the UK outscores Canada on any of these five overall indices, and then only once. So, size plays a part in this story, as we mentioned at the start of this book. As a large country, Canada is doing well.

Size aside, the other conclusions to draw from these data are obvious. First, as we have noted repeatedly, Canada is never in first place among the seventeen nations we are comparing—it is usually in the middle of the pack. By contrast, the Nordic countries—especially Norway, Finland, and Denmark—are usually near the top of the list, as is Switzerland. That said, on these five measures, all seventeen of these countries score similarly, if we consider the world as a whole. Compared with countries in the Global South, these seventeen all perform well on the societal, economic, and political measures we have considered. They all have problems, but they all deal with their problems reasonably well, compared to less prosperous, less stable nations of the world. However, the United States is usually near the bottom of each measure among countries in the Global North.

These charts lead us to several questions: First, what is wrong with the United States? Second, why does Canada always score around the middle of this prosperous, successful pack of nations? Why isn't it in first place? And third, what (if anything) could Canada do to score in first place? Some answers to the second question come quickly to mind. First, we are a colonial settler society with a large, impoverished Indigenous population. Second, we are an immigrant- and refugee-friendly society and our many newcomers need time to integrate. Third, we bear some costs (as well as gaining some benefits) by living next to the powerful and often domineering United States. Fourth, our geographic vastness and regional differences make national programs of improvement difficult if not sometimes nearly impossible.

That said, it is interesting to recognize that Canada and Australia score almost identically on these comprehensive measures. Perhaps this is because, of all the seventeen countries, they are most alike in population size and political history. Canada was the first of the self-governing dominions to be established under the British Crown. Its constitutional arrangements served as an important precedent for those dominions subsequently established, of which Australia was the next in 1901. So, the success factors for both Canada and Australia are similar, despite differences in geography, history, immigration, and demographic diversity. Perhaps this points to the value and resilience of British political traditions and the enduring role of the Commonwealth connection.

On the five measures of well-being outline above, Canada sits comfortably in the middle of the seventeen comparison countries on every measure. How do we explain this? In considering why Canada isn't in first place, we have to return to our chapter-by-chapter assessments of who is doing better than Canada. We will also have to consider how those countries respond to the social problems covered in this book.

What Have We Learned So Far?

To repeat, by studying social problems cross-nationally, we have seen the clear superiority of certain countries over other ones. Repeatedly, Canada has scored in the middle or, occasionally near the bottom. Almost invariably, the U.S. has held the bottom spot for worst performance. At the top, we have repeatedly found the Nordic countries and, occasionally, some of the other northern European countries like Switzerland.

For example, we have seen that, in social benefits in kind, Sweden, Iceland, and Norway lead the pack, with Canada doing poorly. On the measure of poverty, Denmark, Finland, and Iceland have the best scores, while Canada's score is poor. On the Gini index of income inequality, Iceland, Finland, and Norway are doing best, while Canada has one of the worst inequality scores. In efforts to decrease inequality through taxation, Finland, Denmark, and France do best, and Canada does poorly.

With some other measures, the results are more mixed. On social mobility, Denmark, Norway, and Finland lead the pack but Canada does nearly as well. In particular, well-educated children of immigrants do just fine in Canada and better than anywhere else. On youth unemployment, Iceland, Germany, and the Netherlands are doing best, while Canada scores in the middle. In short, Canada does not do well on measures of poverty and income inequality, compared to many Northern European countries. This difference is likely because of the strength of the Nordic social democratic regimes, on the one hand; and the influence of American trade arrangements with Canada, on the other.

Similarly, we have learned that some countries have more social injustice than others. Countries respond differently to social justice issues related to gender, race, and ethnicity. Canada falls in the middle of the pack when compared with other countries on various metrics of gender inequality. Specifically, compared with the Nordic nations, we still have a long way to go. We have much to do in closing gender gaps in income, employment, and political representation, and lessening discrimination against immigrants and racialized groups.

Canada does well, however, on issues of immigrant integration. The gap in unemployment rates between immigrants and native-born Canadians is slight (6 percent versus 6.3 percent). One reason may be that Canadian immigration policies screen applicants for employable skills. They purposely try to fill local labour gaps with immigrant workers, in particular through programs like the Express Entry system for skilled workers (Government of Canada, 2019).

Canada does well compared to other high-income countries in welcoming and integrating immigrants. Changes to immigration laws in the 1960s eliminated racial quotas. In 1972, Canada accepted 7,500 South Asians forced out of Uganda after the coup bringing Idi Amin to power. In the photograph above, Ugandan immigrants line up for a meal at a canteen run by the Canadian government. Canada also sent immigration teams to Uganda to assist in the settlement effort.

Canada's embrace of multiculturalism also means that Canadians accept religious freedom and cultural tolerance, at least in principle. Despite the religious-dress laws passed in Quebec, Canadian politics largely avoid formal Islamophobia. As noted in chapter 3, Canada compares well in the welcome it extends to international immigrants and refugees. By contrast, the Nordic nations (except for Iceland) all have strong radical-right political parties that oppose large-scale immigration. These parties lobby actively for severe limits on immigration and propose discriminatory policies, such as banning Halal meat production.

With crime and victimization, Canada does well on the measure of sexual violence, scoring lowest of the seventeen countries we examined. It is also doing well—fourth best— on cybersecurity. However, it does poorly on human trafficking, better only than the UK, France, and the United States. And Canada has the second-highest homicide rate among countries we considered, behind only the U.S. That said, the actual rate is far closer to the low European rates than to the high American rate. So, with crime and victimization, Canada's overall position is a mix of highs and lows. Canada is not the most dangerous of the seventeen comparison countries, but neither is it consistently the safest. To explain this, we again have to consider our closeness to the United States, and the enormous number of handguns that people smuggle across the U.S.-Canadian border each year.

Countries that consistently perform the best on crime are usually much smaller than those that don't do as well. In small populations, it is harder to get away with a crime. Other things (like GDP per capita) being equal, people in a small, tightly knit community hold one another accountable. People trust others more and feel safer in their community. In small, homogeneous cultures, people also have closer ties to their neighbors. It's easier to feel safe when you have clear expectations of everyone's behaviour. Everyone knows those expectations, because they grew up in the same culture. Unfortunately, some homogenous countries are also racist—or at least exclusionary—and, unless they are Nordic countries, also sexist.

With health and addiction, we see patterns similar to those associated with economic inequality. Among the seventeen countries discussed in this book, large countries like the United States show worse health trends—for example, higher mortality rates—than smaller countries like Norway and Finland. It may be more difficult for large countries like the U.S. to meet the varied needs of a huge, diverse and dispersed population. The U.S. also has a lingering history of slavery and racism that seemingly prevents a fair sharing of healthcare and other social benefits. By contrast, the Nordic countries have universal, publicly funded healthcare. The United States has a largely private healthcare system, which makes care prohibitively expensive for many.

As noted earlier, Nordic countries follow a social-democratic welfare regime. As well, they are sensitive to regional variations in need. Nordic countries all have healthcare systems that allow local governments some latitude in their decision-making. In regions with lower-income populations, and for people who need more-than-average levels of care, the national government beefs up funding. Local governments in these regions play a large role in decision-making and healthcare implementation since they know the local needs best. And remember that income equality also contributes to better health. Lower levels of income inequality than Canada or the rest of Europe help Nordic peoples stay healthier (Christiansen et al., 2018).

We saw in the chapter on accidents that Canada is almost always in the middle of the pack when it comes to accidental injuries and deaths. In the one instance where Canada is

Concerns about traffic injuries and fatalities have led to such enforcement measures as the use of photo radar.

not in the middle, it does worst on spending for people with accident-related disabilities. By contrast, the Nordic nations, Germany, the Netherlands, and the UK all do better in this domain. What we see among the countries that do better than Canada is a public commitment to safety over convenience or profit. These countries put public responsibility for the safety of their citizens above narrow economic interests; doing so leads to safer public and private life.

Canada has sometimes, however, served as a model for injury-prevention policies. For many years, Quebec experienced high accident-related mortality rates because of poorly organized service by first-responders and hospitals (Mock, 2010). However, province-wide improvements were carried out, including pre-hospital triaging, medical care on-scene, and enforcement of trauma-caring capacities at hospitals through an external review board. As a result of these changes, death rates among the severely injured decreased dramatically.

In recent years, Canada has also invested large amounts of money on photo radar cameras to penalize and prevent speeding. Within Ontario, the government is planning to install cameras in more than 700 Toronto locations (City of Toronto, 2020). The cameras are to be installed mainly around schools and in neighborhoods where the speed limits are lower. Canada was also the first country to pass a law (in 2005) that mandates fire-safety standards for all cigarette manufacturers (World Health Organization, 2011). Similar laws followed in the European Union and Australia in 2007 and 2008, respectively. Since cigarettes had been the number one cause of fire-related deaths in Canada, this policy proved an effective way to prevent such injuries and deaths (Government of Canada, 2007).

On environmental issues, Canada lags in comparison with the other nations we have studied. The three leading comparison countries have policies that restrict industrial and corporate actors. They also have strict and ambitious climate policies. For example, they all set goals to reduce emissions, backed up by aggressive reforms such as waste and energy-use taxes. The governments of these countries are also willing to spend the money and effort necessary to address climate change. Beyond that, they focus on preventive actions that tackle the causes of climate change, not just its symptoms.

Explaining our Findings

To repeat, we have learned one powerful thing in the book so far: Canada is a middling core country. On both comprehensive measures of well-being and individual measures of our effectiveness in handling social problems, Canada scores in the middle of the pack.

Canada is not the happiest, healthiest, most incorruptible, developed or stable of the seventeen societies we have examined. It doesn't have the lowest poverty rates, the lowest gender gap in wages, the lowest homicide rate, or the lowest rate of workplace accidents. Nor does Canada have the highest longevity, the lowest addiction rates, or most successful environmental programs. It excels in only one area: multiculturalism. It has a better record of integrating its immigrants than the other countries we have examined. So, how do we explain this set of findings, and what can we do with this explanation, in practical terms? First, let's consider some possible explanations. We will call them, respectively, the Immigration Theory, the X Theory, and the Small Republics Theory.

Our so-called *Immigration Theory* notes that Canada has achieved great success with multiculturalism and immigrant integration. However, we have done so at the expense of success with other social issues, on which we do only moderately well. We have not done better with poverty, gender equality, homicide, and so on precisely *because*, as a nation, we have mainly devoted our funds and energies to making a success of multiculturalism and immigration. Since energies and funds are limited, we could not succeed in all of these areas and so we succeeded in only one: multiculturalism. To do better in the other areas, we would have to invest less energy and money in multiculturalism.

It is (nearly) impossible to prove or disprove this theory that immigration has distorted our priorities, given the data currently available to us. Amy Langstaff and Michael Adams argue in their book *Unlikely Utopia* (2007) that we can credit Canada's multicultural success to our history, values, demographics, institutions, and public policies. No doubt, these account for much of our success with immigration. But why haven't these same qualities helped to succeed with the social problems we discussed in earlier chapters? At best, immigration theory offers only an incomplete explanation of Canada's quandary. To explain it better, we must continue our consideration of possible theories.

Perhaps, some other factor outside the immigration and social problems we have studied—call it X—explains the seeming correlation between success with immigration and (relative) failure in other domains. There may be many candidates for this hidden X, so let's put a few on the table: federalism, capitalism, and regionalism. For example, the reason immigration has succeeded is because it lies constitutionally within the domain of a powerful, well-funded federal government. However, many of the social problems we have studied (e.g., social justice, workplace safety, policing) lie constitutionally within the domain of less-powerful, less well-funded provincial or even local governments.

This is true; however, it is only partly true. Clearly, for example, the federal government has exerted its influence on social justice issues. It has done so through the Charter of Rights and Freedoms. It has also exerted influence on the criminal law and environmental legislation, as well as many special agreements with the provinces. Nowhere has it exerted its spending power more obviously and dramatically than in the area of healthcare. As well, equalization payments to provinces have been effective in flexing federal muscle.

Consider another possible X factor: the role of capitalism. One might propose that the reason multiculturalism has worked as well as it has is because immigrant diversity has been in the financial interest of the Canadian capitalist class. Large numbers of educated and ambitious immigrants contribute significantly to Canadian economic success. By contrast, the Canadian capitalist class has no similar interest in wiping out poverty, achieving gender equality, lowering homicide rates, or improving workplace safety. This is a more compelling argument than the federalism argument. However, though improving the social problems we have mentioned may not increase profits, there is little evidence they will reduce profits much either. Reducing homicide, addictions, poor health, or even the gendered wage gap are effectively profit-neutral for the capitalist class.

One can make a similar argument about the political influence of our neighbour to the south. The U.S. does indeed express views about and exert influence on certain Canadian initiatives, such as marijuana legalization, healthcare, and environmental policies. However,

the U.S. government has little interest in Canada's decision-making on matters of poverty, inequality, accidents, and crime. These issues have no impact on either American decision-making or corporate American profit-making.

Finally, consider a third X factor: regionalism as a political influence. One might propose that multiculturalism has worked as well as it has because it has promoted historic regional differences or, at least, has not disturbed them. Different regions of the country, with different needs and preferences, have largely received different kinds (and numbers) of im-

Canada and the U.S. share the longest undefended border in the world. The U.S. exerts influence in areas such as Canada's trade and environmental policies.

migrants. French-speaking immigrants, for example, have usually gone to Quebec while English-speaking immigrants have usually gone to Ontario, Alberta, or British Columbia. Relatively few of either kind have gone to the Prairies or the Maritime provinces.

Wherever the immigrants have gone, they have (largely) fit in and prospered, although Quebec has proved more resistant to easy assimilation than other provinces. However, the regions have continued to differ, often markedly, in their approach to the various social problems we have discussed in this book. Most especially they have differed in their approaches to environmental issues, provincial taxation, social programs, addictions, and programs such as education and childcare. Thus, regions have continued to differ in their orientation to social problems not because of immigration to Canada but despite it.

In short, none of our three X theories has been persuasive in explaining the seeming link between the success of multicultural programs and the (relative) failure of other programs in Canada. That's not to say that they have nothing to contribute; only, that we shouldn't stop looking yet. So finally, let's now consider three theoretical approaches that, together, make up what we will call the *small republic theory*. We can name these three theoretical approaches the demographic, cultural, and institutional approaches.

The so-called *demographic approach* focuses on a country's population size and diversity. We have already noted that Nordic countries—all of them, countries with small, culturally homogeneous populations—are the best able to mobilize their population to make important changes. By this, we mean changes that solve and prevent important social problems. The so-called *cultural approach* focuses on a country's cultural values and norms. We have already noted that the Nordic countries embrace cooperative values and promote these values forcefully to all citizens and would-be citizens. Finally, the so-called *institutional approach* notes that to be successful, such values must also be translated into public institutions and governmental actions. We have repeatedly noted that the Nordic countries, with their social welfare regimes, most effectively carry out this task. As a result, the Nordic countries are the consistently the most successful in solving and preventing social problems, and in achieving consistently high scores on global measures of well-being.

There is a strong link between these three approaches. Just as certain institutional (or welfare) arrangements may need certain cultural arrangements, so too certain institutional and cultural arrangements may need certain demographic conditions. Put another way, solving important social problems may need a particular combination of demographic, cultural, and institutional changes. So, let us now consider how combining approaches captured under the rubric of small republic theory is so successful.

Solving Problems in Small Republics

Jonas Pontusson (2005) rightly calls the five Nordic countries *social market economies*, and he explains why they do a better job in solving social problems. First, in these countries, businesses have strong relations with the government and work closely with it. Second, they have strong unions and well-institutionalized collective bargaining. This means that employers and workers' unions coordinate their efforts, with help from the government. Third, and as Esping-Andersen pointed out, the social market economies provide extensive social welfare and employment protection. This means that workers cannot be fired without reason, and if they become unemployed, the government offers them financial protection.

The *Nordic model*, also called the *social-democratic regime*, is an umbrella term used to refer to the social and economic policies and cultural and social practices characteristic of the Nordic countries. The shared theme of these policies is a reliance on strong and deep welfare policies. A welfare state is rightly called strong when it is effective and efficient, and deep when it impacts many facets of social life. In the Nordic nations, the state provides high quality, free healthcare, education, social services, and employment protections.

The flags of the five Nordic countries. From left, Finland, Iceland, Norway, Sweden and Denmark.

The Nordic model also incorporates collective bargaining: a well-defined negotiation policy between employers and employees. Collective bargaining works to efficiently monitor working conditions, rewards, and support for workers. Finally, as we have seen, the distribution of income in these countries is relatively equal (Normann and Ronning, 2013).

The Nordic model is grounded in a social-democratic welfare state system, where citizenship guarantees access to state support, regardless of market conditions (Korpi, 2006). Thinking behind the Nordic model holds that every individual, regardless of class or background, is entitled to basic social security (Normann and Ronning, 2013). Everyone pays high taxes to the state, and the state repays them with plentiful social services (Esping-Anderson, 1990).

Further, the Nordic model has long stressed gender equality, and gender equality represents a clear goal of family policies in the Nordic nations (Melby, Ravn and Wetterberg, 2008). Crucially, the Nordic model places an emphasis on work-life balance and on gender equality in parenting. In practice, this means that both partners in a marriage expect to do wage work. This also means public welfare, with extensive childcare service and generous maternity and parental leave schemes. As a result, we see an increased number of women in political elites and gender equality as a strong norm in public debate and politics (Bergqvist et al., 1999).

Canada is better in its welfare-oriented policies than some comparison countries, such as the U.S. But to do even better than that, it must become more Nordic and less American. So, for example, Canada currently provides fewer and weaker welfare policies than the Nordic states, and there is less cooperation between government, business, and the unions. As a result, Canada is less able than the Nordic countries to ensure high employment rates despite comparable rates of economic growth. As we have seen, Nordic societies have adopted successful public policies on homelessness, human capital, and social benefits. If Canada is to improve its standing on homelessness, inequality, and social benefits, it will have to adopt public policies that are similar to those in the Nordic countries. It will also have to redistribute more money, which the state can only finance with higher taxation.

This will not be easy. As previously noted, Canada has a working-age poverty rate of over 10 percent and over 100,000 homeless people. By comparison, social welfare economies like Denmark, Norway, and Finland hover around working-age poverty rates of only 3 percent to 8 percent and proportionally fewer homeless people.

Now, bear in mind that Denmark, Norway, Finland, Sweden and Iceland all have smaller populations than Canada and their GDPs (gross domestic products) are also smaller than Canada's. But with roughly the same GDP per capita, the Nordic states do more for their citizens, with about the same amount of money per person. Canada could easily afford to import Nordic universalism and redistribution if it wanted to achieve greater equality. The reasons for failing to do so are political and values-based more than economic. They are also a result of our nearness to and economic interdependence with the United States. Efforts to change this in the last fifty years have not had much success in part because of free-trade agreements like NAFTA and its successor USMCA, which have promoted economic integration with U.S. policies and interests.

Yet Canada, as a service-oriented economy, would benefit significantly by copying Nordic educational policy, as one example. Canada's primary and secondary schools are highly rated. As a country that is heavily reliant on immigration and attracting skilled workers, Canada could gain from a free post-secondary educational system supplemented by flexible work contracts.

Taxation is another domain in which Canada underperforms, compared to its Nordic counterparts. A redistributive tax system that supports (for instance) free university tuition and provides a wage for students decreases economic inequality. However, in Canada, social benefits are still treated as needs-based welfare supplemented by free healthcare. As Esping-Andersen points out, in social democratic regimes, welfare is not only needs-based but also redistributive. Thus, Nordic economies redistribute more wealth and well-being than Canada. It narrows the gap between rich and poor, and Canada could do better here.

But while economic policies play an important role in shaping inequality, they are also tied to political affairs. As noted, politically, Canada is a federalist state while most of our comparison countries, including the Nordic countries, are unitary. In Canada, the federal government has jurisdiction over the entire country and each provincial government has jurisdiction over particular portions of the population. However, the federal and provincial governments also have different powers and responsibilities—that is, constitutionally distinct areas of jurisdiction, with a few shared ones. This is why there are different welfare schemes and tax rates in British Columbia and Alberta, and different legal ages allowing the consumption of alcohol in Quebec and Ontario. Regional governance plays a key role in Canadian politics, especially in areas of social welfare, education, and healthcare. We see this also in Quebec's unique orientation to immigrants and cultural diversity, as displayed in Bill 21. Without federal programs and equalization payments, the regional and provincial variations would be even greater.

Both models of government, unitary and federal, have benefits and drawbacks. The unitary state is efficient in passing legislation the whole country has to uphold, despite different conditions in different parts of the country. A federalist state, like Canada, with regional distribution of power and governance, allows for the regionalization of policymaking. Thanks to regional governance, Quebec (for example) has been able to preserve its language and Alberta has been able to avoid a sales tax to raise revenue. Regionalized policymaking works best when the needs of a region are distinctive. However, regionalization also makes planning and redistribution on a grand scale more difficult. Differences in provincial and federal taxation stand in the way, as does the problem of coordinating provincial and central governments.

Thus, if the Canadian government wants to reduce economic inequality, it has to get all parties and regional representatives to support a universal model for welfare, redistribution, and education. Otherwise, each province and territory will continue to set its own goals and follow its own strategies to deal with social problems.

Take as an example Canada's failure to set up universal, high-quality daycare. The Finnish system, which provides universal daycare, far outdoes the quality and quantity of daycare available in Canada. If we wanted to, we could achieve universal childcare in Canada too, as we did with medicare and the child tax benefit. But we haven't called on the political will to do so. As a result, today, many Canadian families struggle with childcare costs on top of all their other costs, like rent, food, and transportation. These pressures often force both parents to work full-time. Many Canadian daycare services (outside Quebec, which has a regulated and subsidized plan) are prohibitively costly for middle-class and working-class families. This high cost can force women to leave the workforce, a decision is not voluntary, not be good for Canada's economy, and not always good for the women themselves.

In large part thanks to universal daycare, the Nordic nations also have a much smaller wage gap between men and women than Canada. Specific policies around ensuring gender equality are important here. For example, Iceland ensures that women employees earn the same wage as men employees doing a comparable job (Wagner, 2021). There are legal and financial sanctions in place for companies that fail to comply, and the threat of a fine contributes to the small gender wage gap. In part, the Nordic countries have this kind of policy because they have less gender inequality in political representation. Women hold only 31.7 percent of parliamentary seats in Canada. By contrast, women hold over 40 percent of seats in Sweden and Finland, placing these two Nordic nations at the top of the comparison countries (Lane and Ersson, 2008).

These Nordic strategies hold some appeal for Canadians. In fact, opinion polls show the Nordic model is aspirational—wished-for—in Canada. Drawing inspiration from the Nordic model, Canada could do much to improve gender equality. For one, legislating paternity leave and subsidizing childcare would go a long way to support women's opportunities to work for pay. Further, obliging companies to pay men and women equally, as in Iceland, would help to close the gender wage gap. Finally, setting up gender quotas for political representation would be a good start to increasing women's political participation. However, because the Nordic pattern is not aspirational in the United States, and because of our economic ties to the U.S., Canada can move towards the Nordic model only fitfully.

Tying the Threads Together

Why do the leading countries we have examined do better than Canada in solving and preventing their social problems?

When we look at these leading comparison countries, the Nordic countries, we notice major likenesses. First, they are all small and homogeneous. But Canada cannot easily change its population size or diversity. Second, the Nordic nations have homogeneous value systems, also something Canada would also find hard if not impossible to achieve. Third, the Nordic nations have social-democratic welfare institutions. Canada could move in this direction. However, in doing so, Canada faces conflicting regional sentiments (especially in Quebec and the West), a federalist political structure, and economic interdependence with the United States.

As we have seen, an important feature of the Nordic model is the creation through tax funding of universal social services, including free education and childcare. This model also provides a strong social safety net that prevents abject poverty (Fatima, 2019). It stresses the use of the social safety net to help citizens adapt to changes in the economy. This Nordic model promotes equality for all regardless of their demographic, socioeconomic, or ethnic status (Andersson et al., 2010). Canada could do this, if Canadians wanted to.

The Nordic economies have been able to do this, in large part, because of cultural homogeneity, national unity, and low levels of corruption, which all promote the success of this model (Fatima, 2019). Yet, the recent influx of immigrants and poor global economic conditions has created new problems. This has led many to question the Nordic model's sustainability (Andersson et al., 2010; Mcwhinney, 2019). In response to increased global migration, all the Nordic countries have set up immigrant integration policies. They differ slightly from one another but have one common objective: to promote labour force participation but not civic and cultural integration. In short, they have not adopted a multicultural policy, like Canada's.

Compared to the other Nordic countries, Sweden has the most multicultural policies in place (Kouvo and Lockmer, 2013). The Swedish government has created an integration policy based on three ideas: equality, freedom of choice, and cooperation (Andersson et al., 2010). Immigrants who are permanent residents in Sweden have access to all the same rights and benefits as Swedish citizens. Immigrants can choose whether they want to assimilate into Swedish culture or preserve their native culture. Immigrants also have voting rights in both local and national elections (Westin, 2006).

Supporters of the Sweden Democrats, a right-wing populist party which takes an anti-immigration stance, hold a rally in 2014. The party has steadily increased its popularity over the last twenty-five years, polling 17.5 percent of the vote in the 2018 Swedish general election. Since then, the party has entered into governing coalitions at the local level in several municipalities.

In 1985, the Swedish government changed its integration program to help with refugee resettlement. It stressed the importance of language and job training, and dispersal of immigrants to municipalities with available housing (Westin, 2006). Today, Sweden continues to welcome immigrants, including many refugees. In 2014, there were over 80,000 asylum seekers in Sweden (Swedish Institute, 2019). Yet the Swedish integration program is not fully successful. For example, it sent most refugees to areas with few jobs and high unemployment among native Swedes. This led many refugees to depend on social welfare (Westin, 2006). These programs also faced organizational problems, such as finding qualified language teachers. So, Sweden's policy change did not improve immigrant integration into the workforce (Andersson et al., 2010).

This large influx of immigrants occurred alongside significant economic changes. In 2013, the Swedish Labour Force Survey showed the unemployment rate for people 15 to 24 years old had risen. Income inequality, as measured by the Gini Index, also began to rise, although it remained well below the OECD average of 0.31 (Fredlund-Blomst, 2014). This rise in inequality was one of the fastest in the OECD, creating dissatisfaction in the Swedish workforce.

Finland's immigration policy has been more restrictive than Sweden's. In 2006, in response to increased immigration, Finland passed its own Integration Act. The main principle behind this policy was equal treatment for foreign-born and native-born Finns (Tanner, 2011). The policy stressed equality and freedom of choice, and pledged to help immigrants gain the skills needed to work in Finnish society. The Integration Act also protected the rights of asylum seekers. Thus, immigrants to Finland today have full rights to healthcare, education, housing, employment, and voting (Tanner, 2011). All levels of government have help to ensure the success of this program.

Yet the effectiveness of the plan has been limited, in large part because of language problems and inadequate resources. An OECD report (2015) on immigrant integration into the Finnish workforce found that foreign-born people often have short-term contracts and less favorable working conditions that the native population. It also found that many highly educated immigrants have to settle for low-skilled and low-paying jobs. As well, many Finnish people want to limit immigration to preserve Finnish culture (Tanner, 2011). In large part, they have succeeded.

Norway's integration policies are even more restrictive than those of Sweden and Finland. The main concern driving Norway's immigration policy is that the welfare state has limited resources (Cooper, 2005). Thus, limits must be placed on the number of immigrants accepted. Second, all selected immigrants should have equal legal and practical opportunities (Cooper, 2005). People from other Nordic countries, or from European Union member states, have an easier time immigrating to Norway. Citizens from outside this select circle need a permanent job offer to gain a residence permit (Norwegian Directorate of Immigration, n.d.). To reduce racism and xenophobia and improve the integration of immigrants, the Norwegian government has developed cultural programs such as language training for immigrants, (Cooper, 2005). Immigrants are obliged to take part in such integration programs (Siim, 2013). For example, they must all receive 250 hours of Norwegian language classes and 50 hours of civic education.

However, as in Finland, these policies have failed to guarantee better integration. For example, a study found that in Norway, immigrants from non-Western countries show a higher level of psychological distress than immigrants from Western countries (Dalgard and Thapa, 2007). Immigrants also have a harder time finding jobs, leading to an unemployment rate of 5.0 percent: a much higher rate than that of overall population (1.5 percent) (Statistics Norway, 2019).

In short, Canada is doing better than its comparison countries on all measures of immigrant integration. On this dimension at least, Canadians have nothing to learn from the Nordic countries. They could stand to learn from us.

The Rise of Anti-Immigrant Sentiment

Recently, we have seen a radical shift in European politics, as new far-right populist parties, driven by fear, anger, and the notion of cultural struggle, quickly gain support.

These far-right parties may differ on some issues, but they all have a common goal of protecting their homeland against immigrant multiculturalism. This they hope to do by preserving an ethnically homogenous society (Niklasson and Holleland, 2018). The Sweden Democrats Party, founded in 1988, only started to grow its support in the last few years. In the 2010 general election, only 5.7 percent of Swedish voters supported the party. By 2018, the party's support had grown to 17.5 percent, making it the third-largest political party in Sweden (Elgenius and Rydgren, 2018). That said, the party's share of the popular vote in the 2019 Swedish elections for seats in the European Parliament dipped slightly. Voters' views on immigration in the Nordic countries can be volatile, especially when people face more immediate crises.

The Sweden Democrats oppose the country's current integration policies, arguing that a rise in immigration causes social and economic strains (Sweden Democrats, n.d.). They also reject multiculturalism, which they think threatens Sweden's national identity and social cohesion. The party proposes to restrict immigration and support immigrants who voluntarily choose to return to their home country, rather than stay in Sweden. They also insist on all immigrants gaining the ability to speak Swedish. With these restrictive policies, the Sweden Democrats hope to limit immigration and multiculturalism, thus protecting Sweden's traditional culture.

Finland is another country where right-wing populism is gaining momentum. In 2015, the Finns Party received 17.7 percent of the vote, making it the second-largest party in parliament (YLE, 2015). Like the Swedish Democrats, the Finns Party focuses on anti-immigration policies. It proposes making Finland's immigration policies more restrictive, by lowering the refugee quota and tightening conditions for family reunification (Howell and Sundberg, 2015). It is also the only party in Finland that openly opposes multiculturalism and promises to end the use of public funds to advance multiculturalism (Wahlbeck, 2016). The party proposes that immigrants from outside the European Union only be allowed into Finland when doing so gives the country an economic advantage. It also proposes reserving social services and healthcare mainly for Finns, to prevent non-Finns from taking advantage of such services (Howell and Sundberg, 2015).

Therefore, while we admire the Nordic nations for their progressive social policies, we see they are failing in their policies of immigration and cultural integration. In this respect, they offer no model for Canada, which as a country has committed itself to high rates of immigration and multiculturalism.

Can You Combine Multiculturalism and Equality?

Must an effort to increase social justice and economic equality mean a drop in Canada's commitment to multiculturalism? In other words, could Canada preserve its present multiculturalism while also achieving a Nordic level of social and economic integration?

Banting and Kymlicka (2013: 577) think there is no incompatibility here. They note that most countries that adopted multicultural approaches in the late twentieth century have retained these programs. In fact, many other countries have signed on for multiculturalism in the last twenty years So, it would be wrong to say that, in our seventeen societies of interest, multicultural policies are in general retreat. Often, these countries add the goal of civic integration on top of existing multicultural programs, producing a new blend of diversity and equality. This shows us that liberal forms of civic integration are compatible with multiculturalism, though illiberal and coercive forms are not.

There is no denying the evidence of a backlash against multiculturalism in some European countries, the Nordic nations included. Yet, Banting and Kymlicka (2010: 43) warn us not to look for lessons for Canada in this fact. True, we need to avoid smug complacency that could blind us to the stresses and failures of ethnic relations in many countries, our own included. However, we will draw the wrong conclusion if we "read the Canadian experience through the lens of the European debate."

In particular, we must avoid conflating the multiculturalism debate with discussions about Indigenous people or racial discrimination in Canada. Each of these topics—multiculturalism, Indigeneity, and racial discrimination—has its own history and its own pressure points. We do well to keep these topics separate, as they apply to the Canadian experience.

Taking a finer-grained approach to this question, Soroka et al. (2015) examine the extent to which increases in immigration are related to welfare state retrenchment, drawing on data from 1970 to 2007. They find increased immigration is indeed associated with smaller increases in social welfare spending. These drops in spending growth are smaller and slow—more politically symbolic than economically significant—but they do pile up over time. So, what happened in Finland (for example) has happened elsewhere as well.

That said, countries differ in the extent to which they translate rises in immigration into reduced welfare spending; and they differ in the programs they choose for (symbolic) reduction. Further, countries with steady rates of immigration like Canada are less likely to suffer adverse public reactions (and spending drops) than countries like Germany or the Netherlands, with large and erratic shifts in migration in recent years.

As Kymlicka (2010: 105) notes, the seeming retreat from immigrant multiculturalism has affected some comparison countries more than others. In Canada, public support for

immigrant multiculturalism remains at an all-time high. And in countries that are often cited as examples of a retreat from immigrant multiculturalism, such as the Nordic countries, Netherlands, and Australia, the reasons (and lessons to learn) are complicated. In short, a comparative analysis of multicultural experience shows "a lot of uneven advances and retreats in relation to immigrant multiculturalism, both within and across countries."

For multiculturalism to work, at least two conditions must be met: the de-securitization of state-minority relations; and the existence of a human rights consensus. That is, there must not be a concern that immigrant minorities in general, or one minority group in particular, represent threats to the security of the nation. Second, minorities and immigrants must not be seen as "carriers of illiberal political cultures" for fear they might impose tyranny on the members of their own community.

Representatives of the Italian Canadian community presented the statue "Monument to Multiculturalism" by Francesco Perilli to the city of Toronto in 1985. It stands outside Union Station, the city's main railway terminal. Identical statues are located in four other cities around the world.

Without these two "pivotal" concerns, multiculturalism can play a key role in promoting the spread of citizenship among immigrant groups. And happily, these pivotal difficulties have been absent in Canada, making multiculturalism a successful, widely applauded approach to integrating immigrants. But that is because Canada is uniquely situated and enjoys advantages many other immigrant countries do not.

Thanks to its geographical location, Canada has almost no illegal immigration and preserves good control over its borders. Thanks to the points system it uses to select them, immigrants to Canada are more educated and skilled than immigrants to many other countries, such as the United States (Kymlicka 2010: 110). They are no economic burden to the country and Canadians do not see them as such. And because of Canada's historic French–English divide, immigrants to Canada help to unify the country. They provide a cultural middle ground between the founding cultures and may even be more committed to keeping the country intact than the sometimes-feuding "founding nations."

Thus, Canada's approach has allowed multiculturalism to succeed admirably. However, that has not made Canada a model for immigrant assimilation, any more than another country can necessarily be a model for Canada's social welfare strategy. Much depends on historical accident and good luck. Canada cannot provide a model for how to deal with immigrants in a country where immigration is often illegal or at any rate unselected, for example. That's because such immigrants may be largely low-skilled and therefore disproportionately unemployed and on welfare.

This leads Kymlicka to note that, in planning Canada's future, we need to do more than simply identify attractive and desirable social practices. We cannot simply single out the Nordic countries as exemplars in the handling of their social problems, for example. We need to also "identify the conditions under which those models are viable and to see what can be done to put those conditions in place."

What Does This Mean for Canada?

As we have just seen, the Nordic nations have long benefited from being small, homogenous, consensual societies. Yet as Kymlicka (in Hall and Lamont, 2009: 233) points out in a study of "successful societies," we find ourselves in Canada with a particular ethnic and racial mix of minorities. That is a historical fact. And this will remain the case, since gradual addition and assimilation will change the social composition only slowly. For policymakers, therefore, the crucial issue is how to respond to the ethnic diversity and inequality that exist in our society.

The Nordic success story results from a different mix of historical facts. It is well explained by the demographic, cultural, and institutional perspectives discussed earlier. The Nordic nations are small, much smaller than Canada. Their populations are to a large degree culturally, ethnically, religiously, and linguistically homogenous. Largely because of this, they espouse strong consensual values. This culture of consensus feeds broad support for strong welfare policies. These welfare policies, in turn, mean the state has strong social programs to deal with their social problems. As a result, the Nordic nations report lower levels of inequality, less crime, better health, and more climate action, as we have seen.

These findings suggest a particular path ahead for Canada. They suggest limiting immigration only slightly, if at all, and strengthening economic and employment programs, to create a more cohesive society. On this path, with more cultural cohesion, Canada would be better able to justify raising taxes to pay for better social spending. This spending would help us handle our national social problems, and powerfully contribute to dealing with more international ones.

What if Canada were to adopt this path? What would it cost us? First, the Nordic countries may be a model for Quebec; however, adopting this model would come at a real cost to the rest of the country. Major social and cultural changes would be needed everywhere, perhaps even including Quebec. There would be long-term political benefits to Canada in this, but short-term increases in regional conflict. Reduced immigration, however slight, would also carry economic and political costs.

As noted, radical-right political action has surged in recent years in the Nordic nations, beyond anything seen here in Canada. This radical activism is the product of a narrow national identity. The boundaries of who can and cannot be considered a true member of the national community are strict and rigid. With such definitions of citizenship, these radical groups have made significant electoral gains across the Nordic nations. However, in pushing their anti-immigrant agendas, they have also contributed to rising hate crimes and racial and ethnic intolerance in the Nordic nations. This is, clearly, not a desirable result for Canada, where multiculturalism has, since 1971, been a key part of our economic vitality, social mobility, civic integration, national identity, and international reputation.

However, there may be a workaround—one where Canada could keep its open and multicultural society, but still promote a more collectivist culture. This workaround would be to double down on investment in social programs. Such social programs would help to build a strong collectivist culture, thus promoting cohesion and consensus in our diverse population (Peng and Wong, 2010; Andrews and Jilke, 2016). By investing more in the welfare state, Canada could conserve its multicultural identity, increase consensus, and move forcefully towards fixing our social problems.

Put simply: with enough political will, we could solve more of our social problems and rise in the ranking of nations. What's more, we are already trying to do so. The federal response to COVID-19, flawed though it has been, may set the table for more federal interventions in future. For example, it may promote a wider support for national daycare, pharmacare, dental care, employment training, income support, social housing, and help for the Indigenous and racial minorities—perhaps even a universal basic income.

Economic inequality is one of the social forces that most undermines social cohesion in any society (Vergolini, 2011). Tensions between a society's classes and communities are usually worst when economic inequality is worst and welfare-state protections are least (Edlund and Lindh, 2015). Tensions and conflicts like these undermine solidarity and cohesion in a society. Clearly then, an alternative to limiting immigration to increase solidarity is to reduce economic inequality and hardship.

Equally important would be increasing social mobility; that is, helping second-generation immigrants to do as well as native-born Canadians. The most straightforward way to achieve this is by increasing our investment in social programs. Research has shown that. in countries with high-quality social services, social cohesion and confidence in public institutions is strong. In countries marked by financial strain and a lack of state support, people feel less tied to one another and less confidence in public institutions (Andrews and Jilke, 2016). Thus, social policies that invest in the population result both in more sustainable economic growth and in more social cohesion (Hemerijck, 2012).

Strong welfare states, like those in the Nordic nations, provide all their citizens with an excellent quality of life. Liberal democratic welfare states, like those of Canada and the UK, deliver benefits to individuals based largely on what they pay into them (Esping-Anderson, 1989). The advantage of the Nordic welfare state system, then, is twofold: it treats all citizens equally, fostering cohesion and consensus, and it corrects and prevents social problems.

As we have seen throughout this book, several countries—key among them the Nordic nations—outrank Canada on their handling of a wide range of social problems. The main reason these countries do better is because they invest in programs and policies aimed at solving these problems. Iceland has a smaller gendered wage gap because it mandates wage parity. Finland has more participation by women in politics and the workforce because it heavily subsidizes childcare. Norway is fixing health inequality by setting up programs like Health in All Policies (HiAP). Denmark is tackling climate change by investing heavily in green energy and subsidizing businesses that rely on renewable energy sources. The common theme that emerges here is the importance of a strong welfare state—a state that invests heavily in social programs and in its population.

In short, the Nordic countries have much to teach us about social welfare and the prevention of social problems. However, as we have seen, the emphasis there on cultural and ethnic homogeneity has produced a surge of nativist, radical-right politics. The best way forward for Canada, then, is to double down on public spending. Investing in social programs and welfare benefits will correct key social problems such as economic inequality and poor health. It will also foster feelings of social cohesion, and social inclusion. We must attempt all this while keeping up our traditionally high rates of immigration and refugee resettlement, and while continuing to embrace our homegrown model of multiculturalism. As we have seen, this doesn't solve all Canada's problems, but it will build the groundwork for doing so.

There is no evidence we can find that countries like Canada, with large minority populations, have more difficulty improving their social welfare practices than countries with smaller minority populations. What matters, seemingly, with all population processes is not the amount of change that takes place but the pace of change. When people pace their changes correctly, they give (good) governments and (motivated) citizens time to make the needed preparations. With that in mind, Canada should start moving in a more Nordic direction, where social welfare (and social problem solving) is concerned. Meanwhile, it should preserve its current multicultural outlook, where ethnic relations are concerned.

By bringing together these two winning approaches—welfare and multiculturalism—Canada will show the world it can achieve the nearly unachievable: social openness and socio-economic justice in every particular. This will raise Canada's place in the world and is worth the effort.

Acknowlegements

This book took several years to write and benefited greatly from the help of many people.

We want to first thank our University of Toronto undergraduate research assistants who collected much of the data in this book. In many cases, they researched and drafted summaries of research literature on the various social problems we discuss. Over the course of four years, this group included (in alphabetical order) Ayesha Ahmed, Sin Wah (Sabrina) Chan, Khulan Enghbold, Ori Gilboa, Nicole In, Nikhil Koduvath, Alvina Lai, Erica Liu, Sarah Mercer, Miah Musa, Saiefa Rahman, Victoria Shi, Cem Unlu, Naomi Watson, Qingyu (Juanita) Xiong, and Aida Zarghami.

The leader of this team, who worked on the project from beginning to end, was undergraduate student Angela Abenoja. Angela was simply incredible. Besides doing the other jobs mentioned above, Angela reviewed the team's work each month, suggested improvements, and prepared the charts in this book. So, thank you all, and especially thank you Angela for your magnificent help.

Then, we want to thank colleagues Bob Brym, Jeff Reitz, and Jack Veugelers for their helpful comments and for suggestions to improve the manuscript. Environics Institute founder Michael Adams was an enthusiastic supporter of this project from the beginning and provided useful criticisms of an early draft. As expected, their insights were all critically important for our success. Carl Korody, a friend from outside the academic realm, also provided an early and much-appreciated endorsement of the manuscript, for which we are truly grateful.

Finally, thanks go to our friend and publisher, David Stover of Rock's Mills Press, who critiqued, edited, and prepared this manuscript for publication. As always, David was generous and helpful in every imaginable way. We are deeply indebted to David.

LORNE TEPPERMAN AND MARIA FINNSDOTTIR
Toronto, May 2021

References

Chapter One

Babones, S. (2005). The country-level income structure of the world-economy. *Journal of World-Systems Research*, 29–55.

De Montesquieu, C. (1989 [1748]). *Montesquieu: The Spirit of the Laws*. Cambridge University Press.

Elias, N. (1978 [1939]). *The Civilizing Process*. Oxford: Blackwell. 2 vols.

Esping-Andersen, G. (1990). *The Three Worlds of Welfare Capitalism*. Princeton: Princeton University Press.

Esping-Andersen, G. (1995). *Welfare States without Work: The Impasse of Labor Shedding and Familialism in Continental European Social Policy*. Instituto Juan March de estudios y investigaciones.

Hall, P. A., & Lamont, M. (Eds.). (2009). *Successful Societies: How Institutions and Culture Affect Health*. Cambridge: Cambridge University Press.

Jackson, J. C., Gelfand, M. & Ember, C. R. (2020). A global analysis of cultural tightness in non-industrial societies. *Proceedings of the Royal Society B: Biological Sciences* 287 (1930). https://doi.org/10.1098/rspb.2020.1036.

Chapter Two

Atkinson, A. B., & Morelli, S. (2014). Chartbook of economic inequality. ECINEQ WP, 324.

Gaetz, S., Donaldson, J., Richter, T., & Gulliver, T. (2013). The state of homelessness in Canada 2013. https://www.homelesshub.ca/SOHC2013.

Hastings, G., & Domegan, C. (2013*). Social Marketing: From Tunes to Symphonies*. London: Routledge.

Heisz, A., & Richards, E. (2019). Economic well-being across generations of young Canadians: Are millennials better or worse off? Statistics Canada.

Lamprianou, I., & Ellinas, A. A. (2017). Institutional grievances and right-wing extremism: Voting for Golden Dawn in Greece. *South European Society and Politics*, 22(1), 43–60.

OECD (2019). Inequalities. In *Society at a Glance 2019: OECD Social Indicators*. Paris: OECD Publishing. DOI: https://doi.org/10.1787/bbc751e2-en.

Piketty, T. (2013). *Capital in the 21st Century*. Cambridge, MA: Harvard University Press.

Piketty, T., & Saez, E. (2014). Inequality in the long run. *Science*, 344 (6186), 838–843.

Piketty, T., & Saez, E. (2006). The evolution of top incomes: a historical and international perspective. *American Economic Review*, 96(2), 200–205.

Sharpe, A., & Capeluck, E. (2012). *The Impact of Redistribution on Income Inequality in Canada and the Provinces,*

1981–2010 (No. 2012-08). Centre for the Study of Living Standards.

Stapleton, J., and Yuan, Y. (2019). What's the true cost of food when you're poor? *Policy Options*, April 15.

Statistics Canada (2019). Temporary employment in Canada. *The Daily*, May 14.

Statistics Canada (2015) Low income lines, 2013–2014: Update. Catalogue no. 75F0002M–No. 002.

Chapter Three

Abramsky, T., et al. (2011). What factors are associated with recent intimate partner violence? Findings from the WHO multi-country study on women's health and domestic violence. *BMC Public Health*, 11(1), 1–17.

Alba, R., & Foner, N. (2015). *Strangers No More: Immigration and the Challenges of Integration in North America and Western Europe*. Princeton: Princeton University Press.

Bisello, M., & Mascherini, M. (2017). The gender employment gap: costs and policy responses. *Intereconomics*, 52(1), 24–27.

Blau, F. D., & Kahn, L. M. (2017). The gender wage gap: Extent, trends, and explanations. *Journal of Economic Literature*, 55(3), 789–865.

Boudarbat, B., & Grenier, G. (2017). Immigration in Quebec: Labour market integration and contribution to economic growth. *Canadian Ethnic Studies*, 49(2), 13–32.

Boyce, J. (2016). *Victimization of Aboriginal people in Canada, 2014*. Statistics Canada.

Burczycka, M., & Conroy, S. (2018) *Family Violence in Canada: A Statistical Profile, 2016*. Statistics Canada.

Conroy, S., & Cotter, A. (2017). *Self-reported Sexual Assault in Canada, 2014*. Statistics Canada.

Curry, B., & Doiron, M. (2012). Canada's new immigration rules put premium on young people. *Globe and Mail*, August 21.

Daoud, N., et al. (2013). The contribution of socio-economic position to the excesses of violence and intimate partner violence among Aboriginal versus non-Aboriginal women in Canada. *Canadian Journal of Public Health*, 104(4), e278–e283.

Devries, K. M., et al. (2013). The global prevalence of intimate partner violence against women. *Science*, 340(6140), 1527–1528.

Ellsberg, M., et al. (2015). Prevention of violence against women and girls: what does the evidence say? *The Lancet*, 385(9977), 1555–1566.

Fearon, J. D. (2003). Ethnic and cultural diversity by country. *Journal of Economic Growth*, 8(2), 195–222.

Finnie, R., & Meng, R. (2002). Minorities, cognitive skills

and incomes of Canadians. *Canadian Public Policy/Analyse de Politiques*, 257–273.

Fleras, A., & Maaka, R. (2010). Indigeneity-grounded analysis (IGA) as policy (-making) lens: New Zealand models, Canadian realities. *International Indigenous Policy Journal*, 1(1).

Freidenvall, L. (2003). *Women's Political Representation and Gender Quotas: the Swedish Case*. Stockholm, Sweden: Department of Political Science, Stockholm University.

Heise, L. L., & Kotsadam, A. (2015). Cross-national and multilevel correlates of partner violence: An analysis of data from population-based surveys. *The Lancet Global Health*, 3(6), e332–e340.

Hochschild, A., & Machung, A. (2012). *The Second Shift: Working Families and the Revolution at Home*. London: Penguin.

Jayasuriya-Illesinghe, V. (2018). Immigration policies and immigrant women's vulnerability to intimate partner violence in Canada. *Journal of International Migration and Integration*, 19(2), 339–348.

Jencks, C. (1988). Whom must we treat equally for educational opportunity to be equal? *Ethics*, 98(3), 518–533.

Kosny, A. A., & Lifshen, M. E. (2012). A national scan of employment standards, occupational health and safety and workers' compensation resources for new immigrants to Canada. *Canadian Journal of Public Health*, 103(1), 53–58.

Krug, E. G., et. al. (2002). World report on violence and health. Geneva: World Health Organization.

Lightman, N., & Good Gingrich, L. (2018). Measuring economic exclusion for racialized minorities, immigrants and women in Canada: Results from 2000 and 2010. *Journal of Poverty*, 22(5), 398–420.

Milkie, M. A., Raley, S. B., & Bianchi, S. M. (2009). Taking on the second shift: Time allocations and time pressures of US parents with preschoolers. *Social Forces*, 88(2), 487–517.

OHRC. (2008). Right at home: Report on the consultation on human rights and rental housing in Ontario. Toronto: Ontario Human Rights Commission.

Pendakur, K., & Pendakur, R. (1998). The colour of money: Earnings differentials among ethnic groups in Canada. *Canadian Journal of Economics*, 518–548.

Peressini, T. (2007). Perceived reasons for homelessness in Canada: Testing the heterogeneity hypothesis. *Canadian Journal of Urban Research*, 16(1), 112–126.

Perrault, S. (2015). *Criminal Victimization in Canada, 2014*. Statistics Canada.

Reitz, J. G. (2016). Towards empirical comparison of immigrant integration across nations. *Ethnic and Racial Studies*, 39(13), 2338–2345.

Reitz, J. G. (2018). *Warmth of the Welcome: The Social Causes of Economic Success in Different Nations and Cities*. London: Routledge.

Reitz, J. G., Simon, P., & Laxer, E. (2017). Muslims' social inclusion and exclusion in France, Québec, and Canada: Does national context matter? *Journal of Ethnic and Migration Studies*, 43(15), 2473–2498.

Russell, K. J., & Hand, C. J. (2017). Rape myth acceptance, victim blame attribution and Just World Beliefs: A rapid evidence assessment. *Aggression and Violent Behavior*, 37, 153–160.

Scott, K. M., et al. (2018). Post-traumatic stress disorder associated with sexual assault among women in the WHO World Mental Health Surveys. *Psychological Medicine*, 48(1), 155.

Shalabi, D., Mitchell, S., & Andersson, N. (2015). Review of gender violence among Arab immigrants in Canada: Key issues for prevention efforts. *Journal of Family Violence*, 30(7), 817–825.

Sharma, A. (2001). Healing the wounds of domestic abuse: Improving the effectiveness of feminist therapeutic interventions with immigrant and racially visible women who have been abused. *Violence Against Women*, 7(12), 1405–1428.

Shirwadkar, S. (2004). Canadian domestic violence policy and Indian immigrant women. *Violence Against Women*, 10(8), 860–879.

Statistics Canada (2009) Study: Quality of employment in the Canadian immigrant labour market. *The Daily*. Retrieved from: www.statcan .gc.ca/daily-quotidien/091123/dq091123beng.htm.

Statistics Canada (2013). *Immigration and Ethnocultural Diversity in Canada*. Ottawa: Statistics Canada.

Statistics Canada (2019). Canada's population estimates: Age and sex, July 1, 2019. *The Daily*, September 30.

Stöckl, H., et al. (2013). The global prevalence of intimate partner homicide: A systematic review. *The Lancet*, 382(9895), 859–865.

Vancouver English Centre (2014). *Definitions of Citizenship and Immigration Canada Terms*. Retrieved from: http://secure.vec.bc.ca/citizenship- immigration-terms.cfm.

Watts, C., & Zimmerman, C. (2002). Violence against women: Global scope and magnitude. *The Lancet*, 359(9313), 1232–1237.

Chapter Four

Canada Criminal Investigation Service. (2007). 2006 annual report on organized crime in Canada. *Trends in Organized Crime* 10, 76–88.

Agnew, R. (1992). Foundation for a general strain theory of crime and delinquency. *Criminology*, 30(1), 47–88.

Agnew, R. (1980). Success and anomie: A study of the effect of goals on anomie. *Sociological Quarterly*, 21(1), 53–64.

Agnew, R. (1985). A revised strain theory of delinquency. *Social Forces* 64 (1), 151–167.

Åslund, O., Grönqvist, H., Hall, C., & Vlachos, J. (2018). Education and criminal behavior: Insights from an expansion of upper secondary school. *Labour Economics*, 52, 178–192.

Australian Bureau of Statistics (2018). *Pathways to Justice: Inquiry into the Incarceration Rate of Aboriginal and Torres Strait Islander Peoples* (ALRC Report 133).

Axelsson, P., Kukutai, T., & Kippen, R. (2016). The field of Indigenous health and the role of colonisation and history. *Journal of Population Research*, 33(1), 1–7.

Barner, J. R., et al. (2014). Socio-economic inequality, human trafficking, and the global slave trade. *Societies*, 4(2), 148–160.

Beattie, S., David, J., & Roy, J. (2018). *Homicide in Canada, 2017*. Juristat: Canadian Centre for Justice Statistics, 1.

Bell, B., Bindler, A., & Machin, S. (2018). Crime scars: recessions and the making of career criminals. *Review of Economics and Statistics*, 100(3), 392–404.

Boggess, L. N., & Maskaly, J. (2014). The spatial context of the disorder–crime relationship in a study of Reno neighborhoods. *Social Science Research*, 43, 168–183.

Brookman, F., Mullins, C., Bennett, T., & Wright, R. (2007). Gender, motivation and the accomplishment of street robbery in the United Kingdom. *British Journal of Criminology*, 47(6), 861–884.

Chamlin, M. B., & Sanders, B. A. (2013). Falsifying Merton's macro-level anomie theory of profit-motivated crime: A research note. *Deviant Behavior*, 34(12), 961–972.

Chester, C. R. (1976). Perceived relative deprivation as a cause of property crime. *Crime & Delinquency*, 22(1), 17–30.

Cotter, Adam. (2020). *Trafficking in Persons in Canada, 2018.* Juristat, Statistics Canada.

Dahlberg, M., & Gustavsson, M. (2008). Inequality and crime: Separating the effects of permanent and transitory income. *Oxford Bulletin of Economics and Statistics*, 70(2), 129–153.

De Shalit, A., Heynen, R., & van der Meulen, E. (2014). Human trafficking and media myths: Federal funding, communication strategies, and Canadian anti-trafficking programs. *Canadian Journal of Communication*, 39(3).

Deshpande, N. A., & Nour, N. M. (2013). Sex trafficking of women and girls. *Reviews in Obstetrics and Gynecology*, 6(1), e22.

Ehrlich, I. (1973). Participation in illegitimate activities: A theoretical and empirical investigation. *Journal of Political Economy*, 81(3), 521–565.

Farrell, A., & Reichert, J. (2017). Using US law-enforcement data: Promise and limits in measuring human trafficking. *Journal of Human Trafficking, 3*(1), 39–60.

Featherstone, R., & Deflem, M. (2003). Anomie and strain: Context and consequences of Merton's two theories. *Sociological Inquiry*, 73(4), 471–489.

Feingold, D. A. (2011). 3. Trafficking in Numbers: the social construction of human trafficking data. In *Sex, Drugs, and Body Counts* (pp. 46–74). Ithaca, NY: Cornell University Press.

Fougère, D., Kramarz, F., & Pouget, J. (2009). Youth unemployment and crime in France. *Journal of the European Economic Association*, 7(5), 909–938.

Goodfield, K. (2020). Tow truck turf war leads Toronto-area police to lay nearly 200 charges. CTV News. https://toronto.ctvnews.ca/tow-truck-turf-war-leads-toronto-area-police-to-lay-nearly-200-charges-1.4954888.

Grant, T. (2016). The trafficked: The story behind our investigation into the exploitation of indigenous women and girls. *Globe and Mail*, February 10.

Hanley, J., Oxman-Martinez, J., Lacroix, M., & Gal, S. (2006). The "deserving" undocumented? Government and community response to human trafficking as a labour phenomenon. *Labour, Capital and Society/Travail, capital et société*, 78–103.

Hay, C., & Evans, M. M. (2006). Violent victimization and involvement in delinquency: Examining predictions from general strain theory. *Journal of Criminal Justice*, 34(3), 261–274.

Henry, F., & Tator, C. (2016). *Racial Profiling in Canada*. Toronto: University of Toronto Press.

Hipp, J. R., & Yates, D. K. (2011). Ghettos, thresholds, and crime: Does concentrated poverty really have an accelerating increasing effect on crime?. *Criminology*, 49(4), 955–990.

Hughes, D. (2006). Global sex trade: Modern day slave trade. Presentation given at Brigham Young University, Provo, Utah on March 2, 2006.

Jacobs, B. A., Topalli, V., & Wright, R. (2003). Carjacking, streetlife and offender motivation. *British Journal of Criminology*, 43(4), 673–688.

Janko, Z., & Popli, G. (2015). Examining the link between crime and unemployment: a time-series analysis for Canada. *Applied Economics*, 47(37), 4007–4019.

Kelly, M. (2000). Inequality and crime. *Review of Economics and Statistics*, 82(4), 530–539.

Konrad, R. A., et al. (2017). Overcoming human trafficking via operations research and analytics: Opportunities for methods, models, and applications. *European Journal of Operational Research*, 259(2), 733–745.

Lachaud, J., et al. (2017). A population-based study of homicide deaths in Ontario, Canada using linked death records. *International Journal for Equity in Health*, 16(1), 1–7.

Lappi-Seppälä, T., & Tonry, M. (2011). Crime, criminal justice, and criminology in the Nordic countries. *Crime and Justice*, 40(1), 1–32.

Machin, S., & Meghir, C. (2004). Crime and economic incentives. *Journal of Human Resources*, 39(4), 958–979.

Maskaly, J., & Boggess, L. N. (2014). Broken windows theory. *The Encyclopedia of Theoretical Criminology*, 1–4.

Merton, R. K. (1938). Social structure and anomie. *American Sociological Review*, 3(5), 672–82.

Moon, B., Morash, M., McCluskey, C. P., & Hwang, H. W. (2009). A comprehensive test of general strain theory: Key strains, situational-and trait-based negative emotions, conditioning factors, and delinquency. *Journal of Research in Crime and Delinquency*, 46(2), 182–212.

Murphy, D. S., & Robinson, M. B. (2008). The maximizer: Clarifying Merton's theories of anomie and strain. *Theoretical Criminology*, 12(4), 501–521.

Oberwittler, D. (2019). Lethal violence: A global view on homicide. In *Oxford Research Encyclopedia of Criminology and Criminal Justice*. Oxford: Oxford University Press.

Papachristos, A. V., Brazil, N., & Cheng, T. (2018). Understanding the crime gap: Violence and inequality in an American city. *City & Community* 17(4): 1051–1074.

Pare, P. P., & Felson, R. (2014). Income inequality, poverty and crime across nations. *British Journal of Sociology*, 65(3), 434–458.

Pratt, T. C., & Cullen, F. T. (2005). Assessing macro-level predictors and theories of crime: A meta-analysis. *Crime and Justice*, 32, 373–450.

Reilly, B., & Witt, R. (2008). Domestic burglaries and the real price of audio-visual goods: Some time series evidence for Britain. *Economics Letters*, 100(1), 96–100.

Rogers, M. L., & Pridemore, W. A. (2017). A comprehensive evaluation of the association between percent young and cross-national homicide rates. *British Journal of Criminology*, 57(5), 1080–1100.

Sapers, H. (2013). *Annual Report of the Office of the Correctional Investigator 2012-2013*. Ottawa: The Correctional Investigator.

Schwab, Klaus (2019). *The Global Competitiveness Report 2018*. World Economic Forum.

Shelley, L. (2012). The relationship of drug and human trafficking: A global perspective. *European Journal on Criminal Policy and Research*, 18(3), 241–253.

Smith, K. T., Martin, H. M., & Smith, L. M. (2014). Human trafficking: A global multi-billion-dollar criminal industry. *International Journal of Public Law and Policy*, 4(3), 293–308.

Stewart, D. E., & Gajic-Veljanoski, O. (2005). Trafficking in women: The Canadian perspective. *CMAJ*, 173(1), 25–26.

Stys, Y., & Ruddell, R. (2013). Organized crime offenders in Canada: Risk, reform, and recidivism. *Journal of Offender Rehabilitation*, 52(2), 75–97.

Tauri, J. (2005). Indigenous perspectives and experience: Maori and the criminal justice system. In *Introduction to Criminological Thought* (pp. 129–45). Auckland, N.Z.: Pearson.

Testa, A., Young, J. K., & Mullins, C. (2017). Does democracy enhance or reduce lethal violence? Examining the role of the rule of law. *Homicide Studies*, 21(3), 219–239.

Toronto Star (2021). The GTA's tow truck turf wars rage on. https://www.thestar.com/podcasts/thismatters/2021/01/26/the-gtas-tow-truck-turf-wars-rage-on.html.

Töttel, U., Bulanova-Hristova, G., & Kleemans, E. R. (2012). Research on organized crime in Western Europe—4th research conference. *Trends in Organized Crime*, 15(2–3), 260–265.

Tuttle, J., McCall, P. L., & Land, K. C. (2018). Latent trajectories of cross-national homicide trends: Structural characteristics of underlying groups. *Homicide Studies*, 22(4), 343–369.

United Nations (2009). *State of the World's Indigenous Peoples*, Vol. 1. Department of Economic and Social Affairs.

Von Lampe, K. (2007). The crime that pays: Drug trafficking and organized crime in Canada. *Trends in Organized Crime* 10, 131–134.

Wortley, S. (2003). Hidden intersections: Research on race, crime, and criminal justice in Canada. *Canadian Ethnic Studies Journal*, 35(3), 99–118.

Wortley, S., & Tanner, J. (2004). Discrimination or "good" policing? The racial profiling debate in Canada. *Our Diverse Cities*, 1 (Spring), 197–201.

Wu, D., & Wu, Z. (2012). Crime, inequality and unemployment in England and Wales. *Applied Economics*, 44(29), 3765–3775.

Zimmerman, C., & Kiss, L. (2017). Human trafficking and exploitation: A global health concern. *PLoS Medicine*, 14(11), e1002437.

Chapter Five

Adams, J., et al. (2017). Influencing condom use by gay and bisexual men for anal sex through social marketing: A program evaluation of Get it On! *Social Marketing Quarterly*, 23(1), 3–17.

Aggleton, P., & Kippax, S. (2014). Australia's HIV-prevention response: Introduction to the special issue. *AIDS Education and Prevention*, 26(3), 187–190.

Alexander, G. C., et al. (2020). An epidemic in the midst of a pandemic: Opioid use disorder and COVID-19. *Annals of Internal Medicine*, 173 (1), 57–58.

American Heart Association (2015). Accessed at https://www.heart.org/en/health-topics/heart-attack/life-after-a-heart-attack/lifestyle-changes-for-heart-attack-prevention.

Andersson, T. M. L., et al. (2018). Tackling the tobacco epidemic in the Nordic countries and lower cancer incidence by 1/5 in a 30-year period: The effect of envisaged scenarios changing smoking prevalence. *European Journal of Cancer*, 103, 288–298.

Battiloro, C. (2018). Fentanyl: How China's pharmaceutical loopholes are fueling the United States' opioid crisis. *Syracuse J. Int'l L. & Com.*, 46, 343.

Braam, A. W., et al. (2014). Depression, subthreshold depression and comorbid anxiety symptoms in older Europeans: results from the EURODEP concerted action. *Journal of Affective Disorders*, 155, 266–272.

CAMH. (2020). Vaping: What you and your friends need to know. https://www.camh.ca/-/media/files/vaping-youth-resource-en-pdf.pdf?la=en&hash=12D6F6C-985514C14E94B543DD1CA62216847C660.

Carter, A., et al. (2015). Gay and bisexual men's awareness and knowledge of treatment as prevention: findings from the Momentum Health Study in Vancouver, Cana-

da. *Journal of the International AIDS Society*, 18(1), 20039.

CBC News. (2021). Homeless advocates call on city to do more to help unhoused people as temperature drops. January 25.

CDC (2012). Frequently asked questions about SARS. https://www.cdc.gov/sars/about/faq.html.

Conference Board of Canada (2008). *The Canadian Tourism Industry: A Special Report*. https://tiac-aitc.ca/_Library/documents/The_Canadian_Tourism_Industry_-_A_Special_Report_Web_Optimized_.pdf.

Corsi, D. J., et al. (2014). Trends in smoking in Canada from 1950 to 2011: Progression of the tobacco epidemic according to socioeconomic status and geography. *Cancer Causes & Control*, 25(1), 45–57.

Currie, C. L., et al. (2013). Illicit and prescription drug problems among urban Aboriginal adults in Canada: The role of traditional culture in protection and resilience. *Social Science & Medicine*, 88, 1–9.

European Centre for Disease Prevention and Control (ECDC)/ WHO Regional Office for Europe. *HIV/AIDS Surveillance in Europe 2011*. Stockholm: ECDC. Available from http://ecdc.europa.eu/en/publications/Publications/20121130-Annual-HIV-Surveillance-Report.pdf 2.

Fischer, B., et al. (2018). Patterns, changes, and trends in prescription opioid dispensing in Canada, 2005–2016. *Pain Physician*, 21(3), 219–228.

Government of Canada (2019). *Suicide in Canada: Key Statistics*. Accessed at: https://www.canada.ca/en/public-health/services/publications/healthy-living/suicide-canada-key-statistics-infographic.html.

Grana, R., Benowitz, N., & Glantz, S. A. (2014). E-cigarettes: A scientific review. *Circulation*, 129(19), 1972–1986.

Hawryluck, L., et al. (2004). SARS control and psychological effects of quarantine, Toronto, Canada. *Emerging Infectious Diseases*, 10(7), 1206.

Health Canada (2017). Smoking, 2016. Accessed at: https://www150.statcan.gc.ca/n1/en/pub/82-625-x/2017001/article/54864-eng.pdf?st=GLwpwVws.

Helweg-Larsen, M., & Tjitra, C. (2021). Does ostracism help smokers quit? *Stigma and Health*. Advance online publication. https://doi.org/10.1037/sah0000304.

Helweg-Larsen, M., Sorgen, L. J., & Pisinger, C. (2019). Does it help smokers if we stigmatize them? A test of the stigma-induced identity threat model among US and Danish smokers. *Social Cognition*, 37(3), 294–313.

International Diabetes Federation (IDF). (2017) *IDF Diabetes Atlas*. 8th Ed. Brussels: International Diabetes Federation. http://www.diabetesatlas.org/resources/2017-atlas.html.

Jiwa, A., Kelly, L., & Pierre-Hansen, N. (2008). Healing the community to heal the individual: Literature review of aboriginal community-based alcohol and substance abuse programs. *Canadian Family Physician*, 54(7), 1000.

Kunitz, S. J. (2008). Risk factors for polydrug use in a Native American population. *Substance Use & Misuse*, 43(3–4), 331–339.

Lisa, B., & Jessica, H. (2018). Evidence synthesis: The opioid crisis in Canada: A national perspective. *Health Promotion and Chronic Disease Prevention in Canada: Research, Policy and Practice*, 38(6), 224.

Ma, C., Rogers, J. H., & Zhou, S. (2020, January). Global economic and financial effects of 21st century pandemics and epidemics. *SSRN Electronic Journal*. DOI:10.2139/ssrn.3565646

Marmot, M. (2004). Status syndrome. *Significance*, 1(4), 150–154.

Marmot, M., & Brunner, E. (2005). Cohort profile: the Whitehall II study. *International Journal of Epidemiology*, 34(2), 251–256.

McNeill, A., et al. (2015). E-cigarettes: An evidence update. *Public Health England*, 3.

Mondal, M. N. I., & Shitan, M. (2014). Relative importance of demographic, socioeconomic and health factors on life expectancy in low-and lower-middle-income countries. *Journal of Epidemiology*, 24(2), 117–124.

Oliver, L. N., Peters, P. A., & Kohen, D. E. (2012). Mortality rates among children and teenagers living in Inuit Nunangat, 1994 to 2008. *Health Reports*, 23(3), 1–6. Retrieved from http://www.statcan.gc.ca/pub/82-003-x/2012003/article/11695-eng.pdf.

Pearson, C., Janz, T., & Ali, J. (2013). Mental and substance use disorders in Canada. https://www150.statcan.gc.ca/n1/pub/82-624-x/2013001/article/11855-eng.pdf.

Pickett, K. E., & Wilkinson, R. G. (2015). Income inequality and health: A causal review. *Social Science & Medicine*, 128, 316–326.

Plant, M. A., et al. (2009). The social consequences of binge drinking: A comparison of young adults in six European countries. *Journal of Addictive Diseases*, 28(4), 294–308.

Public Health Agency of Canada (2017). *Diabetes in Canada: Highlights from the Canadian Chronic Disease Surveillance System.* Accessed at:https://www.canada.ca/en/public-health/services/publications/diseases-conditions/diabetes-canada-highlights-chronic-disease-surveillance-system.htm.

Public Health Agency of Canada (2019). *HIV in Canada: Surveillance Report, 2018.* Accessed at https://www.canada.ca/en/public-health/services/reports-publications/canada-communicable-disease-report-ccdr/monthly-issue/2019-45/issue-12-december-5-2019/article-1-2018-hiv-surveillance-report.html.

Public Health Ontario (2019). *The Burden of Chronic Diseases in Ontario.* Accessed at: https://www.publichealthontario.ca/-/media/documents/C/2019/cdburden-report.pdf?la=en.

Rather, L. J. (1985). *Rudolf Virchow: Collected Essays on Public Health and Epidemiology,* Vol. 1-2. Science History Publications.

Rieder, T. N. (2018). There's never just one side to the story: Why America must stop swinging the opioid pendulum. *Narrative Inquiry in Bioethics*, 8(3), 225–231.

Ritchie, H., & Roser, M. (2018). Causes of death. *Our World in Data.*

Sachs, J. D., Layard, R., & Helliwell, J. F. (2018). *World Happiness Report 2018* (No. id: 12761).

Selin, J., et al. (2015). Opioid substitution treatment in Finland and other Nordic countries: Established treatment, varying practices. *Nordic Studies on Alcohol and Drugs*, 32(3), 311–324

Statistics Canada (2017). *Health Fact Sheet: Smoking, 2017.* Accessed at https://www150.statcan.gc.ca/n1/pub/82-625-x/2018001/article/54974-eng.htm.

Statistics Canada (2019). *Canadian Tobacco and Nicotine Survey (CTNS): Summary of Results for 2019.* Accessed at https://www.canada.ca/en/health-canada/services/canadian-tobacco-nicotine-survey/2019-summary.html.

Thomas, G. (2012). *Analysis of Beverage Alcohol Sales in Canada.* (Alcohol Price Policy Series: Report 2). Ottawa: Canadian Centre on Substance Abuse.

UNAIDS (2019). *UNAIDS Data 2019.* Accessed at: https://www.unaids.org/sites/default/files/media_asset/2019-UNAIDS-data_en.pdf.

United Nations (2020). UN chief calls for domestic violence 'ceasefire' amid 'horrifying global surge.' Accessed at https://news.un.org/en/story/2020/04/1061052.

WHO (2003). Update 27: One month into the global SARS outbreak: Status of the outbreak and lessons for the immediate future. Accessed at https://www.who.int/csr/sars/archive/2003_04_11/en/.

WHO (2019). Measures of harm reduction service provision for people who inject drugs. Accessed at: https://www.who.int/bulletin/volumes/97/9/18-224089/en/.

WHO (2020). The top 10 causes of death. Accessed at: https://www.who.int/news-room/fact-sheets/detail/the-top-10-causes-of-death.

WHO (2020). Tobacco. Accessed at https://www.who.int/news-room/fact-sheets/detail/tobacco.

WHO (2018). Alcohol. Accessed at: https://www.who.int/news-room/fact-sheets/detail/alcohol.

WHO (2017). *Depression and Other Common Mental Disorders: Global Health Estimates* (No. WHO/MSD/MER/2017.2). World Health Organization.

World Obesity Federation. (2017). Prevalence of obesity. Accessed at: https://www.worldobesity.org/about/about-obesity/prevalence-of-obesity.

Yourex-West, H. (2015). New rules say Alberta doctors must provide after-hours care. Global News, June 11

Chapter Six

Attwood, D., Khan, F., & Veitch, B. (2006). Occupational accident models: Where have we been and where are we going? *Journal of Loss Prevention in the Process Industries*, 19(6), 664–682.

Beirness, D. J., & Davis, C. G. (2007). Driving after drinking in Canada. *Canadian Journal of Public Health*, 98(6), 476–480.

Bertelli, A. M., & Richardson, L. E., jr. (2007). Measuring the propensity to drink and drive. *Evaluation Review*, 31(3), 311–337.

Blais, É., et al. (2015). Effects of introducing an administrative .05% blood alcohol concentration limit on law enforcement patterns and alcohol-related collisions in Canada. *Accident Analysis & Prevention*, 82, 101–111.

Brown, S. W., Vanlaar, W. G. M., & Robertson, R. D. (2015). *Alcohol and Drug Crash Problem in Canada: 2012 Report.* CCMTA Road Safety Research Report Series. Ottawa: Traffic Injury Research Foundation of Canada.

Chan, J., Parmenter, T., & Stancliffe, R. (2009). The impact of traumatic brain injury on the mental health outcomes of individuals and their family carers. *Australian e-Journal for the Advancement of Mental Health*, 8(2), 155–164.

Dawson, D. A. (1994). Heavy drinking and the risk of occupational injury. *Accident Analysis & Prevention*, 26(5), 655–665.

De Castro Ribas, R., jr., Tymchuk, A. J., & Ribas, A. F. (2006). Brazilian mothers' knowledge about home dangers and safety precautions: An initial evaluation. *Social Science & Medicine*, 63(7), 1879–1888.

Drabek, T. E. (2017). Sociology of disaster. *The Cambridge Handbook of Sociology*, 139–147.

European Agency for Safety and Health at Work, (2010). Economic incentives to improve occupational safety and health: A review from the European perspective, 2010. Available at: http://osha.europa.eu/en/publications/reports/economic_incentives_TE3109255ENC/view.

Fortin, B., & Lanoie, P. (2000). Incentive effects of workers' compensation: A survey. In *Handbook of Insurance*, pp. 421–458. Dordrecht: Springer.

Friehe, T. (2008). Victim interdependence in the accident setting. *German Working Papers in Law and Economics, 2008*(1), 2.

Gallagher, C., & Underhill, E. (2012). Managing work health and safety: Recent developments and future directions. *Asia Pacific Journal of Human Resources*, 50(2), 227–244.

Gjerde, H., et al. (2013). Norwegian roadside survey of alcohol and drug use by drivers (2008–2009). *Traffic Injury Prevention*, 14(5), 443–452.

Government of Canada (2019). Drug-impaired driving. Accessed at: https://www.canada.ca/en/services/policing/police/community-safety-policing/impaired-driving/drug-impaired-driving.html.

Guadalupe, M. (2003). The hidden costs of fixed term contracts: The impact on work accidents. *Labour Economics*, 10(3), 339–357.

Hennessy, T., & Tranjan, R. (2018). *No Safe Harbour: Precarious Work and Economic Insecurity among Skilled Professionals in Canada*. Canadian Centre for Policy Alternatives.

Hilton, M. E. (1984). The impact of recent changes in California drinking-driving laws on fatal accident levels during the first postintervention year: An interrupted time series analysis. *Law & Societyy Rev.*, 18, 605.

Hoofien, D., Gilboa, A., Vakil, E., & Donovick, P. J. (2001). Traumatic brain injury (TBI) 10–20 years later: A comprehensive outcome study of psychiatric symptomatology, cognitive abilities and psychosocial functioning. *Brain injury*, 15(3), 189–209.

Kaestner, R., & Grossman, M. (1998). The effect of drug use on workplace accidents. *Labour Economics*, 5(3), 267–294.

Karjalainen, K., Blencowe, T., & Lillsunde, P. (2012). Substance use and social, health and safety-related factors among fatally injured drivers. *Accident Analysis & Prevention*, 45, 731–736.

Katsakiori, P., Kavvathas, A., Athanassiou, G., Goutsos, S., & Manatakis, E. (2010). Workplace and organizational accident causation factors in the manufacturing industry. *Human Factors and Ergonomics in Manufacturing & Service Industries*, 20(1), 2–9.

Khanzode, V. V., Maiti, J., & Ray, P. K. (2012). Occupational injury and accident research: A comprehensive review. *Safety Science*, 50(5), 1355–1367.

Lovenheim, M. F., & Slemrod, J. (2010). The fatal toll of driving to drink: The effect of minimum legal drinking age evasion on traffic fatalities. *Journal of Health Economics*, 29(1), 62–77.

Mayhew, C., & Quinlan, M. (1997). Subcontracting and occupational health and safety in the residential building industry. *Industrial Relations Journal*, 28(3), 192–205.

Nenonen, S. (2011). Fatal workplace accidents in outsourced operations in the manufacturing industry. *Safety Science*, 49(10), 1394–1403.

OECD (2019). Accessed at: https://www.oecd-ilibrary.org/social-issues-migration-health/public-spending-on-incapacity/indicator/english_f35b71ed-en#:~:text=Public%20spending%20on%20incapacity%20refers,labour%20market%20due%20to%20disability.

Palk, G., et al. (2011). The prevalence and characteristics of self-reported dangerous driving behaviours among a young cohort. *Transportation Research Part F: Traffic Psychology and Behaviour*, 14(2), 147–154.

Parachute (2015). Cost of injury in Canada. Accessed at: https://parachute.ca/en/professional-resource/cost-of-injury-in-canada/.

Public Health Agency of Canada (2019). *At a Glance: Injury Hospitalizations in Canada*. Accessed at: https://www.canada.ca/en/public-health/services/reports-publications/health-promotion-chronic-disease-prevention-canada-research-policy-practice/vol-40-no-9-2020/injury-hospitalizations-canada-2018-2019.html.

Quinlan, M., & Mayhew, C. (1999). Precarious employment and workers' compensation. *International Journal of Law and Psychiatry*, 22(5-6), 491–520.

Quinlan, M., Mayhew, C., & Bohle, P. (2001). The global expansion of precarious employment, work disorganization, and consequences for occupational health: A review of recent research. *International Journal of Health Services*, 31(2), 335–414.

Robson, L. S., et al. (2012). A systematic review of the effectiveness of occupational health and safety training. *Scandinavian Journal of Work, Environment & Health*, 193–208.

Transport Canada (2017). *Canadian Motor Vehicle Collision Statistics: 2017*. Accessed at: https://tc.canada.ca/en/canadian-motor-vehicle-traffic-collision-statistics-2017.

Weisburd, D., & Wire, S. (2018). Crime hot spots. In *Oxford Research Encyclopedia of Criminology and Criminal Justice*.

WHO (2020). *Road Traffic Injuries*. Accessed at: https://www.who.int/news-room/fact-sheets/detail/road-traffic-injuries.

Wundersitz, L. (2019). Driver distraction and inattention in fatal and injury crashes: Findings from in-depth road crash data. *Traffic Injury Prevention*, 20(7), 696–701.

Chapter Seven

Baldé, C. P., et al. (2017). *The Global E-waste Monitor 2017: Quantities, Flows and Resources*. United Nations University, International Telecommunication Union, and International Solid Waste Association.

Bertoldo, R., et al. (2019). Scientific truth or debate: On the link between perceived scientific consensus and belief in anthropogenic climate change. *Public Understanding of Science*, 28(7), 778-796.

Bissett, K. (2018). Conservation deal halts commercial salmon fishing in Greenland for 12 years. The Canadian Press, May 28.

Boyd, M., & Vickers, M. (2000). 100 years of immigration in Canada. *Canadian Social Trends*, 58(2), 2–12.

Brooks, B. W., et al. (2016). Are harmful algal blooms becoming the greatest inland water quality threat to public health and aquatic ecosystems?. *Environmental Toxicology and Chemistry*, 35(1), 6–13.

Brulle, R. J., Carmichael, J., & Jenkins, J. C. (2012). Shifting public opinion on climate change: an empirical assessment of factors influencing concern over climate change in the US, 2002–2010. *Climatic Change*, 114(2), 169–188.

Bush, E., & Lemmen, D. S. (Eds.). (2019). *Canada's Changing Climate Report*. Government of Canada.

Canada's Oil & Natural Gas Producers (2019). Accessed at: https://www.capp.ca/economy/#:~:text=Canadian%20Economic%20Contribution,across%20the%20country%20in%202017.

Capstick, S., et al. (2015). International trends in public perceptions of climate change over the past quarter century. *Wiley Interdisciplinary Reviews: Climate Change*, 6(1), 35–61.

Carmichael, J. T., & Brulle, R. J. (2018). Media use and climate change concern. *International Journal of Media & Cultural Politics*, 14(2), 243–253.

Chung, E. (2018). Shrinking mountain snowpack, drier summers spell trouble for Vancouver water supply. CBC News, March 16.

Comim, F., Kumar, P., & Sirven, N. (2009). Poverty and environment links: An illustration from Africa. *Journal of International Development: The Journal of the Development Studies Association*, 21(3), 447–469.

Conference Board of Canada (2013). *Municipal Waste Generation*. Accessed at: https://www.conferenceboard.ca/hcp/Details/Environment/municipal-waste-generation.aspx.

Dangerfield, K. (2018). Heat wave smashes records around the world: A look at the sizzling temperatures. Global News. August 1. https://globalnews.ca/news/4311444/heat-wave-weatheracross-the-world.

Driedger, A. G., Dürr, H. H., Mitchell, K., & Van Cappellen, P. (2015). Plastic debris in the Laurentian Great Lakes: A review. *Journal of Great Lakes Research*, 41(1), 9–19.

EPA (n.d.). Recycling basics. Accessed at https://www.epa.gov/recycle/recycling-basics.

Fisher, S., Fitzgerald, R., & Poortinga, W. (2018). Climate change: Social divisions in belief and behaviour. In Phillips, D., Curtice, J., Phillips, M. and Perry, J. (Eds.), *British Social Attitudes: The 35th Report*. London: The National Centre for Social Research.

FNHA. (n.d.) Drinking water advisories. https://www.fnha.ca/what-we-do/environmental-health/drinking-water-advisories.

Gennings, C., Ellis, R., & Ritter, J. K. (2012). Linking empirical estimates of body burden of environmental chemicals and wellness using NHANES data. *Environment International*, 39(1), 56–65.

Gleick, P. H. (2014). Water, drought, climate change, and conflict in Syria. *Weather, Climate, and Society*, 6(3), 331–340.

Hamilton, L. C., et al. (2015). Tracking public beliefs about anthropogenic climate change. *PloS One*, 10(9), e0138208.

Hanania, J., Sheardown, A., Stenhouse, K., & Donev, J. (2019, February 24). *Energy Education: Conventional vs Unconventional Resource* [Online]. Retrieved from https://energyeducation.ca/encyclopedia/Conventional_vs_unconventional_resource.

Hanna, R., & Oliva, P. (2016). Implications of climate change for children in developing countries. *The Future of Children*, 115–132.

Hobwana, C., Ngaza, N., & Mapira, J. (2018). Challenges of waste management in Chiredzi, Zimbabwe. *European Journal of Social Sciences Studies*.

Hoornweg, D., Bhada-Tata, P., & Kennedy, C. (2013). Environment: Waste production must peak this century. *Nature News*, 502(7473), 615.

Hornsey, M. J., et al. (2016). Meta-analyses of the determinants and outcomes of belief in climate change. *Nature Climate Change*, 6(6), 622–626.

Hounsell, K. (2018, March 29). Canadian municipalities struggling to find place for recyclables after China restricts foreign waste. CBC News. Retrieved from https://www.cbc.ca/news/technology/garbage-recycling-china-plasticscanada-1.4586602.

Lachapelle, E., Borick, C. P., & Rabe, B. (2012). Public attitudes toward climate science and climate policy in federal systems: Canada and the United States compared 1. *Review of Policy Research*, 29(3), 334–357.

Lampert, A. (2019). Over-exploitation of natural resources is followed by inevitable declines in economic growth and discount rate. *Nature Communications*, 10(1), 1–10.

Lockwood, M. (2018). Right-wing populism and the climate change agenda: Exploring the linkages. *Environmental Politics*, 27(4), 712–732.

Lougheed, S. C., Hird, M. J., & Rowe, K. R. (2016). Governing household waste management: An empirical analysis and critique. *Environmental Values*, 25(3), 287–308.

Luginaah, I., Smith, K., & Lockridge, A. (2010). Surrounded by Chemical Valley and 'living in a bubble': The case of the Aamjiwnaang First Nation, Ontario. *Journal of Environmental Planning and Management*, 53(3), 353–370.

McCright, A. M., Dunlap, R. E., & Marquart-Pyatt, S. T. (2016). Political ideology and views about climate change in the European Union. *Environmental Politics*, 25(2), 338–358.

Mikalsen, K. H., & Jentoft, S. (2003). Limits to participation? On the history, structure and reform of Norwegian fisheries management. *Marine Policy*, 27(5), 397–407.

Morton, A. (2020). Australia's electricity grid could run with 75% renewables, market operator says. *The Guardian*, April 29.

National Marine Fisheries Service (2020). *Fisheries of the United States, 2018*. Accessed at: https://repository.library.noaa.gov/view/noaa/23716.

Orisakwe, O. E., Frazzoli, C., Ilo, C. E., & Oritsemuelebi, B. (2019). Public health burden of e-waste in Africa. *Journal of Health and Pollution*, 9(22).

Perera, F. (2018). Pollution from fossil-fuel combustion is the leading environmental threat to global pediatric health and equity: Solutions exist. *International Journal of Environmental Research and Public Health*, 15(1), 16.

Poortinga, W., Whitmarsh, L., Steg, L., Böhm, G., & Fisher, S. (2019). Climate change perceptions and their individual-level determinants: A cross-European analysis. *Global Environmental Change*, 55, 25–35.

Rochman, C. M., et al. (2013). Classify plastic waste as hazardous. *Nature*, 494(7436), 169–171.

Sherman, L. S., et al. (2015). The use of Pb, Sr, and Hg isotopes in Great Lakes precipitation as a tool for pollution source attribution. *Science of the Total Environment*, 502, 362–374.

Statistics Canada (2020). Waste management industry: Waste disposal, 2018. Accessed at https://www150.statcan.gc.ca/n1/daily-quotidien/200709/dq200709e-eng.htm.

Stegemann, L., & Ossewaarde, M. (2018). A sustainable myth: A neo-Gramscian perspective on the populist and post-truth tendencies of the European green growth discourse. *Energy Research & Social Science*, 43, 25–32.

UNFCC (2018). Canada's INDC submission to the UNFCC. Accessed at https://www4.unfccc.int/sites/ndcstaging/PublishedDocuments/Canada%20First/INDC%20-%20Canada%20-%20English.pdf.

United Nations (2014). Water scarcity. Accessed at https://www.unwater.org/water-facts/scarcity/.

United Nations (2019). World population aging, 2019: Highlights. Accessed at https://www.un.org/en/development/desa/population/publications/pdf/ageing/WorldPopulationAgeing2019-Highlights.pdf.

Van der Pol, T. D., van Ierland, E. C., & Gabbert, S. (2017). Economic analysis of adaptive strategies for flood risk management under climate change. *Mitigation and Adaptation Strategies for Global Change*, 22(2), 267–285.

Verma, R., Vinoda, K. S., Papireddy, M., & Gowda, A. N. S. (2016). Toxic pollutants from plastic waste: A review. *Procedia Environmental Sciences*, 35, 701–708.

Watkins, M. (2013). Some reflections on the making of global capitalism. *Studies in Political Economy*, 92(1), 77–83.

WHO (2020). Ambient air pollution: A major threat to health and climate. Accessed at https://www.who.int/air-pollution/ambient/en/.

World Bank Group (2018). Global waste to grow by 70 percent by 2050 unless urgent action is taken: World Bank Report. https://www.worldbank.org/en/news/press-release/2018/09/20/global-waste-to-grow-by-70-percent-by-2050-unless-urgent-action-is-taken-world-bank-report.

Wynes, S., & Nicholas, K. A. (2017). The climate mitigation gap: Education and government recommendations miss the most effective individual actions. *Environmental Research Letters*, 12(7), 074024.

Zanocco, C., et al. (2018). Place, proximity, and perceived harm: Extreme weather events and views about climate change. *Climatic Change*, 149(3), 349–365.

Chapter Eight

Bilodeau, A., Turgeon, L., & Karakoç, E. (2012). Small worlds of diversity: Views toward immigration and racial minorities in Canadian provinces. *Canadian Journal of Political Science/Revue canadienne de science politique*, 579–605.

Booth, P., & Boudreault, F. (2016). By the numbers: Canadian GHG emissions. Lawrence National Center for Policy and Management.

Breau, S. (2007). Income inequality across Canadian provinces in an era of globalization: Explaining recent trends. *The Canadian Geographer/Le Geographe canadien*, 51(1), 72–90.

Breslin, F. C., Smith, P., Mustard, C., & Zhao, R. (2006). Young people and work injuries: An examination of jurisdictional variation within Canada. *Injury Prevention*, 12(2), 105–110.

Canning, P. M., Courage, M. L., & Frizzell, L. M. (2004). Prevalence of overweight and obesity in a provincial population of Canadian preschool children. *CMAJ*, 171(3), 240–242.

Colin, S., Lidia, L., & Bernard, C. C. (2017). Evaluating compression or expansion of morbidity in Canada: Trends in life expectancy and health-adjusted life expectancy from 1994 to 2010. *Health Promotion and Chronic Disease Prevention in Canada: Research, Policy and Practice*, 37(3), 68.

Corsi, D. J., et al. (2014). Trends in smoking in Canada from 1950 to 2011: Progression of the tobacco epidemic according to socioeconomic status and geography. *Cancer Causes & Control*, 25(1), 45–57.

Filate, W. A., Johansen, H. L., Kennedy, C. C., & Tu, J. V. (2003). Regional variations in cardiovascular mortality in Canada. *Canadian Journal of Cardiology*, 19(11), 1241-1248.

Brzozowski, J. A., Taylor-Butts, A., & Johnson, S. (2006). *Victimization and Offending among the Aboriginal Population in Canada*. Ottawa: Canadian Centre for Justice Statistics.

Kreatsoulas, C., & Anand, S. S. (2010). The impact of social determinants on cardiovascular disease. *Canadian Journal of Cardiology*, 26, 8C–13C.

Lightman, N., & Good Gingrich, L. (2018). Measuring economic exclusion for racialized minorities, immigrants and women in Canada: Results from 2000 and 2010. *Journal of Poverty*, 22(5), 398–420.

Malakieh, J. (2018). Adult and youth correctional statistics in Canada, 2016/2017. *Juristat. Canadian Centre for Justice Statistics*, 1–20.

Marchand, Y., Dubé, J., & Breau, S. (2020). Exploring the causes and consequences of regional income inequality in Canada. *Economic Geography*, 96(2), 83–107.

Palay, J., et al. (2019). Prevalence of mental disorders and suicidality in Canadian provinces. *Canadian Journal of Psychiatry*, 64(11), 761–769.

Ramage-Morin, P. L. (2008). Motor vehicle accident deaths, 1979 to 2004. *Health Reports*, 19(3), 45.

Roberts, J. V., & Reid, A. A. (2017). Aboriginal incarceration in Canada since 1978: Every picture tells the same story. *Canadian Journal of Criminology and Criminal Justice*, 59(3), 313–345.

Roy, J., & Marcellus, S. (2019). Homicide in Canada, 2018. *Juristat: Canadian Centre for Justice Statistics*, 4–33.

Schindler, D. W., & Donahue, W. F. (2006). An impending water crisis in Canada's western prairie provinces. *Proceedings of the National Academy of Sciences*, 103(19), 7210–7216.

Schirle, T. (2015). The gender wage gap in the Canadian provinces, 1997–2014. *Canadian Public Policy*, 41(4), 309–319.

Schirle, T., & Vickers, E. (2015). The 2014 Gender Wage Gap in Ontario. *LCERPA Commentary* (2015-1).

Sharpe, A., & Capeluck, E. (2012). *The Impact of Redistribution on Income Inequality in Canada and the Provinces, 1981–2010* (No. 2012-08). Centre for the Study of Living Standards.

Shields, M., & Tjepkema, M. (2006). Trends in adult obesity. *Health Reports*, 17(3), 53.

Sinha, M. (2013). Family violence in Canada: A statistical profile, 2011. *Juristat: Canadian Centre for Justice Statistics*, 1.

Statistics Canada. (2017). *Human Activity and the Environment 2016*. Catalogue no. 16201X.

Tucker, S., & Keefe, A. (2018). *2018 Report on Work Fatality and Injury Rates in Canada*. University of Regina.

Vanasse, A., Demers, M., Hemiari, A., & Courteau, J. (2006). Obesity in Canada: Where and how many? *International Journal of Obesity*, 30(4), 677–683.

Chapter Nine

Adams, M. (2008). *Unlikely Utopia: The Surprising Triumph of Canadian Multiculturalism*. Toronto: Penguin Canada.

Andersson, R., Bråmå, Å., & Holmqvist, E. (2010). Counteracting segregation: Swedish policies and experiences. *Housing Studies*, 25(2), 237–256.

Andrews, R., & Jilke, S. (2016). Welfare states and social cohesion in Europe: Does social service quality matter?. *Journal of Social Policy*, 45(1), 119–140.

Banting, K., & Kymlicka, W. (2010). Canadian multiculturalism: Global anxieties and local debates. *British Journal of Canadian Studies*, 23(1), 43–73.

Banting, K., & Kymlicka, W. (2013). Is there really a retreat from multiculturalism policies? New evidence from the multiculturalism policy index. *Comparative European Politics*, 11(5), 577–598.

Bergqvist, C., Blandy, T. O., & Sainsbury, D. (2007). Swedish state feminism: Continuity and change. In *Changing State Feminism* (pp. 224-245). London: Palgrave Macmillan.

Christiansen, T., et al. (2018). Healthcare, health and inequality in health in the Nordic countries. *Nordic Journal of Health Economics*. Special issue.

Cooper, B. (2005). Norway: Migrant quality, not quantity. Migration Policy Institute, May 1, 2005. Accessed at https://www.migrationpolicy.org/article/norway-migrant-quality-not-quantity.

Dalgard, O. S., & Thapa, S. B. (2007). Immigration, social integration and mental health in Norway, with focus on gender differences. *Clinical Practice and Epidemiology in Mental Health*, 3(1), 1–10.

Edlund, J., & Lindh, A. (2015). The democratic class struggle revisited: The welfare state, social cohesion and political conflict. *Acta Sociologica*, 58(4), 311–328.

Elgenius, G., & Rydgren, J. (2019). Frames of nostalgia and belonging: The resurgence of ethno-nationalism in Sweden. *European Societies*, 21(4), 583–602.

Esping-Andersen, G. (1989). The demographics of age in labour market management. Working paper. Florence: European University Institute, 1989. EUI Working Papers, 414.

Esping-Andersen, G. (1990). *The Three Worlds of Welfare Capitalism*. Princeton: Princeton University Press.

Fatima, M. (2019). *Development of Forenom's Corporate Social Responsibility Actions across the Nordic Countries*. Bachelor's thesis. Haaga-Helia University of Applied Sciences.

Fredlund-Blomst, S. (2014). Assessing immigrant integration in Sweden after the May 2013 riots. *Migration Information Source*, 16.

Government of Canada (2007). Program estimates the damage of cigarette fires. Accessed at:https://www.canada.ca/en/health-canada/services/science-research/activity-highlights/health-protection-promotion/program-estimates-damage-cigarette-fires-science-research-health-canada.html.

Government of Canada (2019). Eligibility to apply for the Federal Skilled Trades Program (Express Entry). Accessed at https://www.canada.ca/en/immigration-refugees-citizenship/services/immigrate-canada/express-entry/eligibility/skilled-trades.html.

Hemerijck, A. (2012). The political economy of social investment. In *Economy and Society in Europe*. Cheltenham, UK: Edward Elgar Publishing.

Howell, J. P., & Sundberg, T. (2015). Towards an affective geopolitics: Soft power and the Danish notion of "hygge". *Environment, Space, Place*, 7(2), 97–120.

Korpi, W. (2006). Power resources and employer-centered approaches in explanations of welfare states and varieties of capitalism: Protagonists, consenters, and antagonists. *World Politics*, 58(2), 167–206.

Kouvo, A., & Lockmer, C. (2013). Imagine all the neighbours: Perceived neighbourhood ethnicity, interethnic friendship ties and perceived ethnic threat in four Nordic countries. *Urban Studies*, 50(16), 3305–3322.

Kymlicka, W. (2009). The multicultural welfare state. In *Successful Societies: How Institutions and Culture Affect Health*, 226–53.

Kymlicka, W. (2010). The rise and fall of multiculturalism? New debates on inclusion and accommodation in diverse societies. *International Social Science Journal*, 61(199), 97–112.

Lane, J. E., & Ersson, S. (2008). The Nordic countries: Compromise and corporatism in the welfare state. In *Comparative European Politics*, 3rd ed., J. Colomer (ed.). London: Routledge, 2008.

McWhinney, E. (2019). *Canada and the Constitution 1979–1982*. University of Toronto Press.

Melby, K., Ravn, A. B., & Wetterberg, C. C. (Eds.) (2008). *Gender Equality and Welfare Politics in Scandinavia*. Bristol: Policy Press.

Mock, C. (Ed.). (2010). *Strengthening Care for the Injured: Success Stories and Lessons Learned from Around the World*. World Health Organization.

Niklasson, E., & Hølleland, H. (2018). The Scandinavian far-right and the new politicisation of heritage. *Journal of Social Archaeology*, 18(2), 121–148.

Normann, T. M., Rønning, E., & Nørgaard, E. (2014). *Challenges to the Nordic Welfare State: Comparable Indicators*, 2nd ed. Copenhagen: Nordic Social-Statistical Committee.

OECD (2015). Indicators of immigrant integration, 2015: Settling in. Accessed at https://www.oecd-ilibrary.org/docserver/9789264234024-en.pdf?expires=1619885323&id=id&accname=guest&checksum=3F-9F24A8A725B2EF6FA80A6B1BA9E1CD.

Peng, I., & Wong, J. (2010). East Asia. In *The Oxford Handbook of the Welfare State*. Oxford: Oxford University Press.

Pontusson, J. (2005). Varieties and commonalities of capitalism. In *Varieties of Capitalism, Varieties of Approaches* (pp. 163–188). London: Palgrave Macmillan.

Porter, M. E., Stern, S., & Green, M. (2017). *Social Progress Index 2017*. Washington: Social Progress Imperative.

Siim, B., & Mokre, M. (Eds.). (2013). *Negotiating Gender and Diversity in an Emergent European Public Sphere*. London: Palgrave Macmillan.

Soroka, S., Wright, M., Bloemraad, I., & Johnston, R. (2019). Multiculturalism policy and support for the welfare state. *Federalism and the Welfare State in a Multicultural World*, 198, 263.

Swedish Institute (2019). Sweden and migration. Accessed at https://sweden.se/society/sweden-and-migration/.

Tanner, A. (2011). Finland's balancing act: The labor market, humanitarian relief, and immigrant integration. Migration Policy Institute.

Vergolini, L. (2011). Social cohesion in Europe: How do the different dimensions of inequality affect social cohesion? *International Journal of Comparative Sociology*, 52(3), 197–214.

Wagner, I. (2021). How Iceland is closing the gender wage gap. *Harvard Business Review*, January 8.

Wahlbeck, Ö. (2016). True Finns and non-true Finns: The minority rights discourse of populist politics in Finland. *Journal of Intercultural Studies*, 37(6), 574–588.

Westin, C. (2006). Sweden: Restrictive immigration policy and multiculturalism. Migration Policy Institute, June 1.

World Health Organization (2011). Best practices in Tobacco control: Regulation of tobacco products, Canada report. Accessed at https://www.who.int/tobacco/global_interaction/tobreg/Canada%20Best%20Practice%20Final_For%20Printing.pdf?ua=1.

Figure Sources

Data used in the construction of figures was drawn from the following sources.

Chapter One

Figure 1-1: World Values Survey (2017).

Figure 1-2: I. Uz (2015). The index of cultural tightness and looseness among 68 countries. *Journal of Cross-Cultural Psychology* 46 (3).

Figure 1-3: UN Population Fund (2020). *Total population in millions.* https://www.unfpa.org/data/world-population-dashboard.

Chapter Two

Figure 2-1: Organization for Economic Cooperation and Development (OECD) (2019).

Figure 2-2: Statistics Canada (2017b).

Figure 2-3: OECD (2018).

Figure 2-4: Image: Dennis/Wikimedia Commons. Data sources: Global Wealth Databook, Credit Suisse, 2019. Created with Mapchart.net.

Figure 2-5: Credit Bank Suisse (2019).

Figure 2-6: OECD (2015) and World Bank (2018).

Figure 2-7: OECD (2019). *Income inequality.* https://data.oecd.org/inequality/income-inequality.htm; World Bank (2019). *Gini index.* https://data.worldbank.org/indicator/SI.POV.GINI/.

Figure 2-8: OECD (2020). *Social benefits to households in cash, % of GDP.* https://data.oecd.org/socialexp/social-benefits-to-households.htm#indicator-chart.

Figure 2-9: OECD (2017).

Figure 2-10: OECD (2020).

Chapter Three

Figure 3-1: OECD (2019). *Gender wage gap.* https://data.oecd.org/earnwage/gender-wage-gap.htm.

Figure 3-2: World Bank (2018).

Figure 3-3: OECD (2019). *Violence against women: prevalence in the lifetime.* https://data.oecd.org/inequality/violence-against-women.htm.

Figure 3-4: Ibid.

Figure 3-5: Ibid.

Figure 3-6: Gallup World Poll (2017).

Figure 3-7: OECD (2014).

Figure 3-8: Drazanova (2019).

Figure 3-9: OECD (2019).

Figure 3-10: Pew Research Center (2018).

Figure 3-11: Ipsos Public Perspectives (2018).

Figure 3-12: OECD (2015).

Figure 3-13: OECD (2018).

Figure 3-14: OECD (2018).

Figure 3-15: OECD (2018).

Chapter Four

Figure 4-1: Jeandré du Toit/Wikimedia Commons.

Figure 4-2: WHO (2019). *Estimates of rate of homicides (per 100,000 population).* https://www.who.int/data/gho/data/indicators/indicator-details/GHO/estimates-of-rates-of-homicides-per-100-000-population.

Figure 4-3: Prison Policy Initiative (2018). *States of incarceration: the global context 2018.* https://www.prisonpolicy.org/global/2018.html.

Figure 4-4: Prison Policy Initiative (2017).

Figure 4-5: UNODC. (2020). *Global report on trafficking.* https://www.unodc.org/documents/Global_Report_on_TIP.pdf.

Figure 4-6: World Economic Forum Report on Global Competitiveness (2019).

Chapter Five

Figure 5-1: OECD. (2019). *Life expectancy at birth.* https://data.oecd.org/healthstat/life-expectancy-at-birth.htm.

Figure 5-2: WHO. (2020). *Age-standardized rate per 100,000 population by cause, sex, and WHO member state, 2019.* https://www.who.int/data/gho/data/themes/mortality-and-global-health-estimates/ghe-leading-causes-of-death.

Figure 5-3: WHO. (2021). *Probability of dying between age 30 and 70 from any of cardiovascular disease, cancer, diabetes, or chronic respiratory disease, 2019.* https://www.who.int/data/gho/data/indicators/indicator-details/GHO/probability-(-)-of-dying-between-age-30-and-exact-age-70-from-any-of-cardiovascular-disease-cancer-diabetes-or-chronic-respiratory-disease.

Figure 5-4: OECD (2018).

Figure 5-5: Ritchie and Roser (2018b).

Figure 5-6: World Bank (2019).

Figure 5-7: WHO. (2020). *Estimate of current tobacco smoking prevalence (%) (age standardized rate).* https://www.who.int/data/gho/data/indicators/indicator-details/GHO/gho-tobacco-control-monitor-current-tobaccouse-tobaccosmoking-cigarrettesmoking-agestd-tobagestdcurr.

Figure 5-8: WHO (2016). Heavy episodic drinking, past 30 days by country. https://apps.who.int/gho/data/node.main.A1047.

Figure 5-9: WHO (2019). Monitoring Health for the Sustainable Development Goals [Alcohol Consumption]. https://www.who.int/gho/publications/worldhealthstatistics/2019/en/.

Figure 5-10: WHO (2018). Global status report on alcohol and health. [Health Consequences]. Retrieved from https://www.who.int/substanceabuse/publications/globalalcoholreport/en/.

Figure 5-11: Global Burden of Disease Collaborative Network (2017). Global Burden of Disease Study 2017 (GBD 2017) Results. Seattle: Institute for Health Metrics and Evaluation (IHME), 2018.

Figure 5-12: Challcombe (2018); European Centre for Disease Prevention and Control (2018); Australian Federation of AIDS organizations (n.d.); HIV.gov (n.d.); New Zealand AIDS Foundation (n.d.).

Chapter Six

Figure 6-1: World Bank (2019).

Figure 6-2: OECD (2019).

Figure 6-3: ILO (2020, 2019). *Safety and health indicators.* https://ilostat.ilo.org/topics/safety-and-health-at-work/.

Figure 6-4: Ibid.

Figure 6-5: Sources: ILO (2019a); Canada: Government of Ontario, Ministry of Labour (2019); Australia: Wundersitz (2019).

Figure 6-6: ITF (2018).

Chapter Seven

Figure 7-1: OECD (2019). https://stats.oecd.org/Index.aspx?DataSetCode=AIR_GHG.

Figure 7-2: IEA (2018); World Bank (2016). https://data.worldbank.org/indicator/EN.ATM.CO2E.PC.OECD.

Figure 7-3: United Nations Statistics Division (2018).

Figure 7-4: OECD (2020). https://data.oecd.org/air/air-pollution-exposure.htm.

Figure 7-5: OECD (2019); The Conference Board of Canada (2019).

Figure 7-6: U.S. Energy Information Administration (2020).

Figure 7-7: WEC (2016).

Chapter Eight

Figure 8-1: Statistics Canada (2018). Low income statistics by age, sex, and economic family type. https://www150.statcan.gc.ca/t1/tbl1/en/tv.action?pid=1110013501&pickMembers%5B0%5D=1.1&cubeTimeFrame.startYear=2017&cubeTimeFrame.endYear=2018&referencePeriods=20170101%2C20180101.

Figure 8-2: Statistics Canada (2018). https://www.statista.com/statistics/613032/measure-of-income-inequality-in-canada-by-province/.

Figure 8-3: Statistics Canada (2018). (https://www150.statcan.gc.ca/t1/tbl1/en/tv.action?pid=1110019201&pickMembers%5B0%5D=1.1&cubeTimeFrame.startYear=2018&cubeTimeFrame.endYear=2018&referencePeriods=20180101%2C20180101).

Figure 8-4: Maytree (2018, 2019). https://maytree.com/welfare-in-canada/canada/.

Figure 8-5: Conference Board of Canada (2016).

Figure 8-6: Statistics Canada (2019). https://www150.statcan.gc.ca/n1/pub/85-002-x/2019001/article/00018/tbl/tbl02-7-eng.htm.

Figure 8-7a and 8-7b: 2016 Canadian Census.

Figure 8-8: Statistics Canada (2020). https://www150.statcan.gc.ca/t1/tbl1/en/tv.action?pid=1410008301.

Figure 8-9a and 8-9b: 2016 Canadian Census.

Figure 8-10: Statistics Canada (2021). *Self-reported violent victimization among Indigenous people.* https://www150.statcan.gc.ca/t1/tbl1/en/tv.action?pid=3510016801.

Figure 8-11: Statistics Canada (2020). Canadian Centre for Justice and Community Safety Statistics, Homicide Survey, 2020.

Figure 8-12: Allen, M. (2020). Crime reported by police serving areas where the majority of the population is Indigenous, 2018. Canadian Centre for Justice and Community Safety Statistics. https://www150.statcan.gc.ca/n1/pub/85-002-x/2020001/article/00013-eng.htm.

Figure 8-13a and 8-13b: Statistics Canada (2016). Life expectancy, at birth and at age 65, by sex, three-year average, Canada, provinces, territories, health regions and peer groups. https://www150.statcan.gc.ca/t1/tbl1/en/tv.action?pid=1310038901.

Figure 8-14: Statistics Canada (2019). Mortality rates, by age group. https://www150.statcan.gc.ca/t1/tbl1/en/tv.action?pid=1310071001.

Figure 8-15: Conference Board of Canada (2011). Mortality due to heart disease and stroke. https://www.conferenceboard.ca/hcp/provincial/health/heart.aspx.

Figure 8-16: Statistics Canada (2017). Body mass index, overweight or obese, self-reported, adult age groups 18 years and older. https://www.150.statcan.gc.ca/n1/pub/11-627-m/11-627-m2018033-eng.htm.

Figure 8-17: Palay, J., et al. (2019). Prevalence of mental disorders and suicidality in Canadian provinces. *Canadian Journal of Psychiatry*, 64(11), 761–769. https://doi.org/10.1177/0706743719878987.

Figure 8-18: Ibid.

Figure 8-19: Statistics Canada (2019).

Figure 8-20: Tucker, S., & Keefe, A. (2020). 2020 Report on work fatality and injury rates in Canada. University of Regina. https://www.uregina.ca/business/faculty-staff/faculty/file_download/2020-Report-on-Workplace-Fatalities-and-Injuries.pdf.pdf.

Figure 8-21: Ibid.

Figure 8-22: Statistics Canada (2018). https://www150.statcan.gc.ca/t1/tbl1/en/tv.action?pid=3510005101.

Figure 8-23: Statistics Canada (2018). https://www150.statcan.gc.ca/n1/daily-quotidien/191127/t001b-eng.htm.

Figure 8-24: Government of Canada (2018). https://www.canada.ca/en/environment-climate-change/services/environmental-indicators/air-pollutant-emissions.html.

Figure 8-25: Statista (2019). https://www.statista.com/statistics/973790/oil-production-share-in-canada-by-province/.

Figure 8-26: Government of Canada (2018). https://www.canada.ca/en/environment-climate-change/services/environmental-indicators/greenhouse-gas-emissions.html.

Figure 8-27: Statistics Canada (2016). https://www150.statcan.gc.ca/n1/pub/11-402-x/2012000/chap/geo/tbl/tbl06-eng.htm.

Figure 8-28: Statistics Canada (2013). https://www150.statcan.gc.ca/n1/pub/16-201-x/2017000/sec-2/c-g/c-g-2.12-eng.htm.

Figure 8-29: Statistics Canada (2018). https://www150.statcan.gc.ca/t1/tbl1/en/tv.action?pid=3810003201.

Chapter Nine

Figure 9-1: United Nations Development Program (2019).

Figure 9-2: The Fund for Peace (2019).

Figure 9-3: Transparency International (2019).

Figure 9-4: Social Progress Index (2019).

Figure 9-5: OECD (2019).

Photo Credits

Index

About the Authors

Lorne Tepperman is professor of sociology at the University of Toronto. The winner of many teaching awards, including the Dean's Excellence Award, an Outstanding Teaching Award from the Faculty of Arts and Science, and an Oswald Hall Teaching Award given by the Department of Sociology, Tepperman in 2003 also received the Outstanding Contribution Award from the Canadian Sociology Association. Among his dozens of books are *Consumer Society*, a comprehensive introduction to the sociology of consumerism published by Rock's Mills Press in 2021, *Starting Points: A Sociological Journey* (second edition, 2015), and *Habits of Inequality* (with Nina Gheihman, 2013). He appeared on CBC Radio's *Ideas* program to discuss his book *The Sense of Sociability: How People Overcome the Forces Pulling Them Apart* (2011).

Maria Finnsdottir is a Ph.D. student in the Department of Sociology at the University of Toronto. Her most recent research focuses on radical politics and gender inequality, as well as the effects of racial discrimination in Canada.